# Women
# in Anglo-Saxon
# England

There is a tide in the affairs of men
Which, taken at the flood, leads on to fortune;
Omitted, all the voyage of their life
Is bound in shallows and in miseries.

Shakespeare, Julius Cæsar, IV, iii, 217.

There is a tide in the affairs of women,
Which, taken at the flood, leads – God knows where.

Byron, Don Juan, c.VI.ii.

Philosophy, female, with book and sceptre.

# Women
# in Anglo-Saxon
# England

BY CHRISTINE FELL

# and the impact of 1066

BY CECILY CLARK

AND ELIZABETH WILLIAMS

INDIANA UNIVERSITY PRESS

BLOOMINGTON

TO JOANNA MARY AND NICOLA ELIZABETH
*broðordohtrum*

Copyright © 1984 Christine Fell

Manufactured in Great Britain

Library of Congress Cataloging in Publication Data

Fell, Christine E.
 Women in Anglo-Saxon England and the impact of 1066.
 Bibliography: p.
 Includes index.
 1. Women—England—History—Middle Ages, 500–1500.
2. Great Britain—History—Anglo-Saxon period, 449–1066.
3. Anglo-Saxons.  4. Great Britain—History—Medieval
period, 1066–1485.  I. Clark, Cecily.  II. Williams,
Elizabeth.  III. Title.
HQ1147.G7F45     1985     305.4′2′0942     84-48493
ISBN 0-253-36607-0

1   2   3   4   5   89  88  87  86  85

# Contents

## ACKNOWLEDGEMENTS

We are deeply grateful to our friends and colleagues who have read this through and from whose scholarship we have profited: Ray Page, Thorlac Turville-Petre, Leslie Webster and Patrick Wormald. We should like to thank those whom we have consulted on various matters ranging from place-names to picture research: Gordon Anderson, David Bates, Kenneth Cameron, Jayne Cook, Peter Fell, Margaret Gelling, John Insley, Peter Kitson, Lynette Muir, Dorothy Owen, Dominic Tweddle, Kathleen Thompson, Elizabeth Watson and Andrew Wawn. We should also like to record our gratitude to W. A. G. Doyle-Davidson and Mary Orgill whose gifts of books have made our work so much quicker and easier. The Persons from Porlock have been generous in their support. Norma Hazzledine has typed and re-typed with miraculous patience, and our editors Celia Clear and Jenny Chattington have given us every help and encouragement.

## NOTE ON CONVENTIONS

In Old English and Old Norse the symbols þ and ð for 'th' are retained. In Middle English orthography has been partly modernised to avoid the need for translation. We have tried to be consistent in our spelling of personal and place names, but total consistency is impossible. Where, for example, a name is as well known in its modern form as Edith, I have tended to leave it rather than replace it with Old English Eadgyð. Reading lists at the end of each chapter indicate the sources used for that chapter as well as possible further reading, but all texts mentioned in shorthand form in these lists are detailed in full in the bibliography at the end of the book. Citations in capital letters in the reading lists indicate the name under which the work is given in the bibliography.

# Introduction

Nothing could be more calculated to produce a very striking dissimilarity, between the Gothic [i.e. Germanic] nations and the Oriental states, than this exaltation of the female sex to that honour, consequence and independence, which European laws studied to uphold. As the education of youth will always rest principally with women...it is of the greatest importance that the fair sex should possess high estimation in society; and nothing could more certainly tend to perpetuate this feeling, than the privilege of possessing property in their own right, and at their own disposal.

This quotation from Sharon Turner's *History of the Anglo-Saxons* published between 1799 and 1805 is one of the first serious statements by a modern historian about Anglo-Saxon women. Turner's control of the sources, both Latin and Old English, is superb, and he presents a serious and scholarly analysis of the evidence. He has read the charters, the wills and the laws, as well as the literature, some in early editions, some in manuscript. John Mitchell Kemble compiling *The Saxons in England* half a century later, writes about women in very much less detail, and has a rather different set of value judgements to impose:

As an individual, woman was considered a being of a higher nature; as a member of the state, she was necessarily represented by him upon whom nature had imposed the joyful burthen of her support, and the happy duty of her protection, – a principle too little considered by those who with a scarcely pardonable sciolism, have clamoured for what they call the rights of woman. Woman among the Teutons was near akin to divinity, but not one among them ever raved that the *femme libre* could be *woman*.

Within the next twenty years a couple more influential works appeared. In 1862 John Thrupp published *The Anglo-Saxon Home*. Thrupp attacks Sharon Turner with some violence and includes Kemble in his denunciation. He quotes a passage where Turner refers to 'countries [such as Anglo-Saxon England] which have the wisdom and urbanity to treat [women] as equal, intelligent and independent beings' and claims that Turner's views are supported 'by no very great amount of evidence'. He then produces his own attitudes:

In contradiction to the generally received opinion, it may be said, that the Anglo-Saxon women were, at one time, sold by their fathers and always beaten by their husbands; that they were menial servants even when of royal rank; that they were habitually

7

1 'The Summer
Dress and Travelling
Habit of the Ladies
of the eighth
century', a plate from
Joseph Strutt's
*Complete View of the
Dress and Habits of
the People of England*,
published in 1796.
Strutt's illustrations
of Anglo-Saxon
costume are based on
manuscripts but
redrawn in the style
of his own period.

subjected to coarse personal insult; and that they were never addressed, even in poetry, in the language of passion or respect.

Since Thrupp attacks Turner for views unsupported by evidence, it seems unlikely that he would put forward such challenging opposition to them on the basis of no evidence whatsoever. But if Thrupp had evidence for any single one of these assertions I do not know what it was.

*Womankind in Western Europe* by Thomas Wright came out in 1869. It is a book of some charm based upon extensive research. Wright is capable of examining evidence with a judicious eye even in minor detail:

It has been supposed that it was only towards the tenth century that the women of the household gained the right of sitting at table with the men, and that this is evidence of a great advance in their social position. This, however, may be an assumption founded too hastily upon our mere want of knowledge.

True, Wright sometimes draws erroneous conclusions from his evidence, and is moreover inclined to believe what he reads in the 'excellent and interesting volume of [his] friend Mr Thrupp', so the overall picture is a distorted one. Montalembert's *Les Moines d'Occident* published in the same decade is closer to Sharon Turner's views: '[Anglo-Saxon] woman is a person not a thing. She lives, she speaks, she acts for herself'. (La femme est une personne et non une chose...elle vit, parle, agit pour elle-même.)

There are two classes of women which attract particular attention from historians writing about the European Middle Ages, namely queens and saints, not always in Anglo-Saxon society distinguishable. In 1854 Mrs Matthew Hall published her two-volume work *The Queens before the Conquest*, being clearly less concerned than we are today about the ambiguity of the word 'conquest'. She has chapters on British queens (Cartismandua, Boadicea, Guenever) where she is not distinguishing too clearly between the historical and the legendary. On the Anglo-Saxon queens she does not distinguish between the reliability of contemporary sources such as Bede and the information obtained from post-Conquest chronicle and hagiography, but she is by no means alone in this, and she has read almost all the secondary sources available to her, including Turner, with care and attention. She takes from Turner the extremely interesting point (which I have also made use of in chapter 3 below) of the alterations which King Ælfred made to the original in his translation of Boethius in order to stress rather more emphatically the grief of the prisoner's wife. She does not acknowledge a source for the translation of Henry of Huntingdon's verses on Æðelflæd, Lady of the Mercians, so the following version is perhaps to be attributed to her own pen:

> Mighty Elfleda! maiden, thou should'st bear
>    The name of Man: – though Nature cast thy frame
> In Woman's softer mould – yet he could fear
>    Thy matchless might! Let him resign his claim,
> And, maiden do thou change thy sex's name,
>    In grace, a queen – be hence a king in might,
> And ages shall renounce proud Cæsar's fame,
>    To gaze on thine, as on a fairer light!
> So, maiden fare thee well! surpassing queen, good night!

Thomas Heywood's version of the same text published in 1624 in his *History concerninge Women* was closer to Henry's Latin. Heywood translated Henry's *virgo virago* quite literally in his phrase *virago maide*. Between the seventeenth and the nineteenth centuries, however, the word 'virago' had lost any complimentary overtones, and it would have been impossible for Mrs Hall to retain it.

Frances Arnold-Forster, who published her impressive three-volume work *Studies in Church Dedications* in 1899, has a fine chapter on 'Saxon Ladies of High Degree'. The real scholarship of this book is in the Appendices where church dedications are carefully collected and sifted, and we may see which of the Anglo-Saxon female saints had churches dedicated to them before the Reformation and which dedications were part of the nineteenth-century revival of interest. In her chapter of general information we find her efforts to sort out facts from legend become blurred by her delight in the stories. She imposes on these saints a very nineteenth-century vocabulary of femininity. 'In the eight years of her married life Ethelburga had known all a mother's tenderest joys and sorrows'. On young Edith of Wilton she writes: 'A blithe sparkling creature was this fair young princess, this "beloved bird" as the great Dunstan once fondly

2 Ælflæd, Hild's successor at Whitby, not one of the more sparkling of the virgin saints, may owe her inclusion in S. Baring-Gould's *Virgin Saints and Martyrs* to her friendship with St Cuðbert or support of St Wilfrid.

designated her'. But this does not prevent her from occasional vigorous attacks on masculine power-politics and her work as a whole is as remarkable for its range as for its readability.

Written in a very different style is Lina Eckenstein's *Woman under Monasticism*, which appeared three years earlier in 1896. Eckenstein makes her views clear in her Preface:

The right to self-development and social responsibility which the woman of today so persistently asks for, is in many ways analogous to the right which the convent secured to womankind a thousand years ago.

She distinguishes much more carefully than Frances Arnold-Forster does between the reliability of different types of source material, noting on the one hand the importance of charters, letters and early chronicle references and analysing on the other hand the difference in value between the hagiographical writings of the eighth century and those of the eleventh and twelfth. She is fully alive to the difference of attitude to women before and after the Norman Conquest, and equally perceptive of the different phases within Anglo-Saxon Christianity itself. The following paragraph summarises splendidly the early history of women in the religious life:

Most of the women who were honoured as saints in England belong to the first hundred years after the acceptance of Christianity in these islands. A few other women have been revered as saints who lived in the 10th century and came under the influence of the monastic revival...But no woman living during Anglo-Norman times has been thus honoured, for the desire to raise women to saintship was essentially Anglo-Saxon and was strongest in the time which immediately followed the acceptance of Christianity.

We may find exceptions to her generalisations as in St Christina of Markyate but we can hardly quarrel with the analysis otherwise.

The interest of the nineteenth century in the Anglo-Saxon period resulted not only in works of scholarship and works of synthesis but in numbers of historical novels for both adults and children. Many of these have masculine heroes, but Emily Sarah Holt's *Imogen: A story of the mission of Augustine* centres on a British girl who married into an Anglo-Saxon family. It is a rich feast of fine confused reading. I quote sections from it partly to demonstrate the odd mixture of pedantry and error and partly to show how Thrupp's distortions have influenced the popular image.

'Well', said Bertha with a sigh, 'we can only do as we are told. Women – or at least Saxon women – must not think for themselves. British women seem to do'.

Or:

And Imogen remembered, that while British sons entreated their mothers, Saxon sons commanded them.

Or:

It was etiquette for the bridegroom to be carried to bed, helplessly drunk. The generality of Saxon brides would have thought themselves insulted otherwise.

Both here and elsewhere the statements that are made about the subordination of Saxon women, and the relative freedom of 'British' ones, are quite blatant misrepresentations of such evidence as we have. Early Celtic law shows women in a far less favourable position than Anglo-Saxon law.

It is, of course, impossible to do more than take note of a few works on and references to Anglo-Saxon women whether in the nineteenth century or the twentieth, and as works proliferate selection becomes more arbitrary. Two of the most important contributions in this century are those of Sir Frank and Lady Stenton, and, though it inevitably ranges less widely, Wainwright's study of

3 The Victorians were deeply moved by the doubtless apocryphal tale of Godiva. Tennyson turns it into romantic verse:

> She prayed him 'If they pay this tax they starve'...
> He answered 'Ride you naked through the town
> And I repeal it' and nodding, as in scorn,
> He parted with great strides among his dogs.

Æðelflæd, Lady of the Mercians. Sir Frank's seminal paper of 1943, 'The Historical Bearing of Place-Name Studies: The Place of Women in Anglo-Saxon Society', was of major importance in bringing a whole new range of evidence to the subject. The nineteenth century had expert control of law, charter and will, and Sharon Turner had used such material with confidence. But Stenton, who equally controlled this documentary evidence, added to it substantially, in his use of place-name material. Wainwright's paper reminds us how in this area as in others we need to watch the *Anglo-Saxon Chronicle* for its West-Saxon propaganda, and it is important to remember that the suppression of information about female achievement is not necessarily anti-feminist. In the case of the writer of the *Anglo-Saxon Chronicle* it was more probably anti-Mercian, or at any rate a desire that Mercian achievement should not be seen to outshine West-Saxon.

Doris Stenton's *The English Woman in History*, published in 1956, opens with a chapter on 'The Anglo-Saxon Woman' and ends with 'Reaction and the Rise of Modern Feminism'. She was herself a medievalist and therefore able to handle all the early material, not depending on secondary sources, though obviously she makes full use of her husband's work. Since of all the major writers so far Doris Stenton is the only one to have looked at both Anglo-Saxon women and those in succeeding centuries down to the twentieth, the conclusions she came to after such a wide-ranging survey, as she states them in her Epilogue, deserve quoting:

The evidence which has survived from Anglo-Saxon England indicates that women were then more nearly the equal companions of their husbands and brothers than at any other period before the modern age. In the higher ranges of society this rough and ready partnership was ended by the Norman Conquest, which introduced into England a military society relegating women to a position honourable but essentially unimportant. With all allowance for the efforts of individual churchmen to help individual women, it must be confessed that the teaching of the medieval Church reinforced the subjection which feudal law imposed on all wives.

I should have liked to quote more of Doris Stenton's excellent good sense, but must instead concentrate on her last point. There is a major division of views between those works which see Christianity as improving the status of women, and those which see it, as Doris Stenton does, as detrimental. Wright, for example, in the work quoted above, stated unequivocally:

There can be no doubt that for the improvement of woman's position in society she was indebted in a great measure to the interference of the Christian clergy. They laboured to destroy, or at least to diminish, the old patriarchal spirit, and to emancipate the female sex from the too great authority of fathers and husbands.

The situation is not as simple as either of these statements would suggest. Christianity as interpreted by the fathers of the church developed a full set of theories on the inferiority of women, which have been so frequently documented elsewhere that it seems pointless to rehearse them yet again. (Angela Lucas gives an adequate survey of them in her recent *Women in the Middle Ages*.) Yet what is important is not whether such theories existed, or even how often they were repeated, it is the extent of their actual application within society as a whole, both secular and ecclesiastic. Throughout the Anglo-Saxon period they seem to have little practical effect. On the contrary, in the first enthusiasm for Christianity we not only see men and women engaging as equals in the challenge of a new religion and way of life, we see also women specifically asked to take a full and controlling part. No women could have been asked to take on so powerful a role as the early abbesses unless they were used to handling power, but Christianity is certainly not at this stage cramping their range of activity and responsibility.

We see traces of anti-female propaganda in letters or homilies from the pens of clergy and in the penitentials, but these seem to have been ineffectual in practice. Even Wulfstan in the eleventh century is denouncing sexual immorality in general, not women in particular. But the impact of the Norman Conquest, which Doris Stenton summarises so admirably, is almost instantly followed by the impact of the Gregorian reform, when theological concept hardens into canon law, and canon law acquires control of much legislation concerning women. The combination of the new military-based civil law and the increasing effectiveness of anti-female canon law produced a society in which the role of women was very sharply differentiated from that in the pre-1066 era. In the seven chapters following which look at the Anglo-Saxon period, including any modifications made by the Viking settlement, it is possible at any point to look at the practical evidence and the literary evidence side by side. The literary image may be a heightened concept of reality, but it is not divorced from it. In the last two chapters the difference is so great between women in reality and women in literature that they cannot properly form part of a single study. Practically, the status of women deteriorates. In literature it becomes stereotyped. One of the impressions that comes over most strongly from Elizabeth Williams's chapter on the literary image is the extent to which literature deals in conventions and ideals, and the contrast between this and the harsh realities delineated in Cecily Clark's chapter (chapter 8) is illuminating.

Our book is not intended to be on the Middle Ages as a whole, and the balance of it, represented by seven chapters on Anglo-Saxon society and two on post-Conquest society is deliberate. We are looking basically at women in Anglo-Saxon England, and the study of that is not complete without demonstrating the complete shift of pattern, the turn of the tide, within a single century after 1066. As far as possible we have handled all the types of evidence relevant to such a study, and we hope that the book represents what the evidence has shown us, rather than preconceptions imposed on the evidence. The range of source-material is extensive and various, especially for the early period where archaeology has much to contribute.

The nineteenth century had at its disposal a reasonable range of the documentary evidence. A lot of it had been published; interest in Old English had resulted in the appearance of both dictionaries and grammars, and it is impressive to note how many historians of that period could handle the vernaculars with almost as much competence as they could the Latin. In the twentieth century we have refined our techniques of dating and annotating this material, and even occasionally find more. But in the nineteenth century the study of place-names and of archaeology were the hobbies of antiquarians, and neither had been put on a serious scholarly basis. In these fields the twentieth century has made progress, and advanced technology is continually extending the usefulness of archaeology in particular.

There is another area in which technology is allowing us to make great steps forward in our use of the evidence and this is in the analysis of vocabulary. It has long been obvious to archaeologists that find-patterns are up to a point arbitrary, and that distribution maps impose deceptive statistics in areas where chance preservation and haphazard discoveries or destruction play a large part. In the same way the texts that survive from Anglo-Saxon England are a fragment of what existed. In the first place much was destroyed by Viking raids; later the Norman Conquest meant that anything written in Old English became at first unfashionable, fairly soon unreadable and therefore expendable. Hundreds of books must also have perished through Henry VIII's dissolution of the monasteries, especially the ones that seemed of least value or comprehensibility. All things considered, the wonder is that we have as much as we do. This means that our knowledge of Old English vocabulary and the way it could be used depends on the limited number of records that actually contain it. Some quite ordinary words are found once only. Many of the words have survived into Modern English but the meaning may have changed over the centuries. We too readily assume that an Old English word can be translated by the Modern English one that derives from it. One of the commonest examples is *eorl*, for though this is sometimes a status word and can be translated by its modern equivalent 'earl', in the earlier Anglo-Saxon period it meant something more like 'warrior'. Thus if a woman speaks, as she does in one charter I discuss below, in an *eorlic* manner, a manner befitting an *eorl*, we are obliged to hesitate about the precise implications.

But in 1980 the Centre for Medieval Studies in Toronto issued its complete concordance of Old English in microfiche, and this has meant that for every English word that occurs in texts from the Anglo-Saxon period we have full documentation of all the contexts in which it is found, and can see at a glance its range and type and date of usage. Added to this, computer studies now enable us to do much more precise statistical work on semantics and syntax. It is an area in which there is a great deal of work still to be done, and particularly for work in the field of women's studies it is important that we should know exactly how to handle, translate and interpret the vocabulary. It is important in all fields of course, but since many recent articles on Anglo-Saxon women and attitudes to women rest very largely on how the authors read certain key words, there will continue to be scope for much misunderstanding until proper and detailed semantic analysis has been carried out. We now at last have the tools to do this kind of work.

One of the commonest semantic errors that is made by scholars not accustomed to working with words is to assume that the range of a word in one language is the same as its range in another, especially where the languages are closely linked. There are two verbs in Old English, *bicgan* and *agan*, which are commonly translated respectively as 'to buy' and 'to own'. If, instead of probing the precise semantic range of these words in Old English, historians and literary critics assume that conclusions may be drawn from the semantic range of a lexicographer's

Morgan-gife. -gifu. mongen-gife. -gifu. Matutinum donum: Craitinum donum: Donum sc. quod, nomine dotis, novæ nuptæ *postridie nuptiarum* maritus erogare solebat. Sponsalitia largitas. Donatio propter nuptias. Dos nuptialis; Ælfr. gloss. p. 57. R. 13. Hickes. Præf. p. lx. Rettendune þe pær min Morgen-gyfu. *Rottendunum,* quod erat mea dos nuptialis; Testam. Ælfledæ ap. Wott. not. in consp. Hick. p. 29. Lif heo. binnan geaþer fæce. peþe geceoþe. Donne Solige heo þæþe Morgen-gyfe. Si illa (vidua sc.) intra anni spatium virum eligat, tum perdat illa dotem; LL. pol. Canut. 71. Hinc *Germanorum* Morgen-gabe, quæ in legibus antiquis eorum, præcipue vero *Ripuaria, Alamannica, Burgundica, Longobardica,* passim occurrit, & Morgan-geba & Morgan-giba vocatur: De qua tamen scribit *Wacht.* in Gloss. suo, non fuisse, apud priscos Germanos, *totam* dotem, at unam tantummodo dotis *speciem,* quam sc. " novus maritus novæ nuptæ post pri- " mam noctem offerebat tanquam pretium " virginitatis, ut apud *Græcos* Διαπαρθένια. " Hoc munus (inquit ille) apud *Longobar-* " *dos* erat *quarta pars* bonorum mariti, & " a reliquis dotibus passim distinguitur. " Diserte *Greg. Turon.* IX. 20. Tam in " *dote* quam in *Morgane-giba.* In Jure " etiam provinciali *Alaman.* Morgen-gaube " eodem occurrit sensu. Cap. XX." Denique id genus Donationem codicillarem *Saxonice* scriptam, circ. A. D. 1000, videre licet in *Hickes.* Diss. Epist. p. 76.

4 The entry for *morgengifu* in Lye's *Dictionarium Saxonico et Gothico-Latinum* of 1772 shows how fully scholars of that date had probed and assembled their sources.

modern equivalent, it is fairly obvious that this will lead to unscholarly results. There is scope for a full article on both these verbs, but space here only to summarise a little of the material. The verb *bicgan* is used in several contexts, legal and literary, of the marriage contract. The simplest to take as an example here is *cyning sceal mid ceape    cwene gebicgan.* This is commonly translated as 'a king shall buy a queen with property', and conclusions are then drawn from this and other usages of the verb that marriage was simple barter in Anglo-Saxon England, the father selling his daughter to her prospective husband. Yet there is a vast range of evidence (mostly analysed in chapter 3 below) for the fact that the money the bridegroom had to pay (the *morgengifu*) was payment to the woman herself, intended to guarantee her financial security and independence within marriage. *Bicgan* has the meaning 'to pay for' and there is evidence that it could be used in the sense of paying money within a contractual framework. Anglo-Saxon society was very largely governed by such money payments – the *wergild* for example that one had to pay for killing or injuring someone. Thus a more appropriate translation of the above line would be 'a king must pay for the privilege of a marriage contract' and we should thereby avoid all the emotive implications of the word 'buy' in Modern English. Similarly the verb *agan*, 'to own', and especially the present participle *agend*, 'owner', are regularly used as evidence that women were 'owned' in Anglo-Saxon England. Yet a full study of *agend* in particular would show that it could be used of any person in charge of a community, man or woman in charge of an estate, abbess in charge of a monastery, with regard to any of the dependants, male or female, within that community. It does not imply 'ownership' in our sense of the term, nor imply that the dependant was of slave status. But in a society that did not have professional lawyers, insurance agents, trade union representatives and so on the *agend* was the person who, on the one hand, had to accept responsibility before the rest of the world for the crimes of any person within that community, and, on the other hand, to press for full recompense if they were injured.

One of the points which has impressed itself on my mind while I have been writing this book is the extent to which our response to some of the simplest words can blur our understanding of the original. We are, in Modern English, accustomed to read the word *man* as masculine, even though we know that in certain contexts (e.g. 'mankind') it is used of human beings of both sexes. But our primary assumption in most contexts will be that it refers to the male. Old English *mann* however can equally be used of women.

Sir Henry Spelman (1564?–1641) produced a study on *The Laws and Antiquities of England*, published posthumously in 1723. In it he notes that a charter of Edward the Confessor uses the word *man* to refer to a woman:

And King Edward the Confessor granting *duas Mansas*...to Thola Widow of the aforesaid Orc, whom in a Saxon Charter he calleth his *Man*, that is his *Thane*...

The Old English is more clearly unambiguous than Spelman's rendering: *Tole min mann*. It is not an isolated occurrence. A charter of 969 contains a grant of land near Worcester leased for three lives by the bishop to a man called Ælfweard. The main body of the charter is in Latin, the bounds are in English. Then there is a final sentence in English:

Ælfweard wæs se forma man and nu hit stant his dohtor on handa and heo is se oðer man.

'Ælfweard was the first man, and now it is in the hands of his daughter and she is the second man.'

A panegyric in an eleventh-century fragment on the virtues of St Mildrið mentions that she always remembered we were all born of one clay, descendants of Adam and Eve, *ealle of twam mannum comon*. The impossibility of saying in Modern English that we are all 'descended from two men' should make us hesitate over the way we translate the word *mann* elsewhere in Old English. Similarly in the Latin of Domesday Book the word *homo* is properly used for women as well as for men. In Hertfordshire Eadgifu *puella*, 'a girl', held an estate. She was Archbishop Stigand's *homo*. Another woman, Sæhild, the holder of a manor in Buckland, was Earl Leofwine's *homo*. It is also observable in the manumission clauses of wills and in inventories that the word *menn* must be used of people in general, and we may note that the list of Bishop Æðelwold's gifts

5 A detail from the Corpus manuscript of *Psychomachia* by Prudentius. A scribe copying this drawing into another manuscript adds a translation of the Latin caption *þis is þæt hus þær se wisdom oninnan sit. Sapientia*, grammatically feminine in Latin, is translated by the Old English masculine *wisdom*, but drawn as a feminine personification.

to Peterborough in the tenth century distinguishes *wepmen* and *wimmen* and *geonge men*. Whether the *geonge men* were young men or young persons I am not sure, just as I am not sure whether *mega* is properly translated 'kinsmen' in the charter that tells Cyneswið she may leave her land to *swelcum hire mega swelce hit hire to geearnigan wille* ('whichever of her kin is willing to earn it from her'). Quite apart from the fact that *mega* could be genitive plural of the masculine or feminine form, the masculine may be used where the general is implied. Grammatically speaking, the male embraces the female, but where natural gender has taken over from grammatical gender confusion may arise.

Even more likely to lead to mistranslation are the simple words *his* and *him*. Every philologist knows that in Old English these may be forms of the neuter pronoun as well as of the masculine, and they even survived up to a point in early Modern English. The authorised version of the Bible asks us 'if the salt have lost his savour, wherewith shall it be salted?' But the anthropologist Lorraine Lancaster in her article on kinship terminology in Old English assumed that the grammatically neuter word *bearn* could only be used of a son, never of a daughter, and I can only understand this error if she was misled by the grammatical forms of the pronoun. It is a common word for 'child' and used regularly of either sex. That masculine words such as *hlaford*, 'lord', could be used of women is easily demonstrable in individual cases. The difficulty is when we meet generalisations in the plural to 'lords' or 'men' or 'kinsmen'. It is, however, obvious that for the Anglo-Saxons the word *mann* carried the primary sense 'human being' so clearly that it could be used without awkwardness of either sex, and that where it was necessary to distinguish the sexes the terminology was not as in Modern English 'men and women' but *weras and wifas* or *wepmen and wifmenn*.

Terminology of sex is not the only difficult range in Old English, and any translation makes us more and more aware of the extent of work waiting to be done on individual words. Some of it has been done, but does not necessarily make translation easy thereby. The noun 'hide', Old English *hid*, was basically a unit of resource, relating approximately to the amount of land that would support one family. This obviously would vary according to the nature of the land. But an equivalent of 120 acres has been put forward, and since vast numbers of documents discuss land in terms of 'hides' we need some indication of acreage for the purpose of comparisons. The whole problematic question of the nature of land-tenure throughout the period is so complex that as far as possible I have tried to side-step it, but inevitably in referring to land held, land bequeathed, and so on, I have simplified the issues. Some other difficulties whether of terminology or of interpretation we have endeavoured to handle as we come to them.

The written evidence for the Anglo-Saxon period divides into two languages and two alphabets, though there is not a great deal of useful extant material written in the runic alphabet. Anglo-Saxon Latin texts occur throughout the period, starting with Bede's eighth-century history and ending, perhaps, with the Latin of the Norman scribes who, in producing the Domesday survey for William the Bastard are giving us material from the very end of Anglo-Saxon England. Old English texts are of many different types. There are formal documents such as wills, translations from a variety of Latin sources, and the whole range of Old English poetry. Written sources are not only in different alphabets, in different languages and of different types, they vary also in provenance and in date. The Anglo-Saxon period covers a number of centuries, and we cannot ever be quite sure in recounting any one fact from a given place and time, how far it may be relevant for a different part of the country and a different century. The limitations of our knowledge make generalisation and synthesis from a scattering of facts too easy a temptation.

What we have tried to do is as far as possible to confine ourselves to sources within England itself. For the Anglo-Saxon period as such this is fairly easy, and

I have deliberately avoided drawing parallels and analogies with contemporary European cultures. Total consistency has, however, not been maintained. For my chapter on the religious life I have drawn heavily on the Boniface correspondence, even though some of those communicating had taken up residence abroad. On secular women I have on the whole not followed the careers of those English princesses who married into European houses, though some women like Ælfgifu, the Anglo-Saxon wife of King Cnut, established by him as regent in Norway, made a considerable impression on the countries of their adoption. But for the periods where foreigners invade England it is impossible to use English sources only. For the chapter on Viking women I have inevitably drawn on non-English Viking source-material, and for the chapters on England after 1066 Cecily Clark and Elizabeth Williams have drawn on Norman chroniclers and writers of French romance. The post-1066 chapters differ in the dating of their material. Cecily Clark uses mostly evidence from immediately after the Norman Conquest, though with occasional reference to later urban records. Elizabeth Williams inevitably uses literature of the later medieval period, since so little in English survives from the early post-Conquest years.

A type of evidence that I have deliberately avoided is in the Anglo-Saxon penitentials. These are the first formulation in England of a system of Christian penance and punishment for sin which may bear some relation to the society which the missionaries from Rome encountered, but in fact represents a system of codification already formulated in the country of origin. Missionaries do not customarily invent a system to suit the *mores* of the society they have come to convert, they bring their rules with them. The first penitential in Anglo-Saxon England is attributed to Theodore of Tarsus, seventh-century archbishop of Canterbury. He was sixty-six at the time of his appointment to England and, according to Bede, there was some anxiety as to whether he would teach pure Roman doctrine, or attempt to introduce 'any Greek customs which might be contrary to the true faith'. The rules that he had absorbed in the first sixty-six years of his life would be the ones that were handed on, and indeed in many of them we can trace the Continental parallels. Thus, although Theodore has in his section on penalties for homicide a penance for a woman who beats a servant to death (seven years), it would not be rational to conclude that this was a form of indulgence peculiar to Anglo-Saxon women, any more than fornicating with Jews (nine years penance) or heathens (seven years: heathens were presumably more accessible). Though I have not avoided reference to the penitentials entirely, I have considered it too chancy an area to use to any great extent.

Another use of evidence or non-evidence that it has seemed to me proper to avoid is the drawing of firm conclusions from the absence of source-material. It may seem obvious that no such conclusion could be reliable, but where the sources are so limited a number of critics have been tempted. Anne Klinck, in an article on 'Anglo-Saxon women and the law', argues from the fact that Cnut was the first law-giver to specify penalties for adultery that there were earlier unwritten, much worse, penalties. Another recent article by Rosalind Hill on 'Marriage in Seventh-Century England' builds a theory on the payment of *morgengifu*, through the implied scarcity of marriageable women, to 'the sinister probability that some girl children were not allowed to survive'. Yet the only evidence for either abortion or infanticide – and it is mostly in penitentials which I personally do not consider as rigid proof – has not the slightest implication that these crimes bore any relation to the sex of the infant. It is in any case hard to see how abortion could do so. But infanticide in so far as it may have occurred would be more likely to be determined by the difficulty of feeding another member of the family and, equally, in the case of illegitimacy by the expected lack of adequate provision. In so far as the bearing of an illegitimate child may have been considered a disgrace – and we have little evidence on society's attitudes here except in the case of nuns – the sex of the child would hardly have mitigated the situation. In the handling of any kind of evidence we are obliged from time to time to read between the lines. But it is salutary to remember that scholarship does not require us to read only, always and inevitably a history of oppression and exploitation of the female sex. The real evidence from Anglo-Saxon England presents a more attractive and indeed assertive picture.

The three of us who have written this book have all felt at the completion of each chapter that there is material in that chapter alone that could be expanded into a book in itself. An encyclopaedic study of the kind that would result might, however, be more than our readers could bear. But for the omissions, the simplifications and the generalisations that are an inevitable part of any synthesis we apologise. And as Bede said before beginning Book II, doubtless addressing those who had managed to get to the end of Book I, *Lege Feliciter*: 'good luck to the reader'.

## FURTHER READING

All books and articles cited in this chapter will be found under author in the complete bibliography. The Toronto microfiche concordance is listed under HEALEY. One important book not quoted above is Pauline STAFFORD, *Queens, Concubines and Dowagers*, which has a very comprehensive bibliographical section. For an interpretation of the evidence completely at variance with our own, see the article by Anne KLINCK who summarises her views as follows: 'There is a much closer resemblance between the situation obtaining in late Anglo-Saxon England and post-Conquest England than there is between the early and late Anglo-Saxon period. Thus to describe Anglo-Saxon England as a time when women enjoyed an independence which they lost as a result of the changes introduced by the Norman Conquest is misleading.'

# 1. Myth and Legend

We know so little about the Romano-British women who lived in England before the coming of the Anglo-Saxons that it is difficult to assess their way of life except by extrapolating from foreign or late evidence. The villas and cities that are excavated in this country do not differ greatly from cities and villas in other parts of the Roman Empire, and the average woman's life was perhaps dictated more by her social class than either her ethnic origins or the part of that Empire she lived in. The surviving buildings or remnants of buildings, urban and rural, excavated in this country tell us something of the general manner of living. Practical documents tell us a good deal about woman's position under Roman law, and literature – lyric, comic and tragic – gives us a stylised variety of attitudes towards women. But all that would emerge from this is a general survey of women in the Roman Empire, nothing that pertains specifically to Romano-British ones. Even the statues or illustrations in mosaics are more likely to be stylistically based on current fashion in Rome than on local models. If we then look to 'Celtic' material to guide us on the British rather than the Roman aspects of the culture, it may be that both the later Welsh laws, for example, and the myths and poetry preserve social attitudes and values from the earlier period, but we ought not to rely on it. And certainly to draw out some generalisations from 'Roman' and some from 'Celtic' material to produce a composite picture of the Romano-British woman would be chancy indeed.

Similarly, if we were to rely solely on our primary written sources for the Anglo-Saxon settlement we should not be able to deduce very much from them about the women involved. We learn from Bede's *History of the English Church and People*, written in the early eighth century, that Angles, Saxons and Jutes settled in England in the fifth century. The *Anglo-Saxon Chronicle*, compiled in the ninth century, drawing on oral tradition and perhaps also on written annals as well as on Bede's work, has some details to add to the picture. We know in general terms that these people were Germanic, pagan and unlettered. Historians can reconstruct a good deal from the written sources about the political events of this period, the struggles for power between Anglo-Saxon and Briton, and between the invading tribes themselves. But it is on the whole a matter of deduction and interpretation that women came over with these early invaders. Bede, it is true, implies mass-migration when he says that the original province

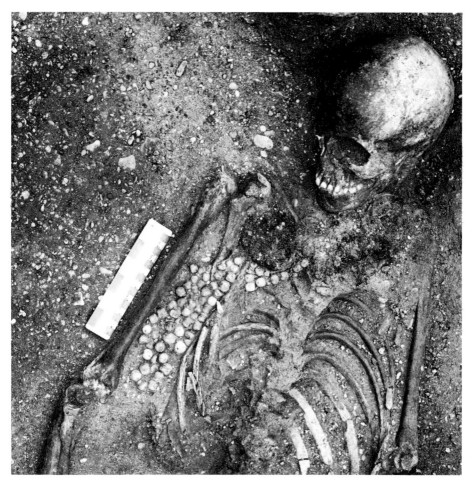

6 The richest female grave in the Anglo-Saxon cemetery at Berinsfield near Oxford shows beads and brooches lying as they were worn at the burial.

on the Continent from which the Angles came 'remains unpopulated to this day', but the actual evidence for this mass-migration is hard to determine. It is largely a matter of inference from later accounts, and from such evidence as that of Anglo-Saxon cemeteries, where though it may not be possible to show that female skeletons were ethnically Germanic rather than Celtic, it is possible to demonstrate that they were buried with Germanic grave-goods. As soon as women are mentioned in the sources there are plenty with Anglo-Saxon names, and place-names too suggest we are dealing with the settlement of family groups. To some extent intermarriage and interbreeding with the resident British population undoubtedly took place, but we have very little evidence for this at the higher

7 Beads from a female Anglo-Saxon grave at Howletts, Kent.

levels of society. Most of the women recorded in the early period have unmistakably Anglo-Saxon names. One important exception is Rienmellt, the British chieftain's daughter who was the first wife of Oswiu of Northumbria. It should be noted that we know of her solely from the *Historia Brittonum*, a ninth-century work attributed to Nennius. Bede tells us only of Oswiu's wife Eanflæd of Anglo-Saxon stock. But Rienmellt is probably the name that a Northumbrian scribe struggled to write down first in his list of 198 queens and abbesses to be remembered in prayer, and rendered as *Rægnmæld*. Eanflæd is the second name on this list.

Both place-name evidence and archaeological evidence imply that there must have been a good deal more intermingling of the races than the written records suggest, but it is clear too that we are primarily dealing with a pattern in which entire Anglo-Saxon families, not merely Anglo-Saxon warriors, emigrated to England and settled. The attitude of Anglo-Saxon women to Romano-British was perhaps somewhat ambivalent. Anglo-Saxons had already encountered the Roman language and customs on the Continent, as is demonstrated by the fact that certain Latin words had already been adopted into their language – especially words for such comforts of life as wine (*win* from *vinum*), prostitutes (*miltestre* from *meretrix*) and for a whole range of domestic equipment. That Anglo-Saxon women also wore imitation keys or girdle-hangers has been taken as evidence that they adopted the Roman matron's fashions. But their attitude to the women whom they met here and called *wealisc* (the word originally meant 'foreign' but survives as modern 'Welsh') seems to have been contemptuous. References to *wealisc* women are usually to slaves, and an ethnic class distinction is suggested in the riddles of the *Exeter Book* between the blonde (*hwitlocced*) daughter of an Anglo-Saxon nobleman and the dark-haired (*wonfeax*) Welsh slave. And apparently Anglo-Saxon men and women made no immediate attempt to inhabit the Romano-British towns and villas or, as far as we can tell, to adopt their life-style in any other major way than by importing foreign luxury goods.

That the arrival of the Anglo-Saxons heralded a pattern of settlement and colonisation seems certain, but the opening lines of the Parker text of the *Anglo-Saxon Chronicle* imply that we are dealing with simple invasion, and subsequently with military conquest:

> In the year of Christ's Nativity 494, Cerdic and Cynric his son landed at *Cerdicesora* with five ships. That Cerdic was the son of Elesa, the son of Esla, the son of Gewis, the son of Wig, the son of Freawine, the son of Frithugar, the son of Brand, the son of Bældæg, the son of Woden.
>
> Six years after they landed they conquered the Kingdom of Wessex. These were the first kings who conquered the land of Wessex from the Welsh. He held the kingdom sixteen years, and when he died his son Cynric succeeded to the kingdom... When he passed away, his son Ceawlin succeeded...

The text continues with which son succeeded which king and how long he ruled down to the accession of King Ælfred, where we are told that this event was 396 years since Ælfred's ancestors first conquered Wessex. In this entire body of information there is one sentence only in which a woman is mentioned. After the thirty-one-year reign of Cenwalh 'his queen, Seaxburg, held the kingdom one year after him'.

It seems that the literate Englishwoman of the ninth or tenth century would have found little historical information in her reading about her female ancestors, and nothing in which she herself might have traced her ancestry back through the female line to some pagan goddess as her male relatives trace theirs back to Woden. But what survives is not necessarily representative of what existed, and there may have been oral traditions in areas where there are no written documents. Certainly the written vernacular and secular poetry is representative of a tradition that began as oral, and in the poetry it is possible to discover a little about Anglo-Saxon aristocratic women and what role they played or were expected to play in society, though the poetry inevitably gives a formal and ritualised picture. Yet the very formality is helpful here because heroic poetry is not susceptible to rapid change and its values and attitudes can up to a point be assumed to be representative of the early culture, the culture that the Anglo-Saxons brought with them. It is, however, not representative of the religious beliefs. By the time the poetry is written down the community is Christian, and though the poems may shed some light on the position of women in a heroic society they cannot tell us much about beliefs and practices in a pagan one. In order to form any kind of impression about the paganism of Anglo-Saxons in general and Anglo-Saxon women in particular we have to collect together a range of haphazard and often enigmatic references. It is not easy to formulate these into a coherent picture, nor to know how far we are entitled to interpret such evidence as we have. Normally accounts of what we do know centre on the masculine deities, Woden, Thunor and Tiw, but in this chapter I propose to examine the meagre evidence for major and minor female deities. It is easier to give their names, however, than to demonstrate the extent of their cults or the practices of their worshippers.

The Roman historian Tacitus, writing in the first century AD, gives us our earliest information on Germanic religion, but it is unlikely that he had first-hand knowledge of the tribes he writes about, and however reliable his sources may have been, it is not easy to judge how far statements made about Germanic tribes in the first century are applicable to the Anglo-Saxons in the fifth. His main piece of information about the religion of northern Germanic tribes concerns, significantly, the worship of a goddess. Her name has a Latin masculine ending, *Nerthus*, but Tacitus says that *Nerthus* is 'Mother Earth', *Terra Mater*. Her worship is centred in a sacred grove on an island where only one priest is permitted to attend her. Tacitus makes it clear that the ceremonies attached to her worship are deliberately kept as mysteries, and that human sacrifice is involved in keeping them so. The slaves who assist the priest in his rituals are subsequently drowned. He also tells us that the goddess's coming is associated with peace. Only the priest knows the times when she is present, and she then travels among the tribes in a covered chariot. While she is on earth all weapons must be put aside. It is reasonable to suppose that *Nerthus* was linked with plenty as well as peace, being in fact a fertility goddess, giving prosperity and good harvests.

We do not meet *Nerthus* in any Anglo-Saxon context, but we do find in an early eleventh-century manuscript a charm to improve land, which is partly a prayer in Christian terminology but contains also an invocation to a being called 'Mother Earth'. The charm opens with the word *erce* three times, a word which appears nowhere else in Old English, but must be some kind of invocation. The charm names 'Mother Earth', *eorþan modor*, asking that God shall grant her fertility, growing crops, barley, the white wheat, and all the fruits of the land in abundance. A second part of the charm again directly addresses 'Earth, mother of men', *folde fira modor*, this time with a *hal wes þu* formula – normally a mode of greeting between humans, signifying 'Be in good health'. In this part Earth is adjured to be filled with food for the use of mankind 'through God's embrace', which can hardly be other than a pregnancy image.

It is not in the least likely that in these later centuries of Anglo-Saxon Christianity a being called 'Mother Earth' could have been the object of any formal worship, but the men and women who used this charm personify, invoke and revere her not as she was worshipped by their pagan ancestors, but within the framework of Christian theology. Late medieval writers, Chaucer for example, similarly have little hesitation in describing Nature on the one hand as 'a noble goddesse' and on the other as 'the vicaire of the almyghty Lord'.

The Old English concept *wyrd* may have undergone a similar transformation. Scholars of the present generation are rightly reluctant to accept that when we meet the word in our reading of Christian Old English poetry it has any lingering pagan overtones. Yet the fact that we have texts from the Anglo-Saxon period in which scribes use *wyrd* as a translation of Latin *Fortuna*, 'Fortune', and, in the plural, of *Parcae*, 'the Fates', suggests that it must have seemed to some Anglo-Saxons a reasonable equivalent to these classical female deities of chance and destiny. *Wyrd* is a feminine noun, and though feminine gender grammatically speaking does not necessarily imply feminine personification the use of the word to translate Latin names of goddesses, and the fact that it is cognate with Old Norse *Urðr*, a female of supernatural status who wove the loom of destiny, does suggest a pagan past in which *wyrd* had a similar function, and was similarly personified. The link with weaving persists in casual references. In the *Rhyming Poem* the Anglo-Saxon poet tells us that *wyrd* 'wove' events. In another text *gewefe*, 'web', and *wyrd* are used side by side as alternative translations of *Fortuna*. But by the time we meet any serious comment in Anglo-Saxon writings on the meaning of *wyrd* it is placed, like Mother Earth, firmly within the Christian God's control. King Ælfred reminds us that what we call *wyrd* is the working of God's Providence, and it is clear that if *wyrd* was ever thought to be a goddess of destiny, she has been put in her Christian place by the time we meet her.

We know one, possibly more, of the goddesses of the pagan Anglo-Saxons by name. The first of these gives her name to Friday. The male gods Tiw, Woden and Thunor are responsible for Tuesday, Wednesday and Thursday, but the first element of Friday is the name *Frig*. We know from Scandinavian sources of a goddess Frigg in their mythology, supreme on the female side of the divine hierarchy, wife to Óðinn (Old English Woden). From English sources, however, our sole statement is the one by Ælfric towards the end of the Anglo-Saxon period, contained in his homily *De Falsis Deis*, 'On False Gods'. Frig was seen by Ælfric as the Germanic version of Venus, though he professes to be drawing his information, and is certainly drawing the forms of his names, from contemporary Viking paganism, not from discarded Anglo-Saxon usage. His slight statement is: 'The sixth day they dedicated to the shameless goddess called Venus, and Fricg in Danish'. At an earlier stage in the same homily where he mentions Venus one scribe adds 'Venus in Latin, that is in Danish Fricga'. A recently discovered charter from the reign of Edgar in the second half of the tenth century has the spelling of the place-name Friden (Derbyshire) in the form *Frigedene*, 'the valley of Frig'. This is an important addition to our knowledge, since although certain other place-names with the first element *Fri* (in some spelling) have been thought to contain the goddess's name, we have not previously had the evidence of an early spelling which substantiated this theory. The only other occurrence of the word in Old English at all is in the compound Friday itself, *Frigedæg*, and the words for Thursday evening, *Frige-æfen*, and *Frigeniht*. The common noun *frig* however is a word meaning 'love' in some sense, probably in the sense of sexual intercourse. It is of rare occurrence, but twice in the Old English poem *Christ* the poet says that the Virgin Mary conceived without *friga weres*, 'the love of man'. That the pagan goddess Frig is denounced by Ælfric as 'shameless' suggests that she was associated in his mind more with sexual promiscuity than sanctified conjugal love, but we have no way of knowing whether that is clerical prejudice, inference from classical allusions to Venus, or accurate representation. It is a sad irony that under Christian theology the day of Frig should become instead a day of fasting and abstinence.

None of the pagan gods are represented in the names of the months but it is a possibility that a pagan goddess gave her name to the Anglo-Saxon word for April. There are a number of references to the name *Eastermonað*, 'Eastermonth', and one clear statement that 'the month called in Latin *Aprilis* is in our tongue *eastermonað*'. The word Easter itself is explained by Bede as the name of a goddess, but he is our only authority for this statement and he is writing well after the establishment of Christianity. His statement is that *Eostre* was the goddess whose rites were celebrated in the month of April, and it is difficult to find a convincing alternative explanation for the name *Eostre* though attempts have been made. A related word occurs in some Germanic dialects for the spring festival, and it was certainly normal early Christian practice to adapt and modify pagan ritual. Yet Bede is not an impartial commentator on paganism, nor is his interest an antiquarian one. What he tells us is normally for a specific Christian purpose, and his comments on *Eostre* may be intended rather to draw a contrast between a false goddess of spring and Christ the sun of righteousness. His other pagan goddess who had a month named after her is yet more dubious than *Eostre*. The month of March, according to Bede was called *Hredmonað*, 'Hredmonth', from the goddess Hreda to whom they sacrificed in this month. We have no other evidence at all for the existence of Hreda, and though it is difficult to find an alternative meaning for *Eostre* there is no such difficulty with the element *hred*, which could easily have the sense of 'fierce' or 'rough', referring obviously enough to the well-known March winds. Our evidence for pagan goddesses thus diminishes, but Bede offers us one other interesting comment. The celebration of the old Anglo-Saxon New Year near the time of our Christmas was a feast called *modranect*, which he properly interprets as 'the night of mothers'. He seems not to know anything more about this feast, but darkly conjectures that the name was given because of the ceremonies which took place. There is nothing that we can add to his information, and no point in adding to his conjectures.

The Old English word *god* has its female counterpart *gyden*, but apart from Ælfric's reference to Frig the word is used mostly of classical goddesses, or in general phrases such as 'heathen gods and goddesses'. But on the fringes of Anglo-Saxon paganism there lurked a number of minor supernatural beings. Elves, on the whole deemed to be malevolent to mankind, could be masculine or feminine, *ælf* or *ælfen*. The feminine form is found mainly in translation of the Latin words for various wood or water nymphs. The terminology for giants, dwarfs and monsters consists mostly of masculine nouns, though this obviously does not preclude the concept of female monsters – witness Grendel's mother in *Beowulf*. The poet of *Beowulf* does not, however, give us any very clear description of Grendel's mother, who is called various names such as *brimwylf*, 'water-wolf', *merewif*, 'sea-woman', and *aglæcwif*, 'terrible woman'. She seems to have some affinity with the female trolls of Scandinavian legend, having something akin to human shape. She is less terrifying than her son Grendel, 'just as the power of women, of a war-terrible woman, is less than that of an armed man', and she is urged on to her attack not simply like Grendel, maddened by the sound of human joy, but by the more comprehensible motive of revenge for the death of her son. The poet calls her *ides*, 'lady', which has suggested to some editors and translators that one proper meaning of *ides* is 'hag', but it is much more likely that the poet is using the word ironically to stress the unladylike qualities of his creation. Her fight with Beowulf in the depths of the lake is not noticeable for restraint.

There are other terrible and terrifying supernatural women about whom we know a little more. Old English offers us four interesting words, *wælcyrige*, *wicce*, *hægtesse* and *burgrune*. The first of these is a word better known to us from its Scandinavian form 'valkyrie'. In both Old English and Old Norse the original meaning is the same, 'chooser of the slain', and Norse traditions make it clear that valkyries were employed by Óðinn to select those who should die on battlefields. The existence of the English form must mean that the Anglo-Saxons had once had a similar tradition, and the word itself must have remained readily comprehensible throughout the Anglo-Saxon period since both its elements were in common use. But we never find it used with the supernatural implications of the Old Norse word. When the Anglo-Saxons meet avenging furies or goddesses of battle in their classical reading, *wælcyrige* tends to be the word they find for their translations, but they cannot always have been entirely clear about the relationships between their half-forgotten pagan background and the half-understood classical one they meet in the borrowed cultures of Rome or Greece. Thus *wælcyrige* is the best they can do for the Furies Allecto and Tisiphone. But when the late Anglo-Saxon homilist Wulfstan expresses horror of *wiccan* and *wælcyrigan* he can mean little enough beyond those thought to practise magic, since the phrase occurs in a list of criminals, such as robbers and fornicators, apparently rampant in contemporary Anglo-Saxon society.

There is a real problem in analysing the concepts underlying these words since in the twentieth century we have fairly clear distinctions in our minds between supernatural beings and humans with supernatural powers, between immortal and gifted mortal, devil, for example, and wizard. This distinction does not seem to have been equally clear cut for the Anglo-Saxon mind. Analogous material from Old Norse shows valkyries in some contexts regarded purely as supernatural attendants on Óðinn, in others as women with an ordinary human family background for their unusual activities.

The classical Fates may be old women but they are immortal old women. When Aldhelm uses the word *Pythonissa* he is referring, not to the priestess of Apollo's oracle at Delphi, but to the woman in *Acts* who 'possessed a spirit of divination', *puellam habentem spiritum pythonem*, but was presumably mortal. Furies are as immortal as fiends. King Ælfred in his translation from Boethius may not be sure whether *Parcae* are Fates or Furies, but he is clear that they are *gydene*, 'goddesses'. Yet the two Old English words *wicce* and *hægtesse* which give us the modern derivatives 'witch' and 'hag' are both used by Anglo-Saxon scribes to translate on the one hand the mortal *Pythonissa* and on the other the immortal Fates, the *Parcae*. Either way the words cannot have meant anything as trivial and debased as their modern equivalents. Compounds in -*rune*, *helrune*, *heahrune* and *burgrune* are similarly suggestive and difficult. The element -*rune* is feminine and implies 'one skilled in mysteries'. Thus *Pythonissa* is glossed not only by the words cited above, but also by *heahrune*, implying the chief of those with such skills, and *helrune*, 'one skilled in the mysteries of hell' or 'of death', which in orthodox Christian manner equates heathen-worship with devil-worship or necromancy. But we also meet the word *helrune* in the poem *Beowulf*, where it is used of devilish beings in general, of Grendel and his kind, without obvious implications of sex. The grammatical fact that the compounds in -*rune* are feminine implies perhaps that in pagan times there were priestesses or prophetesses skilled in mysteries, but we are as usual up against the difficulty of how far grammatical gender can be relied on. The word *wicce*, 'witch', is feminine, but except in the nominative singular it is indistinguishable from its masculine equivalent *wicca*. The two words have the same plural form. Such ambiguities blur the pattern for us. *Burgrune* is the most confusing of all. The element *burg* ought to imply 'fortified settlement', 'town' or 'city'. The word *burgrune* never occurs except in translating the two disparate Latin concepts *Furiae*, 'the Furies', and *Parcae*, 'the Fates'. Can we assume that a *burgrune* was originally some kind of temple priestess, or wise woman of a community? It would be rash to draw firm conclusions from such a fine confusion of evidence, but we have at least one enchanting indication of the powers of the *hægtesse* (plural *hægtessan*), a creature far more formidable than any mere 'hag'.

The tenth-century manuscript BL Harley 585 contains the following charm against elf-shot and *hægtesse*-shot.

> Loud were they, loud indeed, when they rode over the hill;
> They were resolute when they rode across the land.
> Shield yourself now; you may escape this attack.
> Out little spear, if it be in here.
> One stood under the linden-wood, under the bright shield
> Where the mighty women organised their powers
> And they sent the yelling spears.
> I intend to send one back to them
> A flying arrow back against them;
> Out little spear, if it be in here.
> A smith sat, he forged a knife.
> Little iron, severe wound.
> Out little spear, if it be in here.
> Six smiths sat; they wrought death-spears.
> Out spear; not in, spear.
> If there be in here any bit of iron,
> The work of a *hægtesse*, it must melt.
> If you were pierced in skin or pierced in flesh
> Or pierced in blood or pierced in limb
> May your life not be torn away.
> If it were shot of the gods or shot of the elves
> Or shot of the *hægtessan* now I will help you.
> This is to cure you of elves' shooting;
> This is to cure you from the shooting of *hægtessan*.
> I will help you. Be whole now. May the Lord help you.

We wisely avoid much speculation about the links between runes and magic, since these have in the past been made far too often and too lightly, but there is no doubt that in both Old Norse and Old English texts the idea occurs that to have power over runes may include some form of supernatural power. In certain miracle stories when Christian prayers are set against heathen magic the references to the latter use some form of *run* or *runstaf*, 'runic letter'. Whether this tells us anything about the powers a *heahrune* or *burgrune* may be thought to possess is less obvious. Tacitus records in his *Germania* that the *Germani*

8 Humility and Hope being holy, wise and unafraid. A detail from Prudentius' *Psychomachia*.

believed 'there is in women an element of holiness and a gift of prophecy: and so they do not scorn to ask their advice or lightly disregard their replies'. We have no evidence that the Anglo-Saxons in general thought of women as having prophetic gifts, but the precarious survival of a word like *heahrune* and the fact that this is used of the Biblical character possessing a spirit of divination, does suggest Anglo-Saxon familiarity with the concept of women who prophesy.

In Bede, our earliest serious document on Anglo-Saxon paganism, pagan priests are mentioned, but never pagan priestesses or prophetesses. Much later when Ælfric rebukes his hearers for heathen practices he addresses himself to people in general, not distinguishing by sex. When he talks about those to whom such superstitious characters go for charms or advice he occasionally specifies a female *wicce*, but there is little evidence that Ælfric considers the practice of heathen magic and superstition a predominantly female activity or that his 'witch' is the stereotyped crone of later literature. When he complains in his homily 'On Auguries' that men are such fools they will bring offerings to 'earthfast stone or tree or well-spring', 'men' is more likely to mean people in

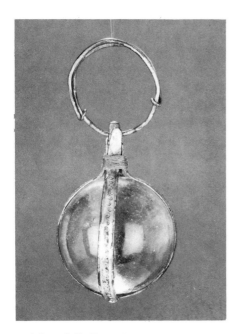 

9 (*above left*) Crystal ball from Chessell Down, Isle of Wight.
10 (*above right*) A beaver's tooth in gold, designed to be worn as a pendant, found among the grave-goods at Wigber Low, Derbyshire.

general than males. Nor does Ælfric offer any indication that stone, tree, or spring were thought to have attendant spirits of either sex, he mentions them merely as inanimate objects 'the dead stone and the dumb tree'. But he has one passage in this homily on the superstitious practices of women in particular, and especially 'witless women'.

He tells us that such women 'go to cross-roads and draw their children through the earth and thus commit their children to the devil'. It is not possible now to recover the significance of such an action to the women who practised it, any more than it is possible to understand exactly what power was attributed to the various charms and amulets found in the grave-goods of an earlier period. Sceptical archaeologists are wary of defining objects as amulets simply because there is no other obvious explanation for their presence among grave-goods, but it does seem quite reasonable to assume that many of the single beads, perforated boar's tusks worn as pendants, crystal balls, and cowrie shells were thought of as having some kind of magical or protective or healing power. This type of object is found in the graves of men, women and children, but mostly in women's graves.

This may, of course, simply mean that women were more superstitious, but it has been suggested that the rock-crystal ball in particular was used in healing rituals and may have symbolised the woman's role as guardian of her family's health. Some wealthy women's graves contain a considerable number of objects of this kind, and it is not impossible that these represent the graves of women who were thought to have, or claimed to have, healing and prophetic powers, and might properly be considered as *burgrunan*, 'wise women of the community'. But there is too much that is speculative here, and as we enter the Christian period we can see clearly how pagan belief degenerates into superstitious practice. Amulets found in graves belong to the pagan period, when graves were furnished; but later literature suggests that they continued to be worn. In the Christian period it was, of course, perfectly respectable to own saintly relics and to attribute to them miraculous powers, and the dividing line between relic and amulet must occasionally have been a difficult one to maintain. Ælfric does, however, put his mind to the problem. In his homily on the Passion of St Bartholomew the Apostle he distinguishes between obtaining one's health from stone or tree and obtaining it from the Holy Cross. Herbs are admissible but only if they are used as medicine not as magic: *Ne sceal nan man mid galdre wyrte besingan*, 'no-one is to sing an incantation over a herb'. In his homily 'On Auguries' he condemns the pernicious habit of devising aphrodisiacs and urges Christian men to shun such *hægtessan* and heathen practices and devil's delusions, offering a neat Christian alliterative conclusion linking the *hægtesse* with both paganism and the devil:

> and forhogian þa hætsan   and ðyllice hæðengyld
> and þæs deofles dydrunga.

He is however writing when Christianity had fully established itself in Anglo-Saxon England, and we cannot tell how much the superstitions he condemns genuinely have their origin in any real pagan belief or practice. There is little other evidence for us to probe concerning the early pagan Anglo-Saxon settlers, their goddesses and lesser female deities, their priestesses or their wise women. When we turn to secular legend to see how these tribes regarded their ordinary mortal women in song and story the material is less elusive.

It is not axiomatic in any period that poetry is composed by men and for men, but we have no evidence for the authorship of most Old English poetry, none at all for that of the secular heroic poetry on which Anglo-Saxons were brought up. References to poets or minstrels in general are to men. In the first century after the settlement there was oral literature only and we can therefore never be quite sure what relation there is between the poetry that was written down after the Conversion, and that which was chanted in hall and at feasting before it. But some continuity there must have been. And since the named characters – men and women – who figure in the early heroic poetry belong not to Anglo-Saxon times, but to a Germanic past, we may assume continuity of interest in such

11. Detail from an illustration in an eleventh-century Psalter to Psalm 45. Verses 9ff. celebrate kings' daughters – seen here in a group lower right: 'And the daughter of Tyre shall be there with a gift...'

people, and some continuity in attitudes to them and the ways in which poetry represents them. Heroic poetry is by nature aristocratic, and will not therefore tell us much about ordinary women and their working lives. Only kings' and chieftains' daughters, wives and sisters are at home in this context.

Superficially, we seem to meet with women of assured status. They wear gold, pour out drink at the feasting, welcome guests, give them gifts. The attractive aspects of the aristocratic life seem similar for lord and lady. Both are ring-givers. In the poem *Beowulf* the queen Wealhðeow honours the hero with magnificent gifts exactly as the king does. In another poem, *Widsið*, which also looks back to a remote past, the poet as it were adopting the persona of a poet, specifically a peripatetic one, says that the king of the Goths gave him a ring of great value. He goes on to say of the queen Ealhild that she too gave him a ring:

> Hyre lof lengde geond londa fela
> þonne ic be songe secgan sceolde
> hwær ic under swegle selast wisse
> goldhrodene cwen giefe bryttian.

'Her glory spread through many lands when I through song had to tell where I knew of a gold-wearing queen distributing gifts.'

The speaker in *The Husband's Message* sends a courteous invitation to his betrothed, a prince's daughter wearing gold, asking her to come to him. He offers her as inducement the fact that he and she together may 'distribute treasure,

35

studded arm-rings to men and comrades'. It is clear that he is offering her the style of giving to which women of her rank were accustomed.

In another kind of poetry traditionally called 'gnomic' we are presented with a series of natural and social platitudes. We learn from them, for example, that masts are found on ships, fish in water and God in Heaven. There are in addition a number of passages which spell out the conventional duties appropriate to a particular sex or status, but there is a problem in translating these. Where the text says *fisc sceal on wætere* it does not make very much difference to the sense whether the verb *sceal* means a fish 'ought' to be in water, or 'it is the nature' of a fish to be in water. It makes a good deal of difference however whether a woman 'ought' to be cheerful, or 'it is the nature' of a woman to be cheerful. It is possible that to the Anglo-Saxon poet this might seem a distinction without a difference. He is, I suppose, describing the woman's behaviour as observed and required in his society.

This gnomic poetry includes one fairly detailed description of the woman's role:

> Cyning sceal mid ceape   cwene gebicgan,
> bunum ond beagum.   Bu sceolon ærest
> geofum god wesan;   guð sceal in eorle
> wig geweaxan,   ond wif geþeon
> leof mid hyre leodum,   leohtmod wesan,
> rune healdan,   rumheort beon
> mearum ond maþmum.   Meodorædenne
> fore gesiðmægen   symle æghwær
> eodor æþelinga   ærest gegretan
> forman fulle   to frean hond,
> ricene geræcan   ond him ræd witan
> boldagendum   bæm ætsomne.

This in my free translation or paraphrase runs:

A king must pay, when he obtains a queen, with cups and with rings. It is proper for both to be generous with gifts. The man of rank is to concentrate on battle, and the woman to thrive, loved by her people; to be cheerful, to preserve knowledge, to be open-hearted in the giving of horses and treasures. At the mead-pouring she will always before a great company first of all greet the ruler of princes with the first cup, present it to the lord's hand; and teach him wisdom for them both together living in that community.

The passage bristles with problems. For example the word I translate 'cheerful' is *leohtmod*, which elsewhere in Old English has a meaning more akin to 'frivolous'. The phrase *rune healdan*, which I think means 'preserve' or 'hand on knowledge', has elsewhere been translated 'keep secrets'. Yet whatever the deficiencies in our understanding of the precise implications, it is clear that the tone here is an admiring and complimentary one. Generosity and wisdom were virtues the Anglo-Saxons esteemed highly. It is also clear that this view of a woman's role is male-centred. She is seen in relation to her lord, to her lord's male companions, his military retinue. The generosity is male-directed. The only phrase that suggests there is a world outside the lord and retainer group is 'loved by her people'. That she had a family or household part to play is not in evidence. Yet the reiterated emphasis on wisdom and advice suggests that she was valued for more than the decorative and ritual role implied by the rest of the passage.

Much Old English poetry is concerned with the vulnerability of the individual, whether this is a man who has lost his lord, an exile, a poet out of favour, a woman separated from her husband, or some other unfortunate. Heroic poetry in particular is much concerned with the vulnerability of the woman cast in the role of *freóðuwebbe*, 'peace-weaver', where it is hoped that a peace-settlement between two hostile tribes or families may be made firmer by a marriage-bond. The emphasis is on the isolation of such an individual in a society where the protection of her own family has been replaced by the dislike and distrust of those in her new environment.

It is Beowulf himself in the poem of that name who most clearly outlines the probable fate of a woman married into a hostile tribe in the hope that her marriage will avert further hostility. He describes a situation where the very presence of a bride and her family attendants serves to stir up the old hatreds and resentments. Thus a woman whose role was designed as that of 'peace-weaver' may find that her mere and innocent presence is a spur to the renewal of hostilities. In such hostilities her situation is normally both passive and pitiable. On the one side will be her husband and any children she may have borne him. On the other will be the kinsmen of her family by blood, her father and her brothers. Wherever her primary loyalties lie, the end result cannot be other than grief for the dead on both sides.

It is, of course, not only women who are caught up in the dilemma of conflicting loyalties, for this dilemma was one explored over and over again by Anglo-Saxon poets, and even occasionally by writers of chronicles. Usually, however, the men seem to be in the more favourable position of being able to make a firm decision: 'They said that no kinsman was dearer to them than their lord and they would never follow his killer' is the clear-cut statement of one group of men reported in the *Anglo-Saxon Chronicle* as having to choose between loyalty to kin and loyalty to lord. The only decision that Hildeburg, the unhappy woman of the Finnsburh episode in *Beowulf*, can make is after her son and her brother have been killed fighting on opposing sides:

> Het þa Hildeburh æt Hnæfes ade
> hire selfre sunu sweoloðe befæstan
> banfatu bærnan ond on bæl don
> eame on eaxle.

'Then Hildeburg commanded her own son to be committed to the flame, his body to burn on Hnæf's funeral pyre, to be placed on that pyre by the shoulder of his uncle his mother's brother.'

37

She can mourn the dead together though she could not prevent their hostility when alive. Her future after this seems purely passive; her kin eventually carry her back, together with vast amounts of treasure taken from her dead husband's home. For them there may be a sense of achievement, but for her the prospects seem bleak enough.

Such a story would not have seemed to the Anglo-Saxon audience the stuff of legend only. Bede in his *Historia Ecclesiastica* gives us enough material to piece together the unhappy history of Osðryð in the late seventh century. We should note, however, that he does not tell it as a consecutive story and his compassion is not – unlike the *Beowulf* poet's – focused on the tragic dilemma of a woman who was ineffectual in the role of 'peace-weaver'. Osðryð, sister of Ecgfrið of Northumbria, was married to Æðelræd of the Mercians. In the Battle of the Trent fought between these two peoples in 679 her brother Ælfwine was killed. Bede tells us that he was only eighteen and that he was much loved by the people of both kingdoms, which suggests that he had spent a good deal of time with his sister and brother-in-law, perhaps trying to strengthen the fragile peace. Eddius, who in his *Life of St Wilfrid* gave both Ecgfrið and Ælfwine the title of 'most Christian kings', implying that young Ælfwine was co-ruler with or sub-ruler to his brother, describes the bitter lamentation in York when the body of the dead Ælfwine was carried home, but has no word of the sister's griefs or loyalties. Bede at the end of his work claims to recapitulate events already dealt with, but in fact informs us laconically for the first time under the year 697 'Queen Osðryð was murdered by her own nobles, that is of the Mercians'. Seven years later her husband retired to a monastery.

## FURTHER READING

General works on Roman Britain tend to be uninformative about Romano-British women, but *The Welsh Law of Women*, ed. JENKINS AND OWEN contains useful analogous material on the Celtic situation. Major Latin sources: for Bede (text and translation) see under COLGRAVE, for Nennius (text and translation) under MORRIS, for Aldhelm, text under EHWALD, translation under LAPIDGE. Major Old English sources: the *Anglo-Saxon Chronicle* is edited by EARLE AND PLUMMER, translated by GARMONSWAY and WHITELOCK. Most poems are in the Everyman *Anglo-Saxon Poetry*, translated by BRADLEY and much of the prose is in the Everyman *Anglo-Saxon Prose*, translated by SWANTON. The best text of *Beowulf* is by KLÆBER, of the poems of the *Exeter Book* in the Early English Text Society volumes by GOLLANCZ AND MACKIE. Charms and remedies are edited by COCKAYNE, and there are useful general books on Anglo-Saxon superstitions by MEANEY, *Anglo-Saxon Amulets and Curing Stones*; and OWEN, *Rites and Religions of the Anglo-Saxons*. I have an introductory chapter on mythology in *The Northern World*, ed. WILSON. The new Edgar charter is being published by BROOKS, GELLING AND JOHNSON.

# 2. Daily Life

The daily life of any woman in Anglo-Saxon England would largely be dictated by the class of society into which she was born, though some women may have married or been sold into other classes. Penal servitude was one way in which women of free status might find themselves relegated to unfree, and in times of bad harvests free-born children may have been sold into slavery as a preferable alternative to starvation. Regional and period differences may also have had a bearing on women's activities, and the cosmopolitan society of tenth- and eleventh-century Northumbria was probably less stable in its class distinctions than eighth-century Kent. Money, then as now, may have made for distinctions between classes, but would also have made a difference to the degree of hardship or comfort within them. Differences between rural and urban society may not have been as pronounced as in some cultures, but must have existed. It is not difficult to get some idea of the public activities of wealthy and high-ranking women, though even there, whether in convent or in court, it is not always easy to get a picture of the day-to-day routine patterns of existence. With women of the lower classes the routine patterns are all we can hope to glimpse, but since they are not the stuff of chronicles, legend or public record, evidence is hard to come by.

The ordinary words for woman in Old English are *wif*, 'wife' or 'woman', its compound *wifman* which gives us the Modern English word 'woman', and *cwen/cwene* from which we derive 'queen' and the obsolete or dialectal 'quean'. *Wif*, which is the most common, occurring regularly in such phrases as *weras and wifas*, 'men and women', is obscure in origin, not present, for example, in the earliest known form of the Germanic languages, Gothic. It could be etymologically connected with the words for 'weaving' and this would certainly make good sense in so far as the duties of cloth-making seem to be the ones most consistently linked with the feminine role. The contrasting male connotation is 'weaponed' and the alliterating phrase *wæpman and wifman* (in singular and plural forms) is almost as common as *wer and wif*. Boys and girls are sometimes distinguished as *wæpnedbearn* or *wifcild*, and wills and charters occasionally specify whether property is to go to the male or female line of the family distinguishing between *wæpnedhand*, *sperehand*, *wæpnedhealf* or *sperehealf*, and *wifhand*, *wifhealf* or *spinelhealf*. Whether the element *wif* links with 'weaving'

12 Two ivory pin-beaters
from Faversham, Kent, and a
decorated spindle-whorl from
Whitby.

or not, *spinel* certainly links with spinning, and these terms suggest that in the
early stages of their culture Anglo-Saxons distinguished male and female roles
as those of the warrior or hunter and of the cloth-maker. Such distinctions persist
up to a point in the general picture we gain of their society. It places a good
deal of emphasis on the fighting qualities of the male, and many glimpses that
we get of great ladies show them at the occupations of weaving, spinning or
embroidery. As the *Exeter* gnome has it: '*Fæmne æt hyre bordan geriseð*' ('The
place of a woman is at her embroidery'). Grave-goods are abundant but
sometimes hard to interpret. So-called thread-boxes made of bronze are found
in seventh-century Anglo-Saxon women's graves, and these contain thread,
sometimes pieces of cloth, and sometimes needles. They have been called
variously sewing-kits, herbal-kits, and relic-boxes. The bits of cloth in them are
sometimes of high quality but too small to have been of much practical use, and
their inclusion among the grave-goods may have been as a record of the owner's
skills or symbolic of her household role. Spindle-whorls are another common
feature in women's graves. Clay ones are normal, but some beads of glass or
faceted crystal have also been thought to be spindle-whorls possibly belonging
to richer women or those of higher rank. Weaving-batons are also found. Those
that survive are of iron and presumably were an indication of wealth since the
ones normally in use must far more commonly have been made of wood, like
some preserved in waterlogged contexts on the Continent. But clearly the regular
presence of thread-boxes, spindle-whorls and weaving-batons in female graves
indicates a strong link in the culture between women and cloth-production.

The range of activities involved in cloth-making might up to a point have been
distinguished by class, simple weaving and spinning presumably having few
associations with status, whereas the production or elaboration of sophisticated
textiles involving the use of more expensive materials would usually be carried
out by those who had both the leisure and the money to devote to non-basic
skills. The distinction would, however, be unlikely to be preserved in a complex

and rich civilisation where both fine secular garments and elaborate church vestments were required in quantity, and women in control of large households obviously would want slaves to be trained in fine work of this kind. In the household of a free-born woman of *ceorl* status we may assume that cloth-making was a simple matter of keeping the household adequately clothed, with the main emphasis on durability and warmth in the garments produced. In the household of large estate-owners – many of whom were women – though the mistress of the house and her daughters and other women of her family may have prided themselves on the quality of work they could produce, whether for personal adornment or as gifts to churches and churchmen, they would also have the unfree women of their household trained in these skills. Who took the credit for the work finally produced may be left to conjecture.

Wynflæd in her will of the tenth century bequeathed two female slaves to Eadgifu her granddaughter. These are *ane crencestre and ane semestre*. The word *crencestre* occurs only here, but the first element *crenc* links with other words used in cloth-manufacture, and the *semestre* was a woman with sewing or embroidery skills. We cannot recover the meanings more precisely than this, and the *crencestre* may have had quite specific tasks distinct from those of the ordinary weaver.

The termination of a word in Old English in -*stere* usually represents a feminine occupational suffix and these words, not always present in Old English contexts, sometimes survive as occupational surnames or common nouns into Middle and Modern English. The word 'spinster' in the sense of 'one who spins' is first found in Middle English but presumably derives from a non-recorded Old English form. A group of such words link with the production of cloth. The Modern English nouns 'seamster' and 'spinster' originally referred to women responsible for embroidery and spinning. The surnames Webster, Folster (OE *fullestre*), Dyster and Lister referred respectively to the processes of weaving, fulling and dying cloth. It is obvious that as the grammatical forms of Old English came to be used with less precision these words would also describe men engaged in these occupations, and even as early as the eleventh-century will of Ælfric the word *seamestre* appears to be used of a male tailor, just as an eleventh-century manumission refers to a man as *Liueger se bacestre* (baker). But it is equally obvious that a group of words of this kind originally represented a connection between women and the various skills of cloth production.

That the mistress of the house could be the supervisor of such work as well as engage in it herself is implied by the statement in the *Liber Eliensis* that the lady Æðelswið in the eleventh century, rejecting the idea of marriage, retired to Coveney and with her *puellulae* spent her time at embroidery with gold thread and at weaving. Four named pieces of work are all priestly vestments. The white chasuble that she made with extraordinary skill with her own hands and at her own expense is singled out for specific comment. A white headband beautifully embroidered is mentioned later in the inventory of Ely's possessions as having been made by her, and is listed among a number of other headbands (*infulae*) where the giver rather than the maker is usually specified. The fact that the writer bothers to comment on something made 'with her own hands' implies perhaps that most of the work was done by or expected to be done by the *puellulae*. I am at a loss to know what this diminutive signifies. Translations usually say that she retired with her 'maidens' but whether we should consider these to be girls of free or unfree status is not clear. The diminutive may be indicative of rank. A charter of 814 from Denewulf Bishop of Worcester grants land (over two hundred acres) to a woman called Eanswið on the condition that she mends, cleans and adds to Worcester's ecclesiastical vestments. Whether this refers solely to altar-cloths and hangings or whether it includes ceremonial garments is not evident, but for a church the size of Worcester no one woman could have coped with such a major undertaking. It was obviously a requirement from the whole household, as other estates were required to pay rent in goods. Two of the entries in the Domesday survey give us very similar insights. In the Wiltshire record there is a good estate of moderate size described at Knook:

Leofgyð holds Knook. Her husband held it before 1066; it paid tax for $3\frac{1}{2}$ hides. Land for $2\frac{1}{2}$ ploughs, which are there, with 1 slave; 4 villagers and 4 smallholders. A mill which pays 15 shillings; meadow 5 acres; pasture $\frac{1}{2}$ league long and 1 furlong wide. Value £3. Leofgyð made and makes gold-thread embroidery for the king and queen (*aurifrisium regis et reginae*).

It looks as if Leofgyð's husband died fighting on the wrong side at Hastings but this has clearly not affected her status as employee. On the other hand a £4 estate at Swindon has apparently been forfeited: 'Leofgyð held it before 1066'. At Oakley in Buckinghamshire there were two hides of land held before 1066 by Ælfgyð *puella*, 'a girl'. *Puella* must imply that she was both young and unmarried. 'These hides she could grant or sell to whom she would, and from King Edward's household revenue she had $\frac{1}{2}$ hide herself which Godric the Sheriff assigned to her for as long as he should be Sheriff, so that she might teach his daughter gold-thread embroidery work'. Clearly such skills were highly valued and the craftswoman well paid. The tradition survives into late Middle English. In the poem *Piers Plowman* some women are assigned the coarse job of sewing sacks for the wheat, wives and widows are advised to spin wool and flax, but:

> Ye, lovely ladies, with your long fingers
> That ye have silk and sendal to sow when time is,
> Chasubles for chaplains, churches to honour.

There are two texts in particular which give us some slight assistance in determining both the household needs in the way of equipment for cloth-making, and some of the general finished products that would be required. The Old

English word for the man in charge of an estate is *gerefa* ('reeve') and the account of the duties of the *gescadwis gerefa*, 'the discriminating reeve', is preserved in a manuscript collection of legal texts. Among the descriptions of the various matters a reeve must supervise are several involving the growing of plants for making and dying cloth. *On længtene...mederan settan, linsed sawan, wadsæd eacswa* ('in spring...set madder, sow linseed and woadseed too'). Linseed, the seed of the flax plant, is required for the making of linen; madder and woad provide respectively red and blue dye. In autumn the woad requires further attention: *on hærfeste...wad spittan*, an activity which evidently required a special tool since a *wadspitel* is subsequently referred to as a necessary piece of gardening equipment. The words *spittan* and *spitel* are clearly used of some process and implement in the harvesting or preparation of woad, but are not precise enough for us to recover very easily their exact meaning in this context. It is however obvious that the woad, flax and madder harvests were of considerable importance.

Also in this text are two lists of household or general equipment needed on an estate. The first includes the following section: 'and fela towtola; flexlinan, spinle, reol, gearnwindan, stodlan, lorgas, presse, pihten, timplean, wifte, wefle, wulcamb, cip, amb, crancstæf, sceaðele, seamsticcan, scearra, nædle, slic'. It is not possible to produce an accurate translation of all the words in this list: *and fela towtola* which begins the section might literally mean 'and many flax-spinning or linen-working utensils', but since a number of the objects cited are used in weaving not spinning, such a translation does not accurately reflect the contents of the subsequent list. An alternative, less exact, rendering might be 'many objects used in cloth-production'. Some of the objects are clear enough, even to us. A *spinle* is evidently a 'spindle' and *nædle* a 'needle'. The Anglo-Saxons distinguished between a *gearnwinda* and a *reol*, a 'yarn-winder' and a 'reel'. *Scearra*, 'shears', have been mentioned before in the total list, but here obviously refer to ones used in cutting cloth. Different types of comb are carefully distinguished. *Wulcamb* is obviously to be translated 'wool-comb', and these were used to comb the fibres before they were spun. It has been suggested that we have evidence of wool-comb warmers from a site in Essex. Heating the combs would melt the lanolin and make the process less arduous. *Pihten* is also a comb, but one that was used in the actual weaving. The loom itself is not named as an entity but various parts of it are named. *Stodlan*, for example, may refer to the side-posts of a warp-weighted loom, and we have evidence for the use of these in Anglo-Saxon England from the number of loom-weights that are found on settlement sites. The *crancstæf* may have been the object that Wynflæd's *crencestre* was skilled in using, but whether the translation 'distaff' is possible, or whether it refers to some other part of the cloth-making process is less clear. We would expect *presse* to have something akin to its modern meaning of 'cupboard, clothes-press', but we have no archaeological or pictorial evidence

13 In this illustration to Psalm 62 the curtains and furnishings presumably reflect Anglo-Saxon ecclesiastical usage.

for such an object at this period, and it is uncertain what else the word might refer to. Perhaps it was a tool for smoothing and pressing cloth. Yet our inability to make total contact with the words on this list, or to be sure at any point what known weaving processes they relate to, need not obscure the cumulative importance of such a detailed collection. The compiler of the manuscript, the moment he thinks of cloth-making, and whether or not he personally had a precise understanding of the processes involved, instantly produces a list of twenty objects which the work-room must be equipped with. He may have missed some out. His lists elsewhere are not noticeably comprehensive.

A second list of useful equipment later in the same text includes various types of chest, *cyst* and *myderce*, for storing clothes or other goods. Wynflæd leaves to Eadwold (probably her grandson) two chests, *mydercan*, 'and in them a set of bed-clothes, all that is needed for one bed'. To her granddaughter Eadgifu she also leaves two *mydercan* 'and in them her best bed-curtain [?] and a linen cover and all the bed-clothes which belong to it'. Other chests are in the household in plenty. There are two large chests and a *hrægleyst*, which may be a clothes-chest, but *hrægl* is used also of soft furnishings; there is also a *towmyderce* which may contain any kind of weaving or spinning equipment, and perhaps is something as vague as 'work-box'; and there are two old chests.

Wynflæd's will is not the only one which specifies this kind of bequest and it is clear that the soft furnishings of the wealthy household would have filled any number of chests. Bed-clothes, table-linen, seat-covers and wall-hangings are specified. They are more normally mentioned in the wills of women than of men and it is in particular in the wills of three women, Wynflæd, Wulfwaru and Æðelgifu that we get the fullest indication of range. Æðelgifu, whose will survives in a tenth-century manuscript, specified that her best wall-hanging and seat-cover were to be given to the foundation at St Alban's, but in a later paragraph of her will the other household furnishings are distributed among kin or women of the household. Wulfwyn received a wall-hanging, a seat-cover and all the best bedsteads; Leofsige was to have 'three wall-hangings, the best of those that are left', two seat-covers and two bedsteads. Godwif and Ælfgifu each get two chests, but their contents are not specified. Wulfwaru left wall-hangings and bed-linen to one son, wall-hangings and table-linen to another.

The absence of such provision in men's wills does not reflect an absence of interest in the bequests of comparatively small items of personal property including personal clothing. One bishop's will specifies who is to inherit his various elaborate chasubles: 'and I grant to Odgar the yellow chasuble that I bought in Pavia'. A man called Æðelwold specified who was to inherit each of his two fur robes. But it is clear that the bed-covers, table-linen and wall-hangings which were made by the women of the household were also up to a point thought of as female property. What is surprising about some of the bequests is the leaving of a single object to the household women in common. Wynflæd's will contains the curious provision 'and there are also wall-hangings, one of which is worthy of [Æðelflæd], and she can give away the smallest [or least in value?] to her women'. Wulfwaru similarly grants to all her household women in common 'one good chest, well-decorated'. It is, of course, possible that the women were entitled to sell the object and share its value, but the alternative suggestion of a community in which these bequests were intended to enhance the comfort or luxury of the women's quarters cannot be ruled out.

Bequests of clothing which are a fairly common feature of both men's and women's wills tend to refer to the more cherished garments. No-one for example specifies shoes or gloves in bequests. There is not a lot of evidence on the extent to which gloves were made or worn, and shoes would on the whole be the product of a specific craftsman. Women may have occasionally worked with leather, but we have no evidence for any other than the male leather-worker at this period, and the man called the 'shoe-maker' would have been involved in the general production of leather-work, not of shoes only. This aspect of clothing the household was not the woman's prerogative or burden, as far as we can tell.

The general non-survival of textiles means that we have very little tangible evidence of the ordinary household furnishings. Such as do survive tend to be scraps from grave-goods or occasional elaborate pieces, such as the beautiful tenth-century embroidery preserved in St Cuðbert's tomb. Grave-goods from Viking-Age Norway include wall-hangings, but the earliest one from England is the post-Conquest Bayeux tapestry. This may reflect the type and style of wall-hanging made earlier in Anglo-Saxon England in its range of colours, type of subject, and method of production. The colours, though now partially faded, show the kind of muted effects produced by vegetable dyes. The method of production is wool embroidery on a linen background. The subjects of such hangings may well have been events in which ancestors or near kin were thought to have played a glorious role. The East-Saxon leader Byrhtnoð was killed at Maldon in 991. His defeat and death form the basis of a heroic poem, 'The Battle of Maldon', but we are told also in the *Liber Eliensis* that his widow gave a wall-hanging depicting his deeds to Ely in his memory.

The literary evidence indicates that wall-hangings in Anglo-Saxon England were produced in great numbers and must have added considerably to the cheerfulness of the accommodation. Whether seat-covers were merely strips of cloth or some form of cushioning is not evident, though one of the sections of the Bayeux tapestry shows a covered seat which has been described as 'cushioned'. Another section perhaps gives us a sketchy idea of what contemporary bed-hangings looked like, though it must be remembered that late-eleventh-century pictorial evidence is not necessarily a good guide to the Anglo-Saxon period as a whole. We have no evidence at all that I know of for the design of Anglo-Saxon table-cloths, though doubtless these were as much advertisements of high-quality skills as any other work. An attractive eleventh-century drawing of an Anglo-Saxon party, however, does actually show one in use.

The other main area of household activity in which we would expect women to be involved is in the preparation and provision of food but here we have so little actual evidence of any kind that such an assumption requires a good deal of qualification. Textual reference to the preparation of food is meagre. Grinding of meal in a secular society appears to have been the work of female slaves. The

14 King Edward cushioned and curtained on the Bayeux tapestry.

15 A table-cloth elegantly draped.

early laws óf Æðelbert of Kent make it clear that the king's grinding-slave is not among thosc least valued. If a man lies with a virgin who is the king's property, compensation is fifty shillings; if she is a grinding-slave it is twenty-five shillings; if she is of the third class (whatever that is) it is twelve shillings. An eleventh-century manuscript contains a charter reference to a mill where *sume þare munecena comon to grindanne*, 'some of the nuns used to come to do their grinding', though it is doubtful even in a monastery or nunnery to what extent such chores would be shared in the community and to what extent class distinctions would still be operative. Among the *Rectitudines*, a text that specifies rights and duties of estate workers, there is only one woman named among the male workers, the swine-herd, ox-herd, forester, and so on, and she is the cheese-maker. Her state is as follows:

Cys-wyrhtan gebyreð hundred cyse, and þæt heo of wringhwæge buteran macige to hlafordes beode; and hæbbe hire ða syringe ealle butan þæs hyrdes dæle.

'The cheese-maker is entitled to a hundred cheeses, and is to make butter for the lord's table from the whey (whey-cream, perhaps?); and she is to have all the buttermilk except for the herdsman's share.'

A slave is named in a manumission as *Leofgifu þa dægean*, 'Leofgifu the dairy-maid', and an unnamed *dæge* is among the slaves singled out as a useful bequest in Æðelgifu's will. In one of the riddles of the *Exeter Book*, however, churning butter seems to be a male servant's task, and on large estates, where pressures of time and weather would mean that men and women shared generally in many tasks as they needed to be done, it is improbable that jobs were rigidly allocated according to sex. The reeve of the *Gerefa* text who worries about getting everything right for his *hlaford* (who is just as likely to have been female as male) does not at any point say who is to do the various jobs, he simply lists by season what is required to be done. When the weather is unfit for fieldwork there are other things that one can get on with: 'put up buildings...pull up weeds...make tables and benches...clean floors, or whatever else might be useful'. It is likely that women as well as young boys and girls would be involved in any tasks (such as weeding or cleaning floors) that did not demand maximum physical strength. The reeve does not at any point specify who does the cooking or even that there is cooking to be done, though he has a list of kitchen equipment. He does, however, imply that he has personal control over the kitchen economy, an area that we might have been inclined to assume was the housewife's domain. Nothing must go wrong in so far as he can prevent it, 'not meat or fat, cheese or rennet'. The food supplies under his control from the estate – apart from the obvious grain, meat and dairy products – include vegetables, beans and grapes. Broad-beans were an important item, especially during Lent. *Rectitudines* specifies the minimum supplies that a female slave was entitled to:

VIII pund cornes to mete, I sceap oððe III peningas to wintersufle, I syster beana to længtensufle, hwæig on sumera oððe I pening.

'Eight pounds of corn for food, one sheep or three pennies for winter provision, one sester of beans for spring provision, whey or one penny in summer.'

This is less than the comparable provision for the male slave, but we are reminded several times in the text that there were a number of traditional privileges – including Christmas and Easter and harvest bonuses – although these varied in detail from estate to estate. One such list of privileges occurs in the paragraph after the one listing basic supplies for a female slave. Both the *Rectitudines* and the *Gerefa* texts make it very clear that anyone involved in estate management was obliged to think not only of duty to the lord but also of the traditional rights of the people on that estate, in that part of the country.

The question of who did the cooking is one that is dealt with at some length in a document commonly called Ælfric's *Colloquy*. This is basically a work of fiction intended to assist pupils in their learning of Latin. It purports to be a conversation among a number of craftsmen and was composed in the early part of the eleventh century. The original Latin text has been furnished with an Old English gloss. All the speakers are apparently male, and in a monastery it would be normal for provision of food to be handled by men, but the 'craftsmen' do not appear to be talking about work within the confines of monastic life. The speakers concerned with food are the salter, the baker and the cook. The master who is asking questions of the others interestingly inquires whether society actually needs the cook. The pupil in the role of 'cook' has the answer that without him you will find yourself eating raw meat, raw vegetables, and deprived of good soup. The master's answer is that this is scarcely an 'art' since 'we can boil the things that need boiling and roast the things that need roasting for ourselves'. The old English word *seoþan*, 'boil', translates the more general Latin *coquere*, and though *brædan* here translates *assare*, 'to roast', it is elsewhere used in Old English to translate Latin verbs with the more general meaning of 'to warm'; sophisticated culinary processes are not implied by either word.

This is the only occasion in the *Colloquy* where a statement of this kind is made and I think it throws a good deal of light on contemporary attitudes. Ordinary preparation of food was apparently not considered as requiring particular skills, and it seems quite likely that in the general economy it was the job of anyone who either had time to spare from other duties or was too infirm for more strenuous activities. The 'cook's' answer in Ælfric's *Colloquy* is, significantly, not a defence of his skill, but a defence of the class system: 'If you drive me out, so that you may do that [i.e. prepare the food yourselves] you will all be slaves and none of you be lord'. Old English *coc* is a masculine noun and I know of no feminine equivalent. Wynflæd bequeathes in her will to Eadgifu her granddaughter a number of slaves including *Ælfsige þene coc*, ' Ælfsige the cook'. Ælfsige is a masculine personal name.

Old English has both masculine and feminine nouns for bakers, *bæcere* and *bæcestre* both presumably in fairly common use, surviving in the occupational surnames Baker and Baxter. Again in an area which we might have expected to be female-dominated this is not the case, and the *bæcere* of Ælfric's *Colloquy* is clearly describing a secular not merely a monastic situation when he says without his craft every table would look empty, and that his products are not only strengthening for men, nor do the little ones, *litlincgas*, despise them. The woman who in one of the riddles of the *Exeter Book* is apparently making dough is the only indication we have of a woman specifically involved in this range of domestic work, though we have already noted the grammatically feminine *bacestere* used of a man in an Exeter manumission (p. 41).

It is customary to assume that Anglo-Saxon women were associated with both the serving and the preparation of drink. The evidence for the two activities is of different kinds. There survive as surnames a group of words with the feminine occupational suffix connected with brewing and serving ale in Brewster, Malster, and Tapster. Middle English literature tends to give us merry pictures of women who ran ale-houses, but we have none such from Anglo-Saxon England, and no evidence that I know of that brewing was thought of as a particularly feminine domestic skill. The reeve of the *Gerefa* text was concerned about the growing of vines, and insisted moreover that kitchen equipment should include a *beorbyden*, a vessel for holding strong drink (not beer, probably fruit wine). Vast quantities of ale were produced and needed in all households but we have no surviving description of who did the actual work. The serving of drink on the other hand is documented in all formal heroic poetry as the duty not merely of the 'woman', but of the 'lady'. In *Beowulf* it is the queen herself, not a serving woman, who offers the cup to her husband and her guest. There are plenty of similar depictions. Bede gives us an attractive picture of a woman serving drink in a context where it looks more like ordinary domestic hospitality than the formal ceremonial of the heroic poetry. The wife of a nobleman having been cured of an illness 'brought the cup to the bishop and to the rest of us, and continued to serve us all with drink until dinner was finished'. Early laws, however, while still implying that the pourer of drink is female, indicate that a man might have a woman other than his wife fulfilling the role of 'cup-bearer'. The seventh-century law of Æðelbert refers to female slaves or servants with the office of *byrele*, 'cup-bearer'. The *byrele* of an *eorl* was of somewhat higher value than the *byrele* of a *ceorl*, and it is certainly worthy of note that the *ceorl*, the lowest-ranking free farmer, was considered to be a man whose household boasted a cup-bearer. But Bishop Ælfric in the eleventh century, who, as we have already noted, had a male tailor, was served also by a male cup-bearer, Æðelric, to whom he left four pounds in his will.

Single-sex monasteries and nunneries may to some extent have made it difficult to persist in upholding simple distinctions about the duties pertaining to the male or female role, if indeed such existed, even though a fair amount of work for such communities was presumably done by both men and women of lay status. It is clear that the kitchens of monasteries were run by men, perhaps the gardens of nunneries by women. One particular area in which monastic skills may have altered habitual modes of thought is in healing. The compilers of the *lœcedomas*, the collections of medical advice in various manuscripts, may have been monks though it is by no means impossible that they include literate or learned seculars. One important text surviving in a mid-tenth-century manuscript has a number of masculine names associated with it. Bald was apparently the owner, Cild the scribe. There are various references in the manuscript to sources, some written, some apparently oral. The phrase *Oxa lœrde þisne lœcedom*, 'Oxa taught [us] this cure', probably refers to teaching by word of mouth. Elsewhere the scribe uses the phrase *gewritu eac secgeaþ*, 'also writings say', implying a range of reading. One complex passage ends with the words *þis eal het þus secgean ælfrede cyninge domne helias patriarcha on gerusalem*, 'Dominus Helias, patriarch at Jerusalem, ordered all this to be said to King Ælfred'. It is possible to see a considerable influence on these writings from known Greek and Latin medical texts that were in circulation; but it is also clear that the Old English is by no means a simple series of translation and copying exercises, and that it includes a lot of practical and local knowledge. Even the frequent use of such phrases as *englisc hunig*, 'English honey', *englisc moru*, 'English root', perhaps parsnip, *wealisc ealu*, 'Welsh ale', and *englisce gewyrta*, 'English herbs', indicates a tradition of healing-patterns outside the classical ones. The remedies themselves are all directed towards a totally anonymous and unnamed person practising the art of healer, that is to say it is impossible to tell whether they are directed at a man or a woman, or indeed at the general reader. Some of the remedies require surgery, but most of them are simple matters of producing herb drinks or ointments. Anyone in the kitchen could have managed *Wið bryne: wad gecnua, wyl on buteran, smire mid*, 'for a burn pound up woad, boil it in butter, and smear it on'. Similarly anyone suffering from earache could probably have coped with his or her own cure if all it involved was to take garlic, onion, goose-fat, melt them together and squeeze into the ear. But many of the cures are more complicated and would require someone trained in their knowledge and application. How widely such remedies as these were used is impossible to tell.

One remedy in Bald's manuscript contains careful and sensible instructions on the capacity of different bodies to bear surgery, distinguishing between the bodies of man, woman and child, of the manual and sedentary worker, of the old and the young: *Micel gedal is on wæpnedes and wifes and cildes lichoman*, 'there is a great difference between the bodies of man, woman and child'. Other remedies deal specifically with female medical matters. A long passage on what to do if the woman's monthly bleeding has stopped need not be interpreted as an attempt at abortion, but is more likely to be a medical response to malnutrition. It is a perfectly sensible list of practical matters such as warm baths, warm poultices and hot herb drinks, the herbs being fairly rich in iron content. The following eminently rational advice is offered to pregnant women:

Georne is to wyrnanne bearneacnum wife þæt hio aht sealtes ete oððe swetes oþþe beor drince; ne swines flæsc ete ne naht fætes; ne druncen gedrince, ne on weg ne fere; ne on horse to swiðe ride þy læs þæt bearn of hire sie ær riht tide.

'A pregnant woman ought to be fully warned against eating anything too salt or too sweet, and against drinking strong alcohol: also against pork and fatty foods; also against drinking to the point of drunkenness, also against travelling; also against too much riding on horseback lest the child is born before the right time.'

Not all the advice in this medical manuscript is equally sensible. Some of it is nonsense, and some of it is superstition. The advice that a woman may hope to conceive a child if she binds twelve grains of coriander seed to her left thigh clearly falls into the second category. But many of the herbs used were still being used by, for example, Culpeper in the seventeenth century and for similar cures, though Culpeper argues for the various properties of each herb in a more scholarly manner than the Anglo-Saxon text. His statement for example that

16 Pride depicted as a woman (*ventosa virago*) riding recklessly. In Anglo-Saxon manuscripts of the Latin text *Psychomachia* by Prudentius which describes battles between Vices and Virtues, all equally personified as feminine, the distinguishing feature of the illustrations is that Vices are shown unveiled.

woad 'cools inflammation' and 'takes away...fretting humours' shows quite clearly why the Anglo-Saxons used it in the treatment of burns.

There are in the other Anglo-Saxon medical compilations a range of cures for various female ailments, some of them taken direct from classical sources, others apparently pure folklore. From Apuleius is translated the advice *wið tittia sar*

17 A remedy against the bite of poisonous spiders, *wiþ attor coppan bite*, appropriately illustrated.

*wifa*, 'for painful breasts'; from Sextus Placitus comes the cosmetic invitation to use ivory pounded with honey as a facial treatment for removing blemishes. A collection of recipes from no known source contains several charms including the following for a woman who regularly suffers from miscarriages. Since the verse form is normal English, the content is more likely to represent native than classical superstition:

...and þonne þæt wif seo mid bearne and heo to hyre hlaforde on reste ga þonne cweþe heo

> up ic gonge
> ofer þe stæppe
> mid cwican cilde
> nalæs mid cwellendum
> mid fulborenum
> nalæs mid fægan.

'and when the woman is pregnant and goes to her husband's bed she is to say

> I go upward
> Step over you
> With a living child
> Not a dying one
> One which will come to full term
> Not one which is doomed.'

It is also suggested that she may take part of her child's grave, wrap it in black wool, and sell it to merchants. Why anyone should be prepared to buy this remains a mystery, but it is clear that these charms may well have had beneficial psychological effects.

The medical texts cover a depressingly wide range of ailments that must have affected all members of society. There are the common ones such as earache, toothache, headache and so on, and a number of others where it is more difficult to be sure of the precise meaning of the Old English words. *Circuladl*, 'the circle disease', is no doubt shingles. A number of salves for wounds and burns remind us of the commonplace hazards. One, for example, distinguishes with careful precision three different types of herbal ointment to be used for (1) burns, (2) scalds, and (3) sunburn. The frequent sensible suggestions for getting rid of lice and various other parasites, making use of astringent herbs such as wormwood, remind us also of the general hygiene problems that both men and women would constantly need to cope with. Frequent remedies for pain of various kinds, especially pain in the joints, probably relate to the wide prevalence of osteoarthritis in men and women, for which we have the evidence of archaeology. It is clear from the skeletal remains that the onset of this disease was much earlier in the Anglo-Saxon community than it is now, and this in turn suggests for women as well as men a harsh environment and an early life of hard physical work. The high mortality rate among women which is demonstrated by statistical analysis

18 This group of entertainers appears to be illustrating Psalm 42, verse 4: 'the multitude that kept holyday'.

of the remains in Anglo-Saxon cemeteries presumably partly reflects the hazards of pregnancies, miscarriages and childbirth, but it has also been suggested that one major cause was inadequate amounts of iron in the diet. Even if men and women were on exactly the same range of food (and it was noted earlier that the cheese-maker received somewhat less in the way of provisions than the men) insufficiency of iron is a greater danger to the female than the male.

It is not easy to tell whether there was any lighter side to life for the average Anglo-Saxon woman. There is a small group of words and references suggesting that some women had a place in society as entertainers, but we cannot be sure whether such women were privately employed in households, or whether there was any scope for them as part of a travelling group. The common Old English nouns for fiddler, dancer and singer all occur in both masculine and feminine forms, so that we have the words *fiðelestere*, *hleapestre* and *sangestre*. But such words are found mainly in glossaries translating a Latin original, and not in any helpful context which might provide us with more useful information. The noun *wifhearp*, 'a woman's harp', is found once only. One of the riddles in the *Exeter Book* describes a bird that may be the jay or the jackdaw. Its last lines are:

> Saga hwæt ic hatte
> þe swa scirenige    sceawendwisan
> hlude onhyrge.

'Say what I am called, who, like an actress, loudly mimic the ways of a clown.'

This implies some scope for women as comic entertainers, and in Domesday we have a reference to one Adelina *joculatrix* who held land in Hampshire. Adelina is not however an Old English name, and it is to be presumed that she came over in the train of the Normans, and that her lands were a reward for her talents.

How one should translate *joculatrix* I am not sure. Its male equivalent *joculator* is usually translated 'jester', but it may mean no more than 'entertainer' or even 'singer'. A charming Latin love poem in an eleventh-century Cambridge manuscript refers to a female singer in private employment:

> Ibi puer et docta puella
> pangunt tibi carmina bella.
> Hic cum plectro citharam tangit
> Illa melos cum lira pangit.

'Here a boy and an educated girl compose lovely songs for you; he touches the harp; she makes melodies...'

It is true that this poem probably does not originate in England, but the English manuscript into which it has been copied has something of the nature of a school textbook, and it is clear that the idea of a woman in this role was not alien to the Anglo-Saxons.

Even to suggest that women may have had these opportunities requires us to press a very small amount of evidence into service, and conclusions from it are necessarily tenuous. But it is encouraging to note that scope for the exercise of such talents probably existed in secular life, and was not confined to composing or singing hymns in nunneries.

## FURTHER READING

Wills referred to in this chapter are in the volume *Anglo-Saxon Wills* by WHITELOCK, except for the separately published *Will of Æthelgifu* by WHITELOCK, 1968. The voluminous work on charters cannot all be cited here, but a guide to editions, translations, commentaries, and authenticity of individual documents is *Anglo-Saxon Charters* by SAWYER. The Laws, including the texts of *Gerefa* and *Rectitudines*, are edited by LIEBERMANN with a German translation. English translations of some laws are by ATTENBOROUGH, translations of *Gerefa* and *Rectitudines* are in SWANTON's *Anglo-Saxon Prose*. SWANTON also has a translation of Ælfric's *Colloquy*, which is edited in the Methuen series by GARMONSWAY. The *Liber Eliensis* is edited by BLAKE. The excellent series of Domesday volumes is under the general editorship of John MORRIS. The medical material is edited by COCKAYNE and some of it also by GRATTAN AND SINGER. Some useful recent articles include BULLOUGH AND CAMPBELL, 'Female Longevity and Diet in the Middle Ages'; and CAMERON, 'The sources of medical knowledge in Anglo-Saxon England'.

# 3. Sex and Marriage

Almost from the time the Angles and Saxons arrived in England in the fifth century there is clear and sensible legislation for the rights of women in their society. The seventh-century laws of Æðelbert of Kent, for example, are full of important material, though often expressed so laconically that we are obliged to tease out the meaning that was doubtless self-evident to the compilers. Yet law-codes as a whole constitute a range of evidence that can be, and sometimes has been, used rather too glibly and indiscriminately.

The laws of early England survive haphazardly from different periods and from different areas of the country. It is easy for us, looking back, to make one of two basic errors. One is to assume that all pre-Conquest Anglo-Saxon society is the same society and that the laws of one century and region reflect attitudes common to the whole of Anglo-Saxon England from the sixth century to the eleventh. The other is to assume that successive dates represent progress, and that the laws of Ælfred of Wessex in the ninth century represent a natural development from those of Æðelbert, to be superseded and improved on in their turn by eleventh-century law-codes.

This is not the case. It is of course self-evident that Kent, Wessex and Northumbria at any stage in Anglo-Saxon history may have certain well-defined distinctions in law and practice which relate back to early unrecorded differences. More significant is the fact that throughout the Anglo-Saxon period the Church was gaining a stronger and stronger influence over the law-codes, and what was in the earlier period reflective of what one might loosely term Germanic attitudes, becomes more subject to Christian Roman dogma. Yet at the same time as the weight of the Church was being brought to bear, especially in the south, in the mid-to-northern areas of England Germanic attitudes were given unexpected support from the Viking invasions and settlements. What was true of Northumbria in the eleventh century, therefore, might be thought to reflect a good deal more closely on the *mores* of the newly converted Vikings than of the Anglo-Saxons in general. While it is obviously difficult to avoid generalisation altogether, these are important qualifications which should be borne in mind.

As far as marriage is concerned the financial aspects are made quite clear in law and in charter. The money that the prospective husband must pay is the *morgengifu*, literally the 'morning-gift'. This could be a very substantial amount

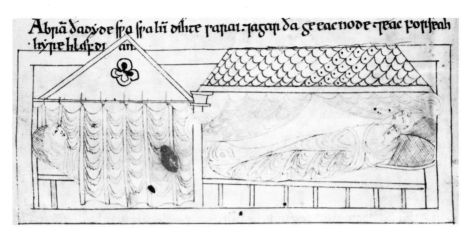

19 Anglo-Saxon illustration of a Biblical *ménage à trois*. Abraham sleeps with his wife's maid, and his wife sleeps alone.

in money and land, and it is paid not to the father or kin, but to the woman herself. She then has personal control over it, to give away, to sell or bequeath as she chooses. Æðelðryð in the time of King Ælfred sold an estate of five hides of land, over five hundred acres. She had received the land as her *morgengifu*. A number of men's wills make it clear that certain property is owned by the wife because it was granted to her as her *morgengifu*. The amount of land that formed a *morgengifu* or part of one is suggested by the surviving place-name evidence. Sussex field-names such as Mayfield, Morgay Farm, Morgay Wood, all contained originally the compound *morgengifu*, as their early forms show. The compound, which is frequent in Sussex and Essex, is found in at least six other counties. But perhaps the earliest *morgengifu* on record is Bamburgh in Northumberland, if we believe what the *Historia* ascribed to Nennius tells us. It claims that the seventh-century king Æðelfrið gave the place to his wife, Bebbe, from whom it has since been named.

The *morgengifu* was not the only property the wife had a right to, but different laws divide the matrimonial estate in different ways. They do, however, make it clear that within a marriage the finances are held to be the property of husband and wife, not of husband only. There are wills and charters which make it equally clear that a statistically significant proportion of donations and bequests are made by both man and woman. According to the laws of Æðelbert a woman had the right to walk out of a marriage that did not please her, though I do not find this particular freedom reiterated in the later laws. Since, if she took the children with her, she was also entitled to take half the property, she seems to have had reasonable independence and security.

Marriage agreements were drawn up between kin but this does not imply that the girl had no rights or say in the matter. It is fairly obvious that where substantial transactions were involved she would require the services of her older kin as legal and financial advisers. There is no indication that any direct profit accrued to the girl's family and no indication that her wishes were not considered, although parents occasionally allowed their prejudices to show. The most charming example of an anxious parent is in the will of Leofflæd in the eleventh century, whose daughter Leofwaru was to have the estate at Wetheringsett provided she remained chaste until her marriage. It is pleasant to record that she fulfilled the condition.

Survival of documents is a precarious matter, but we are fortunate in having two Old English marriage contracts of the early eleventh century. I quote the first section of both of them. The remaining sections deal mainly with the witnesses.

1. Here in this document is stated the agreement which Wulfric and the archbishop made when he obtained the archbishop's sister as his wife, namely he promised her the estates at Orleton and Ribbesford for her lifetime, and promised her that he would obtain the estate at Knightwick for her for three lives from the community at Winchcombe, and gave her the estate at Alton to grant and bestow upon whomsoever she pleased during her lifetime or at her death, as she preferred, and promised her 50 mancuses of gold and 30 men and 30 horses.

2. Here is declared in this document the agreement which Godwine made with Brihtric when he wooed his daughter. In the first place he gave her a pound's weight of gold, to induce her to accept his suit, and he granted her the estate at Street with all that belongs to it, and 150 acres at Burmarsh and in addition 30 oxen and 20 cows and 10 horses and 10 slaves.

It is certainly clear in the second of these that we are dealing with acceptance of the suit by the woman herself, not by her kinsmen on her behalf. A text on the betrothal of a woman, which is perhaps to be dated to the late tenth century makes it very clear what this bridegroom's legal obligations are, and what the responsibilities of the bride's kin are. Virtually every clause of the agreement is concerned with protecting and safe-guarding the woman's interests. The marriage must be 'agreeable to her'. The bridegroom must undertake to maintain her properly as his wife; he must make a direct payment or gift for her acceptance of him; he must make a contractual agreement on what he will leave to her if she outlives him. Her kinsmen are to undertake the negotiations on her behalf. If she is going to any distant region of the country away from immediate contact with her kin, they insist on an assurance that if she gets into legal difficulties they will be allowed to handle any fines or compensations that she might be required to pay, if she cannot do this herself.

It is, however, proper to record that the Anglo-Saxon laws were not so entirely obsessed with protecting women's rights that they did not occasionally make provision against the exploitation of the vulnerable male. Æðelbert 77 records that a marriage contract shall stand if there is no dishonesty, but if there is deception the woman must return to her kin, and the bridegroom receive back the money he has paid her. This clearly provides protection for any unfortunate husband who may have paid out a substantial *morgengifu*, only to find himself fathering another man's child.

One aspect of the laws which remains fairly consistent throughout the period is the care taken to ensure that a wife shall not be held guilty for any criminal activity of her husband. It is first observable in the seventh-century laws of Wihtred of Kent, and is most clearly defined in the eleventh-century laws of Cnut. Number 12 of the laws of Wihtred reads: 'if a man sacrifices to devils without his wife's knowledge he is liable to pay all his goods; if they both sacrifice to devils they are liable to pay all their goods'. Here as elsewhere in the laws the woman's independence is recognised, and there is no suggestion that her finances were under masculine control, or that their goods were regarded as held in common. The seventh-century laws of Ine of Wessex similarly differentiate carefully between the guilt of a woman who is her husband's accomplice and the innocence of one who is unaware of her husband's actions. Law number 7 on theft neatly divides the family responsibilities: 'If anyone shall steal, in such a way that his wife and children know nothing of it, he shall pay sixty shillings as fine: but if he steals with the knowledge of all his household they are all to go into slavery'. Another of Ine's laws allows a wife to clear herself by oath from responsibility for her husband's actions. Ine 57 deals with the question of stolen cattle being brought home. If they are seized the man is obliged to forfeit his 'share' – presumably of the household finances, but since the wife had no choice in the matter, she is not held responsible. 'If she dares to declare on oath that she has not tasted the stolen food she shall retain her third'. The division suggests that the household finances were assumed for legal purposes to be two-thirds those of the man, one-third those of the woman, but it is not really as simple as that, and there are many other circumstances which affect this balance.

It is in the late laws of Cnut that the distinction between male and female responsibilities in the matter of stolen property is most clearly analysed. In Cnut 76 the woman is not guilty – since clearly she cannot forbid her husband to place in his house what he pleases – unless the stolen property is found in one of the three places for which she holds the keys. These are specified as the *hordærn*, *cyste* and *teag*. We cannot recover the exact meaning of these words but it is fairly probable that *hordærn* is something like a store-room; that *cyste* is a largish chest, and that *teag* is the little box used for money or jewellery or small precious things.

Thus, from the beginning to the end of the period the laws recognise an element of financial independence and responsibility in the wife's status. This is also borne out by the archaeological evidence. Women's graves contain both

20 Girdle-hangers
from Soham,
Cambridgeshire.

keys and the key-shaped objects commonly referred to as 'girdle-hangers'. Girdle-hangers have no obvious functional use and can only be symbolic of some aspect of the status of their owner. The most obvious interpretation is that they represent economic control of the household. Grave-goods of this kind are inevitably found only in the early period since furnished graves belong to pagan not Christian contexts, and the girdle-hanger is specifically in Anglian areas.

A recent survey of a Kentish cemetery offers the interesting conclusion that female skeletons buried with keys are not the same as those buried with jewellery, and that this distinction may reflect a position of housekeeper as separate from that of the lady of the house. This distinction obviously can only have applied within rich communities. There is, however, one law among those of Æðelbert which quite specifically refers to a woman's economic responsibility. Æðelbert 73 reads: *Gif friwif locbore leswæs hwæt gedeð. xxx scll' gebete.* This has been translated in a variety of ways, but all editors and translators have assumed unthinkingly that *locbore*, literally 'lock-bearing', means 'having long hair', and the fine to be paid is for some sort of unacceptable sexual behaviour. I have argued elsewhere a case for a complete retranslation of this law, taking the word *locbore* to mean literally 'in charge of the locked places', paraphrasable as 'carrying the keys'. The fault *leswe* for which the fine is to be paid cannot be shown to have anything to do with sex, and can be shown to have something to do with loss or cheating. This is the only place in the laws of Æðelbert where a woman is required to pay a fine, and it makes obvious sense to see this as the other side of the picture in which she is freed from responsibility for her husband's theft. This law, in my interpretation, requires the free woman who has economic privileges to pay a heavy fine for any major abuse of her responsibility.

Most of the other references to women in the laws deal either with provisions for inheritance, or with illicit sex and adultery in various contexts and social classes. The provisions regarding inheritance are particularly interesting, since once again they show a good deal of concern for the economic status of a widow. There is no question in Anglo-Saxon law of estate and property passing automatically to an eldest son, with the widowed mother left dependent on his provision. Any humane society is concerned with protecting its more vulnerable members. The phrasing to which we are accustomed in the Christian context is 'care for the fatherless and widows' and we see throughout the Anglo-Saxon period a range of concern over various aspects of widowhood. The later laws are concerned with inheritance and economic problems; the church is dubious about second marriages. But in the early laws of Æðelbert numbers 75 and 76 are clearly designed to protect the widow. Law 75 specifies the compensation to be made for abducting widows of various classes of society. The verb 'abducting' sounds perhaps unreal, but the law is cryptically expressed. I take it to mean that a man who removes a widow from the protection of her kin (whether kin by blood or law) without an appropriate contract is required to pay an appropriate compensation. Law 76, equally laconically, says that if the widow is *unagen* the compensation is to be doubled. *Unagen* can only mean if she is without protecting kin. Thus, as her vulnerability increases, so also does the amount of fine to be paid.

That widows may be forced into second marriages is a matter of concern to later law-givers in the Anglo-Saxon period. Æðelræd's 1008 code is explicit that a widow remain unmarried for twelve months, and then choose as she herself wishes. Cnut's laws, which repeat Æðelræd's, spell out the inheritance problems and offer a somewhat drastic solution: 'if she chooses a husband within the year's space she is then to forfeit... all the possessions which she had through her former husband', but the obvious corollary to this is that as the widow she was entitled to a considerable share of the inheritance. She clearly does not forfeit her own independently held property. The emphasis on the rights of the widow to choose the life-style she wants is stressed again in subsequent clauses of Cnut 73. A widow is never to be consecrated as a nun too hastily, and neither a widow nor a maiden is ever to be forced to marry a man whom she herself dislikes. Of course, the fact that such legal protection is considered necessary obviously means that the vulnerability of widows allowed some families to be unscrupulous, and where rich inheritances were concerned the rights of the individual may easily have been subordinated to the desire for money and property. Nevertheless, the codes from Æðelbert to Cnut are notable for their humane and sensible provision for the widow's interests.

It is clear that within the legal family framework the rights of maidens, wives and widows were protected, and that women in the upper classes at least were potentially powerful. But it is also fairly clear that attitudes to women were more stringently dominated by their class than their sex, and the degree of protection afforded operated within a rigid hierarchical pattern.

The class distinctions of Anglo-Saxon society are complex. A man is assessed according to a financial scale, which basically represents the amount of money to be paid if he is killed. Many of the laws however do not specify the precise status of the victim, they use general terms for the free-born male such as *ceorl* or *friman*. A major distinction is between slave and free, though there are different classes even within slavery. For women the situation is even more complex; they may be slave or free; they may be virgin, married or widow; they may be assessed within different classes according to their compensation rights. The laws of Æðelbert are sometimes detailed and precise about the rank of the woman; sometimes laconic to the point of ambiguity.

A major area of legal responsibility is the protection of women against rape or seduction, and all the law-codes have fairly full provision. These are, however, offences that are viewed more or less seriously according to the class of the victim. Æðelbert 14 and 16 offer the following carefully thought-out distinctions: if a man lies with the *byrele*, 'cup-bearer' or 'serving-maid' of an *eorl* he is to pay twenty shillings compensation; if however she is the *byrele* of a *ceorl* – the lowest rank of free-man, as *eorl* is the highest – then the compensation is only six shillings. If he lies with a slave-woman of the second class the compensation is fifty *sceattas*; if with one of the third class, thirty *sceattas*. The *sceatt* was, perhaps, a twentieth part of a shilling in Kent at this period. A woman's rank therefore makes a considerable difference to the fine of her seducer. Throughout the laws there are places where it is unclear whether we are talking about a *ceorl's* 'wife' or a female servant. It is also unclear in some instances whether fines are paid to the woman herself, or to some male kinsman, guardian or owner. In the case of slaves the compensation doubtless went to the owner, as it did if a male slave was injured. It is necessary here to distinguish between slaves of either sex being viewed as property and women being viewed as property. I find no evidence of the second assumption, and a reasonable amount of evidence that when free women were injured in any way, they themselves – not their kin or their guardians – were the recipients of the appropriate compensation.

I have used the word 'seducer' in spite of its Victorian overtones, because it is necessary to find some way of distinguishing this offence from that of rape. Anglo-Saxon law is quite clear about these distinctions. The laws of Ælfred in

21 A clerk and Ælfgifu. The indelicate nature of the allusion and gesture is reinforced by the drawing in the lower border.

particular go into considerable detail on the scale of fines for various types of sexual assault. This is particularly interesting because the same law is equally detailed on injuries inflicted by men on each other; and it is thus possible to set up some sort of equation to see how seriously sexual offences were regarded.

Section eleven of Ælfred's laws is entitled *be cirlisce fæmnan onfenge*, which requires some such clumsy translation as 'assaults on women of *ceorl* status'. The first three provisions are as follows: if a man takes hold of her breast compensation is five shillings; if he throws her down but does not lie with her compensation is ten shillings; if he lies with her compensation rockets to sixty shillings. The woman of *ceorl* status is a free woman, and the most notable point in this law is the unambiguous use of the pronoun *hire*, 'her', in the phrase *hire gebete*, 'compensate her', i.e. it is the woman herself who is specified as the recipient of the compensation. We may compare in the same law the compensation for raping a *ceorl's* slave-woman. The notable differences are that here the compensation is paid to the *ceorl* himself, and is only five shillings. In addition to the compensation, however, there is a fine of sixty shillings imposed, which shows the severity with which rape was regarded where rape of a slave comes more expensive than seduction of a free-woman.

How do the injuries to a *ceorl* compare with the injuries to a woman of the same class? A ten-shilling injury to a *ceorl* is to bind him when he is innocent of any offence. A sixty-shilling injury is to bind him and shave him like a priest. But in the case of sexual assaults on women it may be impossible for the offender to get away merely with financial compensation: the laws of Ælfred state that a man may fight without legally incurring any penalty if he finds another man with his wife, daughter, sister or mother, 'behind closed doors or under the same blanket'. And in Ælfred's laws also the penalty for a slave who rapes a female slave is castration.

The penalties for adultery as distinct from fornication become much harsher towards the end of the Anglo-Saxon period. Æðelbert 31 shows excellent good sense in its provisions: 'if a freeman lie with a freeman's wife let him pay for it with her *wergild*, and provide another wife out of his own money and bring her to the other's home', which looks like a straightforward statement of the rights of divorce, remarriage and financial compensation. Such attitudes were firmly attacked by the church, and it is in the ecclesiastical laws, and in the letters of various missionaries and clerics, that we find the most violent attacks on freedom of sexual behaviour. But this hardly in itself accounts for the particularly unpleasant harshness of Cnut's laws, a harshness which I do not find paralleled in any early Anglo-Saxon material. It is possible that he was prompted by the greater severity of the Continental attitude. Cnut 53 reads: 'If a woman during her husband's life commits adultery with another man...her legal husband is to have all her property and she is to lose her nose and her ears'.

There is, however, evidence from other sources that before Cnut a straight-forward financial penalty was the norm. In the early eleventh century during King Æðelræd's reign a charter records that an estate is forfeited because of fornication by the woman who held it. About a century earlier there is another charter record of a *þegn* called Ælfred who forfeits an estate for adultery. The document which records this is not contemporary but historians claim that the story of Ælfred's behaviour is likely to be authentic. Ælfred leased the estate from his kinsman Bishop Denewulf. When he was found to have deserted his wife and to be living in open adultery, not only did he lose his tenancy of the estate, but Bishop Denewulf had to pay a considerable sum to recover it himself. The existence of charters of this nature does not argue very strongly for the prevalence of a 'double standard' with regard to male and female sexual morality.

Virtually no evidence survives from Anglo-Saxon England for organised prostitution. The words *portcwene* and *miltestre* are both usually rendered as 'prostitute'. The latter is in any case a loan-word from Latin *meretrix*, and tends to occur only in translations from Latin texts. Similarly, the compound *miltestre hus*, 'brothel', is found once in a Latin–Old English word-list glossing *lupanar*.

henfrolc punopad bureogalnir rahid on hripe cpærre

22 *Luxuria* (Indulgence), from Prudentius' *Psychomachia*, in her chariot attracting admiration. The illustration does not entirely convey the allure of the text:

> delibuta comas, oculis vaga, languida voce,
> perdita deliciis, vitae cui causa voluptas...

> 'hair perfumed, eyes wandering, languid voice,
> lost to delights, a life lived only for pleasure...'

*Portcwene*, usually found translating Biblical references to harlots, is also preserved in a place-name, Portinscale, Cumberland, which is a compound of Old English *portcwene* and Old Norse *skáli*, 'hut', as the early forms *Porqueneschal* and *Portewinscales* show, but though this may be evidence for the Viking north-west, it is scarcely so for that of Anglo-Saxon England as a whole. Letters from ecclesiastics and homilies refer to harlots and concubines, and we even have a tenth-century charter of King Edmund's which includes in the witness list *ego Ælfgifu concubina regis*. (Her name occurs after all the members of the royal family, including the king's mother, and also after the bishops, but before the nobility.) Boniface lamented earlier not only that kings indulge in too much sexual freedom, but also that among the Englishwomen who made pilgrimages to Rome far too many ended up as harlots in foreign towns. But none of this implies prostitution on any organised basis, and the only legislation is so worded that we cannot be sure whether the references are to prostitution or lax morals in general. There is one statement which occurs virtually without alteration in three eleventh-century law-codes and also in the notes for a sermon *be hæðendome*, 'against paganism', surviving in a York manuscript of the Gospels. Wulfstan is almost certainly the author of the statement in all its forms, and therefore it may be held to reflect the views of one eleventh-century moralist:

Gyf wiccean oððe wigelearas, horingas oððe horcwenan, morðwyrhtan oððe mansworan innan þysan earde weorðan agytene, fyse hy man georne ut of þysan earde and clænsie þas þeode...

'If witches or sorcerers, adulterers or prostitutes, murderers or perjurers are discovered in this land, they are to be driven from this country and the people cleansed...'

But the problems of translation are acute. The only word that is definitely feminine is *horcwen*, and it is really not possible to be sure whether it should be translated 'whore', 'prostitute', 'fornicator', or 'adulteress'. The plural *wiccean* could and probably did refer to both male and female witches; *horing* is a masculine noun and presumably refers to promiscuous people in general. In his *Sermo Lupi* (Sermon of the Wolf) Wulfstan also associates *myltestran and bearnmyrðran and fule forlegene horingas*, 'prostitutes and child-murderers and foul, fornicating adulterers', in a comprehensive denunciation. The two nouns *horing* and *horcwen* do not occur anywhere else in recorded Old English, and Wulfstan's use of them is probably influenced by Norse, which has a fuller range of compounds on *hór*, including *hórkona*. Wulfstan's particularly frenzied response is prompted by his association of sexual laxity with Viking paganism, and the influence he thought this was having on the country as a whole. The evidence, for what it is worth, is rather for promiscuity than prostitution, and though the latter presumably existed it has left little trace in the records.

Neither sex nor marriage is central to Old English literature, and romance plays a very small part. Heroic literature, however, reveals occasional glimpses of the role of wife, daughter or betrothed, some of them surprisingly ambivalent. In *Beowulf* Hroðgar's queen appears to be a woman of poise and assurance, *goldhroden*, 'wearing gold', a *freolicwif*, a 'noble woman'; yet her name, Wealhðeow, means 'foreign slave' and its meaning must have been instantly understood by any Anglo-Saxon audience. The name, not surprisingly, is not recorded elsewhere in Old English, and indeed must be thought of as descriptive, rather than as a baptismal name. The transition from foreign slave to queen was not a commonplace of Anglo-Saxon society as far as we can tell from the records, but it was a readily imagined possibility. The *Beowulf* poet, having made his point by choice of this name, never elaborates on it, but we have an interesting parallel in the career of one Anglo-Saxon woman who progressed from slavery to queenship (and from there to sainthood). Balthild, whose biography was written shortly after her death in the late seventh century, was born in England and brought as a slave-girl to Gaul. Subsequently the Frankish king Clovis II married her, and she acquired considerable power and influence at his court. As we find in many Old English writings on women, she is praised for her wisdom. She founded monasteries, one of which was Chelles, where she retired towards the end of her life, to be venerated for her devotion and asceticism. Memory of her earlier status doubtless prompted one particular aspect of her charity – the redemption of captives, especially those of her own race.

The prospect of slavery for the women of a defeated tribe is recognised in Old English and Old Norse literature, and along with this recognition there is a recurrent ambivalent attitude to slavery. On the one hand there is the perennial class-consciousness which assumes the slave to be a stupid and inferior being. The tone of one of the riddles of the *Exeter Book* has something of this superiority: the subject of the riddle describes itself, and the answer is the ox. Its hide can be made into ropes which 'bind fast the dark Welsh, and sometimes better men'. Ox-hides are also used as bed-coverings, so 'sometimes a black-haired Welshwoman, brought from far away, a stupid drunken slave-girl holds me in the dark nights'. On the other hand, it is obvious that those enslaved may have been of high birth and rank in their own tribe, and the comment which the woman Unnr makes in the Old Icelandic *Laxdœla saga* offers us a contrast to the patronising tone of the riddle: 'You are well aware that I have given Erpr son of *jarl* Meldun freedom; it was very far from my wish that a man so well-born should endure the name of slave'. Wealhðeow presumably made an equally good impression in captivity. But the Anglo-Saxon and Norse poets were well aware of the uncertainties here. The Old English version of *Genesis* tells us:

> Sceolde forht monig
> blachleor ides   bifiende gan
> on fremdes fæðm;   feollon wergend
> bryda and beaga,   bennum seoce.

'Many a frightened, white-cheeked woman had to go trembling into a stranger's embrace: the defenders of wives and rings fell, fatally wounded.'

We may compare the verse of the Norse poet Valgarðr celebrating one of the victorious skirmishes of Haraldr harðráði, in which he describes the women being driven to the ships after the men have fled, and adds the harsh realistic detail of the fetters biting greedily into their flesh. The ultimate fate of these women was perhaps to be that of the 'stupid drunken slave-girl' in the riddle, but society certainly recognised the possibility that it could alternatively be that of Wealhðeow.

The woman who was born great or achieved greatness is shown in heroic literature as sharing in the ceremonies of the hall, courteously honouring warriors and distributing rings, and it is difficult for us to get behind this glittering façade to look at the pleasures or realities of marriage. But in other literature, particularly in the so-called elegiac poetry other patterns tentatively emerge. Pleasures of companionship between the sexes and pleasures of sex are lightly evoked. In *The Husband's Message* the speaker, having overcome misery 'does not now lack any pleasure, neither of horses nor of treasures nor of mead-joys (*meododreama*) nor of any treasures on earth appropriate to the status of an *eorl* (*eorlgestreona*) if, daughter of a prince, he may also obtain you'. The message urges the woman, in loving terms, to let no man hinder her from her journey, but to keep her vow firmly in mind – it is not clear whether the vow is betrothal or marriage, nor whether the message is from lover or husband – and to set out to join him in a foreign land. It is noteworthy that no third party's intervention is mentioned or sought for. This is not a message from the man to his or her kin, though some commentators on Anglo-Saxon society insist that all betrothal and marriage contracts are between suitor and father, with the woman's wishes or consent barely noted. It is perhaps improper to try and extrapolate too much from so enigmatic a poem. But the tone of it does suggest a direct commitment to an individual, not a political alliance.

References to the relationship between retainer and lord in Anglo-Saxon society almost always put the stress on friendship, whereas post-Conquest society is more hierarchically minded. For an Anglo-Saxon retainer his lord is his *winedrihten*, his 'friend-lord'. In the same way we regularly find the terms *freond*, 'friend', and *freondscype*, 'friendship', in texts describing the relationship of lovers, or of husband and wife. *Freond* has perhaps not exactly the semantic range of modern English 'friend', but it would be difficult to pinpoint any precise distinction. Etymologically, *freond* starts out as the present participle of the verb *freogan*, 'to love' or 'to like' or 'to honour'. It is regularly used without sexual implications, translating Latin *amicus* in a number of contexts. In the poet's lament in *The Dream of the Rood* he complains that he has outlived powerful friends and protectors. This declaration *nah ic ricra feala / freonda on foldan* is followed by the hope that Christ will be his friend: *Si me Dryhten freond*. The development of *freond* in Old English is significantly different from that of the cognate word in Old Norse, for in Old English there are frequent phrases where 'friends' and 'kinsmen' are distinguished, whereas in Old Norse the word *frændi* becomes the standard term for kinsman.

In Old English, then, *freond* is used of a relationship of 'loving' or 'liking' usually outside the kinship bonds and I think there remains a certain ambiguity when it is used of affection between men and women. It is not always clear whether the implications are those of desire rather than companionship or vice versa. In *Juliana* the implications might seem to be mostly sexual. Juliana, with the usual virgin martyr's contempt for matrimony, rejects the *freondrǽden*, 'affection' or 'desire'(?) of her suitor. The suitor himself uses *mǽglufu*, 'love of a woman', and *freondrǽden* as synonyms:

> heo me on an sagað
> þæt heo mæglufan   minre ne gyme
> freondrædenne.

'She has said to me that she does not value my love or affection.'

But when her father points out that the rejected suitor, being a man of property, would be *to freonde god*, 'a useful friend', the force of this must be that he would be a good man to have on one's side.

In the Old English *Genesis* Abraham and his wife Sarah are journeying to Egypt. Abraham worries about the effect Sarah may have on the Egyptian males, and urges her to pretend that she is his sister. He fears that some man who desires Sarah may kill him in order to obtain her. The phrase describes a man who looks on Sarah with *freondmynd*. Obviously 'desire' seems a more appropriate translation than 'friendly affection', but when immediately afterwards Abraham tells Sarah to say that she is his sister if men ask about the *freondlufu*, 'relationship', between them, *freondlufu* self-evidently means something more like 'bonds of affection'.

Whether the relationship in *The Husband's Message* is that of lovers or of marriage, what he asks the woman to remember is *freondscype*. In *The Wife's Lament* whether the *freond* is husband or lover depends on which interpretation of the poem one follows, but either way she is explicitly referring to a close and loving relationship.

> Ful oft wit gebeotedan
> þæt unc ne gedælde   nemne deað ana
> owiht elles.   Eft is þæt onhworfen,
> is nu fornumen   swa hit no wære,
> freondscipe uncer.

'Often the two of us vowed that nothing should divide us, except for death only, nothing else. That has changed now; it has gone, our friendship, as if it had not been.'

Pleasures of friendship here must also be euphemistic for pleasures of lovers when she contrasts her own solitary state with that of those 'friends' who are living, loving, sharing a bed.

There is one cryptic text in the gnomic poetry which is perhaps the nearest that Old English literature gets to the romantic view of love.

> Ides sceal dyrne cræfte
> fæmne hire freond gesecean   gif heo nelle on folce geþeon
> þæt hi man beagum gebicge.

An approximate translation might be: 'A lady, a woman shall with secret skill search for her friend, if she does not wish that a man should obtain her with rings', i.e. if she does not like the marriage contract offered to her. I am not sure of the implications of *on folce*. Its literal meaning is 'among the people' but I do not know which kin-group or social group it refers to. Nevertheless, this text quite clearly urges women to independence of action, and should be remembered when we are being encouraged to believe that women were viewed only as pawns in dynastic games. *Wulf and Eadwacer*, another enigmatic poem, appears to deal with the triangle of woman, lover and husband. The plot is not clear but the emotions are conveyed superbly:

Wulfes ic mines widlastum    wenum dogode
þonne hit wæs renig weder    ond ic reotugu sæt.
Þonne mec se beaducafa    bogum bilegde
wæs me wyn to þon    wæs me hwæþre eac lað.
Wulf min Wulf,    wena me þine
seoce gedydon    þine seldcymas
murnende mod    nales meteliste.

'I waited for my Wulf with far-wandering hopes; when it was rainy weather, and I sat desolate. When the man bold in battle put his arms round me it was a joy to me but it was also pain. Wulf my Wulf, it is my longing for you that has made me ill; not hunger, but a grieving mind, and your rare visits.'

It is not necessary to grasp the minutiae of the legend underlying the poem, to respond to the overtones of passive misery, isolation, separation from the beloved and longing for him. When in the final lines the woman appears to be harshly denying the marriage bond and hurls at Eadwacer the words:

þæt mon eaþe tosliteð    þætte næfre gesomnad wæs
uncer giedd geador:

'that can easily be torn apart which was never joined – the song of us two together'

we appear once again to be within the romantic view of marriage rather than the practical. Her statement is devoid of logic or accuracy. One can hardly tear something apart unless it is joined together. The metaphors are incongruously yoked. The suggestion of violently rending cloth in *tosliteð* links uneasily with the word for song or story, *giedd*. The denial of intimacy in the sentence structure is contradicted by the intimate personal pronoun *uncer*. The emotional implications of the statement are, however, perfectly clear, and the violence of the emotional effect is heightened by the linguistic incongruities. There is little enough of this kind of poetry in Old English. *Wulf and Eadwacer* and *The Wife's Lament* are the only two to explore this complex emotional range. But remembering once again how little survives, it becomes important to stress that this evidence does exist.

In the poetry so far we have looked only at the heroic and 'elegiac', with slight glances at the hagiographic. These all appear to deal with the woman of aristocratic status, and she is the one we should expect to find in literature of this period. But there are also here and there domestic glimpses of what one might term the working woman as distinct from the heroic woman. A particularly charming picture is presented to us in the *Exeter* gnomic poetry. Here we have a description of the Frisian wife welcoming home her husband:

Leof wilcuma
frysan wife    þonne flota stondeð.
Biþ his ceol cumen    ond hyre ceorl to ham,
agen ætgeofa,    ond heo hine in laðað;
wæsceð his warig hrægl    ond him syleð wæde niwe,
lið him on londe    þæs his lufu bædeð.

'Her loved one is welcome to the Frisian woman when his ship is at anchor. His boat has arrived, and her man has come home, her own provider; she brings him in, washes his sea-stained clothes, and offers him fresh ones; she gives him on land what his love asks of her.'

There is one other type of poetry which deals with sex and this is the riddle genre. Most of the riddles are straightforward but there is one group where the game is that of the *double entendre*. The maximum amount of sexual innuendo is packed into the verse, though the answer is perfectly innocuous. What is notable about these is their lightness of tone – so distinct from the high seriousness of much Old English poetry. The answer to Riddle 25 may indeed be an 'onion' or a 'leek' or even 'mustard' as various scholars have suggested, but the description is clearly intended to suggest the penis. Thus the arrogant opening line: *Ic eom wunderlicu wiht   wifum on hyhte* ('I am a wonderful creature, for the delight of women'), suggests a rough good-humour in the attitude to ordinary domestic relationships, balancing the formal stereotypes of the aristocratic poetry.

These riddles tend to occur in small groups scattered among the others. Riddles 61, 62 and 63 are all richly suggestive. Formal answers offered for 61 are 'helmet' or 'shirt'; for 62 'poker' or 'gimlet', for 63 'beaker' or 'flute'. The first two are splendidly vulgar as distinct from the third, which uses rather the vocabulary of romance in describing kisses, privacy, pressures of fingers and delight of both participants. Two riddles use the vocabulary of intercourse to describe domestic duties. Number 45 refers to a boneless object which increases in size under the skilled handling of 'a proud bride'. The proper answer is 'dough'. Riddle 54 is perhaps the most graphic comedy among them. The likely answer is 'churn' and the vivid presentation of the actions and energy involved in churning butter gain considerably from the sexual suggestiveness of the language:

> worhte his willan,   wagedan buta.
> Þegn onnette;   wæs þragum nyt
> tillic esne;   teorode hwæðre
> æt stunda gehwam   strong ær þonne hio,
> werig þæs weorces.

'He had his way, and both of them were shaking. The man worked hard. His capable servant was useful at times, but strong as he was, he always tired sooner than she did, exhausted by the task.'

Literature and law alike suggest that the woman's role within marriage in Anglo-Saxon England had, at any rate for the free-born, immense potential. There are other types of evidence that offer a less attractive picture. Homilies and letters from the pens of clergy and missionaries thunder against polygamy and incest. It is a range of evidence I find difficult to assess. Incest, of course, covers marriages between far wider degrees of kin than those of the nuclear

23 Chastity decapitating Lust, a scene from Prudentius' *Psychomachia*.

family, and there are many relationships which seem to us to offer no barrier at all to marriage, but which might be frowned on by ecclesiastics. The following revealing story is told in a plaintive letter by the missionary Boniface written to Nothelm, Archbishop of Canterbury in the eighth century:

Further, I would like your advice as regards a sin which I have unwittingly committed by allowing a certain man to marry. It happened in this way. The man, like many others, had stood as godfather to the child of another man and then on the father's death married the mother. The people in Rome say that this is a sin, even a mortal sin, and state that in such cases a divorce is necessary. They maintain that under the Christian emperors such a marriage was punishable by death or exile for life. If you find that this is considered so great a sin in the decrees of the Fathers and in the canons or even in Holy Scripture, tell me so, because I would like to understand and learn the authorities for such an opinion. I cannot understand how spiritual relationship in marriage can be so great a sin, when we know that through Baptism we all become sons and daughters, brothers and sisters in the Church.

Both before and after the Viking raids, reproaches are levelled at the English for their 'pagan' habits of marrying their kin, or of keeping other women in addition to their lawful wife. It is difficult to know how far these are generalisations, and sometimes, especially in the homilies of Wulfstan, difficult not to believe that delight in rhetoric rather more than devotion to accurate representation has dictated the violence of the accusations. Letters from Popes and Continental bishops to Anglo-Saxon kings tend to focus on individuals of high rank and the morals of their courts, and documented scandals inevitably are reported only if those concerned are of political importance. Unhappy and dramatic histories, then as now, were more likely to make the headlines than happy and uneventful ones. Away from the feuds at court that occupy so much of the historian's attention, and allowing for a certain range of exaggeration in pulpit rhetoric, we are entitled to assume that the average Anglo-Saxon wife was both valued and respected, enjoying economic and marital rights, her independence safe-guarded and her interests protected. One might also look here at King Ælfred's view. When he translates that part of Boethius's *Consolation of Philosophy*, where Philosophy points out to Boethius that he should take comfort in his misery from the thought that he still has a wife living who loves him and grieves for him, Ælfred makes certain additions to the original in his translated version. I print these additions in italics:

Hu ne liofað þin wif eac?...Sio liofað nu þe, *þe anum*, for ðam þe hio nanwuht elles ne lufað buton þe. *Alces godes hio hæfþ genoh on ðys andweardan life, ac heo hit hæfð eall forsawen ofer ðe anne; eall heo hit onscunað, for þæm þe heo þe ænne næfð; þæs anes hire is nu wana.* For þinre æfweardnesse *hire þincð eall noht þæt hio hæfð, for þæm* hio is *for þinum lufum* ormod *and fulneah dead* for tearum and for unrotnesse.

'Surely your wife is still living?...She lives now for you, *only for you*, because she loves nothing else except you. *She has every luxury in her present life, but she has neglected it all, except for you alone, she shuns it entirely, just because she is without you. That is her only lack.* Because of your absence *everything that she has seems nothing to her, because* she is despairing *for love of you, and very nearly dying* in tears and sadness.'

Such comments certainly seem closer in attitude to the world of *The Wife's Lament* than that of dynastic alliances.

## FURTHER READING

On laws in general see *Further Reading*, chapter 3. Text and translation of the marriage arrangements are in *Anglo-Saxon Charters* by ROBERTSON. There are also translations of these and of selected law-codes including the one concerning betrothal in *English Historical Documents*, ed. WHITELOCK. Translations of poems can be found in BRADLEY's *Anglo-Saxon Poetry*, texts of riddles are in the volumes of the Early English Text Society edition of the *Exeter Book* (GOLLANCZ). There are individual editions of *The Dream of the Rood* by SWANTON and by DICKINS AND ROSS, and of *Genesis* by TIMMER, but all poems may be found in the volumes of *Anglo-Saxon Poetic Records*, edited by KRAPP AND DOBBIE. Some discussion of the archaeological material is in MEANEY, *Anglo-Saxon Amulets and Curing Stones* and in Sonia Hawkes' contribution to the volume *Excavations in West Kent*, edited by PHILP. An interesting article on Balthild is by Nelson in *Medieval Women*, ed. BAKER. Place-name evidence is scattered through the volumes of the *Place-Name Society* but a useful starting-point is *English Place-Name Elements* by SMITH, or *English Place Names* by CAMERON.

# 4. Family and Kinship

In the Icelandic *Gísla saga*, written in the thirteenth century and based on events of the tenth, we are given a very vivid insight into the difficulties of a Viking Age family which is moving away from a pattern of rigid kinship loyalties into a society where actions may be governed also by affections within marriage or friendship. The hero of the saga, Gísli, is the one who has most emotional difficulty in accepting that such change is either possible or desirable. In the early part of the story he kills one of his sister's suitors, and so far from expecting her to be disturbed or distressed by this, he makes it clear later that the reaction he anticipated was gratitude: 'I have shown her more than once that her honour was as important to me as my own'. When family quarrels escalate to the point where he kills her husband, and she has to choose whether to protect her brother by silence or precipitate vengeance for her husband by speech, she chooses the latter course, and Gísli is bitterly shocked by what seems to him kinship betrayal. He contrasts her behaviour with that of a legendary heroine who killed her own husband in vengeance for the death of her brother. Yet Gísli himself by the end of the saga is valuing the love and comradeship of his wife above that of his brother and sister. The saga-writer's evident concern with these shifting patterns gives us a very full and clear awareness of the tensions that inevitably result from such a social development.

It is a development that must have taken place very much earlier in Anglo-Saxon society and we do not have it documented in the same way. Heroic poetry preserves awareness of conflicting loyalties, of women needing to decide whether their support goes primarily to the family they were born into or the family they marry into, but not all times are times of feuds and hostilities, and not all marriages require the bride to take the role of 'peace-weaver'. Within the legal framework and comparatively centralised authority that developed in Anglo-Saxon England a woman's rights and her future as she moves from one family to another are carefully protected. It is not, as in some societies, that she moves from the 'authority' of a father to that of a husband. On the contrary, she retains within her marriage the support of the family she was born into, and should she be childless one of the laws of Æðelbert (81) specifies that her property, including the *morgengifu* her husband gave her on her marriage, reverts to her kin, her *fæderingmagas*. It is clearly her rights that are being protected here. We have

24 Defending the family home. A scene from the Franks Casket.

no records from Anglo-Saxon society of wives being repudiated because they were barren, and in a society that sets no particular store by primogeniture the need for a direct male heir does not become obsessive. If this does – though I think it unlikely – refer to repudiation, it allows the woman to return to her kin with financial support and some standing. By bringing her *morgengifu* she enriches her family. If, as is more probable, the law concerns a woman who dies childless, her property goes to support her own kin, not her husband's. That her husband does not inherit clearly places her in a much less vulnerable position. The laws of Æðelbert date from the seventh century, and this is the period before men and women of wealth had acquired the literate habit of leaving their property by will.

We do not in the wills of the later Anglo-Saxon period see any exclusive preference given to men as heirs. Many men leave property of value to their female kin, their mothers, sisters, daughters and remoter kinswomen, as well as to their wives. It is impossible to use the surviving evidence as a statistically significant sample, and it might perhaps be argued that men were under less pressure to leave wills when they had sons to inherit, or that daughters as heirs were in a slightly more vulnerable position, needing the protection and security of the written document. Something of this is suggested by the will of Wulfgeat. The only male kinsman specified among the bequests is a grandson. Otherwise Wulfgeat leaves property to his wife, his two daughters and a 'kinswoman'. 'And he asks his lord for the love of God, that he will be a friend to his wife and daughter.'

There is a provision in the will of Wulfric which shows similar and touching concern, and deserves quoting in full. It is not clear why the woman is his 'poor' or 'unfortunate' daughter, though some sort of illness or injury is perhaps implied. The insistence on her not forfeiting the bequest, and on her retaining the 'lordship' of it, as well as Wulfric's appointment of a protector, are all provisions that are not paralleled in any other recorded bequest:

Ic geann minre earman dehter þæs landes æt Elleforda, and þæs æt Acclea, mid eallon þam þe þær nu to herð, þa hwile hire dæg bið: and ofer hire dæg ga þæt land into þare stowe æt Byrtune. And heo hit nage mid nanne þinge to forwyrcenne ac hæbbe heo ðone bryce þa hwile þe heo hit geearnigean cann. And ga hit syððan into þæra stowe æt Byrtune forþon þe hit wæs mines godfæder gyfu. And ic wille þæt Ælfhelm si hire mund and þæs landes. And þæt æt Tamwurðin hire to nanon þeowdome ne nanon geborenan men, buton þæt hie þone ealdordom hæbbe.

'I grant to my unhappy daughter the estate at Elford and that at Oakley with everything which now belongs there, as long as she lives; and afterwards the land is to go to the monastery at Burton. And she is not to have it on any such terms that she may have to forfeit it, but she is to have the use of it so long as she can cope (?) with the duties. And afterwards it goes to the monastery at Burton because it was my godfather's gift. And I wish that Ælfhelm shall be protector of her and of the estate. And the land at Tamworth is not to be subjected to any service, nor to any man born, but she is to have the lordship.'

We are not even told her name, and she is by no means the major legatee. Ælfhelm, who inherits much more, was probably her uncle. What comes over with absolute clarity is her father's anxiety to secure her future and his fears for her because of some unspecified disability. It is, however, from another part of Wulfric's will that we get one of the clearest indications that women – wives and daughters – inherited and held property independently and separately from husband or father. Wulfric leaves several estates to Morcar; one estate to Morcar's wife, and another estate to Morcar's daughter. We are not told what his relationship was to this family other than that the daughter of Morcar was the god-daughter of Wulfric. The attractive personal concern Wulfric shows in the provisions for his own daughter appears again in the provisions for his god-daughter, who receives not merely an estate but also 'the brooch which was her grandmother's'. An interesting parallel to Wulfric's concern for his daughter and his appointment of a male protector is in the will of Æðelgifu, who is evidently concerned about the vulnerability of Leofsige, her chief legatee, and anxious to secure the protection of a powerful woman for this male heir. He may have been a minor when the will was drawn up: 'she asks her lady...to watch over him, and let him serve the prince, and do not let anyone rob him of his lands'.

King Ælfred is the man who outlines most clearly for us, not merely his personal preferences in the matter of heirs, but also the range of choice open to Anglo-Saxons. His grandfather, he tells us, bequeathed his land in the male line and not in the female line, *on þa sperehealfe næs on þa spinlhealfe*. Ælfred himself chooses to follow this in certain respects but not all. He leaves estates to all his children, both sons and daughters, but he arranges for the male descendants to have the opportunity of buying back the land from the women if they wish to do so. The implications are clearly that the grandfather had full choice in the matter. We should not assume from Ælfred's statement that the choice his grandfather made was unusual or untypical, or that it was in any way abnormal to prefer male to female heirs, but we should accept that Ælfred would not be analysing the matter with such care if primogeniture were the accepted pattern. King Ælfred says also that he asked the assembly to tell him what was 'national law' (?), *folcriht*, in the matter of inheritance, and that they assured him he had the right to give to 'kinsman or to stranger', *swa gesibre hand swa fremdre*. This freedom of choice is reiterated in the number of charters that grant land to named individuals 'and whoever [they] shall choose for [their] heir'. Bishop Wærferð of Worcester grants land to Cyneswið his kinswoman and she may bequeath it to *hire bearna sumum swa hweolcum swa heo ðonne wille*, 'one of her children, whichever one she pleases'. It is in fact quite noticeable how often wills and charters in their reference to heirs deliberately use the words *bearn* or *cild*, 'child', not specifying by sex. A careful statistical survey of the evidence here would be instructive.

Another Ælfred who names himself by the Latin title of *dux* and was in fact a contemporary of King Ælfred leaves a much more substantial amount to his daughter than his son. His will is complex and makes arrangements for some property to go to kin on his father's side, some to kin on his mother's side, using precisely that terminology *fedrenmega* and *rehtmeodrencynn*. He is not here naming individual legatees, merely specifying which side of the family is to inherit certain lands. His daughter Ælfðryð is referred to in connection with his wife Werburg as *uncer gemene bearn*, 'the child of us both'. She is clearly the

25 A scene illustrating Psalm 131: 'as a child that is weaned of his mother'. She appears to be giving him a ring.

major legatee, and his son Æðelwold gets much less, some of it according to his sister's preferences: 'she is to give him whichever she pleases either the estate at Horsley or that at Longfield'. Since she is so clearly specified as legitimate we are naturally left wondering if the son may have been illegitimate. It is possible that he was the child of an earlier marriage, or that he was already established on his estates, before the composition of the will. But since Ælfred expresses the hope for a closer male heir illegitimacy seems the likeliest explanation.

An interesting inheritance quarrel is recorded in an early eleventh-century Herefordshire family. We know nothing about the prosperity and land-holdings of the named son Edwin at the time when he sued his own mother, *his agene modor*, for a piece of land. The wording suggests a sense of shock in the scribe making the record. The mother, however, is not merely shocked but furious: *gebealh heo swiðe eorlice wið hire sunu*; 'she became very angry with her son', literally 'in the manner appropriate to an *eorl*, "noble"'. (*Eorlic* is not a common word, but it usually implies commendation. Beowulf promised to act with *eorlic* courage.) She then made a verbal grant in the presence of witnesses, which we may assume was a common way of making a bequest in the absence of a written will:

Her sit Leoffled min mage þe ic geann ægðer ge mines landes ge mines goldes ge rægles ge reafes ge ealles þæs ðe ic ah æfter minon dæge.

'Here sits Leofflæd, my kinswoman, to whom I leave both my land and my gold, my furnishings and my clothing and all that I own.'

We are not told in what degree Leofflæd is 'kinswoman', but the word implies something less close than sister or daughter. The mother (we are not told her name) then asked for it to be reported at the shire-meeting that she had left her property in this way *and minon agenan suna næfre nan þingc*, 'and not a thing to my own son'. This was done and approved by the meeting, but Leofflæd's husband had the sense to have the matter placed on record so that his wife's claim should be secure.

The woman may have acted in a way appropriate to an *eorl* even if it is not entirely obvious that she acted in the way appropriate to a mother. But since we are not given the full background here and since her decision was upheld we may take it she had full right to do as she did. We do not, however, have very much evidence from Anglo-Saxon England for women in the maternal role, and in so far as we are shown parental love or grief it is not customary to single out the mother as showing any more obvious emotional reaction or involvement than the father. The *Beowulf* poet shows us one woman mourning a dead son, another involved in deep anxieties for the future of her living ones, but Hildeburg's grief as her son is placed on the funeral pyre is given no more lines than the suffering of a father later in the poem who sees his son hang on the gallows, a sport for ravens. A poem in the *Exeter Book* called by modern editors

78

*The Fates of Men* refers twice to a mother's reaction to the loss of her child by violent death: *modor bimurneð*, 'the mother grieves', when the wolf, *har hæðstapa*, 'the grey prowler of the moors', kills her son, and *reoteð meowle*, 'the woman laments', the death of a child through fire.

The beginning of the poem is however one that presents a charming picture of a close and loving family:

> Ful oft þæt gegongeð    mid Godes meahtum
> þætte wer ond wif    in woruld cennað
> bearn mid gebyrdum    ond mid bleom gyrwað.
> Tennaþ ond tætaþ    oþþæt seo tid cymeð,
> gegæð gearrimum,    þæt þa geongan leomu,
> liffæstan leoþu    geloden weorþað.
> Fergað swa ond [fedað]    fæder ond modor
> giefað ond gierwaþ.    God ana wat
> hwæt him weaxendum    winter bringað.

'It happens very often through the power of God that a man and a woman bring a child into the world and clothe it in colours. They encourage it and amuse it until the time comes, as the years pass, that the young limbs full of life are grown. Father and mother thus support it and nourish it, make gifts to it and clothe it. God only knows what the years will bring to the growing child.'

I have rather carefully chosen 'it' in my translation (though the plural 'they' is equally possible) in contradistinction to one accepted translation which uses 'him' throughout, and translates *him weaxendum* as 'to the growing boy'. But *bearn* 'child' is a neuter noun used for both sons and daughters, and *him* is the proper grammatical form of the neuter pronoun as well as the masculine one. What gifts most young children received from their parents is a matter for guesswork, but King Edward reports that his birth-gift from his mother was the estate on which he was born: *swa Ælfgifu Imme min moder on minre frumbirde dæiæge to forme gyfe hit me gæf.* The letter is preserved only in a late copy and some of it is probably spurious, but that detail is possibly authentic, since there would be little point in a later scribe inventing anything so personal.

Delight at the birth of a child is not confined to delight at the birth of a son. It is true that in heroic poetry women who, looking back, realised that their sons had turned out to be heroes were thought to have exceptional cause for rejoicing. Beowulf is told that the woman who gave birth to him has cause to say that God was good to her in the matter of child-bearing:

> Þæt hyre Ealdmetod    este wære
> bearngebyrdo.

Even poor Beadohild was thought by the poet of *Deor* to find, in being the mother of a hero, consolation for her brothers' deaths and her own rape. But against this we may look at Bede's story of the conversion of Northumbria:

On the same night, the holy night of Easter Day, the queen had borne the king a daughter named Eanflæd. The king, in the presence of Bishop Paulinus, gave thanks to his gods for the birth of his daughter; but the bishop, on the other hand, began to thank the Lord Christ and to tell the king that it was in answer to his prayers to God that the queen had been safely delivered of a child, and without great pain. The king was delighted with his words...

The child Eanflæd was the first of the Northumbrians to be baptised.

A mother's rights concerning her children are specified in a number of the early laws. Æðelbert 79 makes it clear that if a woman wishes to leave her husband there is no automatic ruling on custody. If she takes the children with her, she is also entitled to half the property. If she leaves the children with their father then the amount of property she may take is lessened accordingly. The slightly later Kentish laws of Hloðhere and Eadric legislate for the mother's right to keep her children in the event of her husband's death. The situation envisaged here by the legislator must be one in which the paternal kinsmen wish to provide for the child but not necessarily for the mother, who might want or be required to return to her own kin. The phrasing of this law is one of the few early ones that asserts firmly *riht is*, 'it is right' or 'it is just'. 'If a man dies, leaving a wife and child, it is right that the child should stay with the mother, and one of the child's paternal relatives, who is willing, be appointed protector to look after the property until the child is ten years old.' (Ten is the age at which children acquire adult responsibility in the early period, though later laws move the age to twelve.) The laws of Ine reiterate the mother's right to keep her child, and make provision for maintenance: 'if a man and wife have a child and the husband dies, the mother keeps the child and brings it up: she shall be provided with six shillings for its care, a cow in summer and an ox in winter; the kinsmen are to look after the

26 A section from *Deor*, in the *Exeter Book*:

'Beadohild was not so bitter at heart
For the death of her brothers as her own trouble,
When she knew clearly that she was pregnant.'

ui tollenf pane. et utre aque. ipofuit fcapule agar. et tdidit ei pueru.

o' et puer deficeret filr:

27 Anglo-Saxon illustration of Abraham's farewell to Hagar and their son.

property till the child is grown up.' It should perhaps be stressed that the word in both laws is *bearn*, 'child', not 'son', though in the manuscript the first of these two laws slips into the masculine form *he* rather than the neuter *hit* in the last clause. This has caused most translators to write 'he' and 'his' throughout.

It is surprisingly, perhaps, from one of the riddles in the *Exeter Book* that we get the fullest glimpse of a woman in the protective maternal role. The cuckoo riddle describes how a woman extends to a child not her own the same kindness, love and protection that she gave her own children. That this, in the event of one who fosters a cuckoo, is mistaken generosity is a neat parallel to the irony of Wealhðeow's statement in *Beowulf* that her nephew Hroðulf will be good to her sons 'if he remembers what we two did for his delight and honour while he was yet a child'. But whereas the tone of the heroic poetry is formal restrained irony, the riddle evokes briefly the warmth and compassion of the protective woman, the *friðemæg*.

The foster-relationship which is so clearly a part of Viking society may have been more common in Anglo-Saxon England than the documents tell us. The various words for foster-relationships occur so often that the concept was obviously a familiar one, but most of the places they are used are in translations of Latin texts, or metaphors with spiritual connotations, and do not give us any insight into the way fostering worked in society. As we see it in Old Norse

28 Psalm 113, verse 9: 'he maketh the barren woman to keep house and to be a joyful mother of children'.

literature the system was that of sending well-born children to be brought up away from home, usually in the household of one of lower rank than the parents. William of Malmesbury said that Æðelstan was brought up at the court of his father's sister Æðelflæd, but we simply do not know how prevalent such a practice may have been. It is difficult to know whether the term 'foster-mother' is used of a woman in whose house one was brought up, or if it meant 'nurse', specifically 'wet-nurse'. The latter seems the most likely interpretation in some contexts. One of the laws of Ine specifies the servants a man may take with him when he moves. These are, significantly, his reeve, his smith and his *cildfestre*, where the term must mean 'children's nurse'. What precisely the prince Æðelstan meant in his will is less obvious:

Ic geann Ælfswyðe, minre fostermeder, for hire myclon geearnungon, þæs landes æt Westune, þe ic gebohte æt minon fæder, mid þridde healf hund mancuson goldes, be gewiht.

'I grant to my foster-mother Ælfswyð, for her great deserts, the estate at Weston, which I bought from my father for 250 mancuses of gold, weighed out.'

In the letter supposedly by King Edward the Confessor confirming the grant to St Peter's Westminster which was made by *Tosti eorll and Leofrun his wif min fostermoder*, 'Earl Tostig and his wife Leofrun, my foster-mother', the wording is ambiguous, and there are in any case problems about the authenticity of this writ. The use of the term 'foster-mother' is one of the few details in it that stands out as unlikely to be invention.

We may note here also that Ine's humane laws cover provision for the fostering of foundlings, *to fundenecildes fostre*, and also protection for the unacknowledged illegitimate child. The main protection for man, woman or child in Anglo-Saxon England was their *wergild*, the fine that had to be paid if they were killed. Even the unacknowledged bastard has – according to Ine – that protection, but whereas the father or other kin would normally be the recipient of the fine, a father that has not acknowledged the living child is not permitted to benefit from its death. The *wergild* goes to the lord of the estate or the king, either of whom would be the proper protector of the disadvantaged. The *wergild* of men and women of the same class was identical, at any rate according to the laws of Æðelbert, and I know of no indication that the *wergild* status of a woman changed on her marriage. Pregnant women are protected by double *wergild* rights – full *wergild* for themselves, and half for the child they carry, the half to be determined according to the father's status.

We do not have much evidence to go on for the fate of the deprived or disadvantaged, the orphan girls or boys, the bastards and the stepchildren. That the fate of stepchildren was conventionally held to be harsh may be suggested by the fact that *steopcild* regularly translated Latin *orphanus*, 'orphan', notably in various Biblical contexts. It is therefore pleasant to be able to record the attractively efficient arrangements made in the mid-eleventh-century will of Ketel: 'And I and my stepdaughter Ælfgifu have made an agreement about the estate at Onehouse, that whichever of us shall live the longer, is to have as much land as the two of us have there. And if death befalls us both on the way to Rome, the estate is to go to Bury St Edmunds for me and for Sæflæd [his wife ?] and for Ælfgifu, but the men are all to be free.'

Another section in the will of the same Ketel draws our attention to the relationship of brothers and sisters. He has made with his sisters efficient arrangements not dissimilar to the one he has made with his stepdaughter. Both his sisters Gode and Bote are to inherit estates if they live longer than he does. On the other hand, if he should outlive them he points out that they have arranged for him to inherit estates (presumably of equivalent value) from them. We do not have the wills of Gode and Bote, and many arrangements of this kind would be purely verbal agreements. But we notice some kind of concern here that estates that were originally in the same family and separately inherited should be brought together again. Another legal arrangement concerning the purchase of an estate in Kent is recorded in an eleventh-century charter. Godric of Bourne bought the estate at Offham from his sister Eadgifu with full rights to give or bequeath it to whoever he wished. Obviously not all arrangements between brothers and sisters were left as verbal ones: there were three copies made of the document recording this transaction.

In the early years of Anglo-Saxon England we occasionally see royal brothers protectively defending family honour, much as *Gísla saga* initially defined the fraternal role. Bede tells us the story of Penda King of Mercia who drove Cenwealh of Wessex from his kingdom because Cenwealh had repudiated his wife, Penda's sister. In the early years of Christianity where women were powerful both as royalty and as abbesses we occasionally get indications of a sister's role as adviser. A Peterborough addition to the *Anglo-Saxon Chronicle* tells us that Wulfhere endowed the monastery on the advice of a number of excellent people including his brothers and the archbishops, but naming also his sisters Cyneburh and Cyneswið. That a sister might be the recipient of *wergild* is told to us in an eleventh-century document on the founding of St Mildrið's monastery in Thanet which preserves a miraculous tale of how Eafe chose the site of the foundation as *wergild* for her murdered brothers.

In the later material we meet brothers and sisters on a more prosaic and practical basis. The will of Wulfwaru in the late tenth century leaves an estate to be divided between her elder son and younger daughter, but 'they are to share the main residence (*heafodbotl*) between them as fairly as they can so that each of them shall have a reasonable part of it'. We are not told whether either of them was married or expecting to be, but I suppose the implication to be that they were not. An amusing division of family duties occurs as part of a grammar lesson in a text by Ælfric. He is explaining the use of the Latin vocative and giving parallel examples in Latin and English. I quote the Old English only:

eala ðu fæder min, lær þinne sunu; eala ðu min modor, scryd ðinne sunu;...eala ðu ure swuster syle us drincan. ET CETERA

'Father, teach your son; mother, clothe your son; sister, give us something to drink.'

Tacitus writing about the *Germani* in the pre-Anglo-Saxon period claimed that among them the sons of sisters were as highly honoured by their uncles as by their fathers. It could not be statistically demonstrated that in the recorded Anglo-Saxon period brothers felt a greater degree of protectiveness and concern for their sisters' sons than for their brothers' sons, but we do get a range of evidence for a degree of affection and responsibility for the extended family, the nephews and nieces and remoter kin. Up to a point we are baffled by the simple use of the word *mæg*, 'kinsman'. It is used of ancestors, of relatives by blood and relatives by marriage, of close kin, sometimes, as parents or brothers, or of remoter degrees of kinship. But in the closer degrees the words are more specific than ours. The Old English etymon of 'nephew' exists in the form *nefa*, but it is not often used. Anglo-Saxons prefer to specify as 'sister's son' or 'brother's son', 'sister's daughter' or 'brother's daughter'. Bede tends to think in these terms even when writing Latin and uses *filius sororis* regularly where *nepos* would have been perfectly possible.

One significant story told us by Bede concerns a man called Imma, who was taken captive after a battle between Mercians and Northumbrians. Bede is interested basically in the miraculous element of the story, the loosening of the captive's chains. Eventually Imma finds himself in the south, and he makes his way to King Hloðhere of Kent *qui erat filius sororis Ædilthrydae reginae...quia et ipse quondam eiusdem reginae minister fuerat*, 'who was the son of the sister of Queen Æðelðryð, because [Imma] had himself formerly been a *þegn* of that queen.' The degrees of protection spread far when the *þegn* of a Northumbrian queen could expect assistance from her nephew in Kent.

There are references in literature and chronicles to sisters' sons who fought beside and for their mothers' brothers. The best-known example is in the poem *The Battle of Maldon*, where:

> Wund wearð Wulfmær,    wælreste geceas
> Byrhtnoðes mæg:    he mid billum wearð
> his swustersunu,    swiðe forheawen.

'Wulfmær, kinsman of Byrhtnoð, son of his sister, was wounded and died; he was savagely cut down with swords.'

In the record of the *Anglo-Saxon Chronicle* for 1054 one version tells us that Earl Siward fought a battle in Scotland, and though he lived *his agen sunu* was killed. The D text of the *Chronicle* which is usually better informed on northern affairs writes: *Ac his sunu Osbarn. and his sweostor sunu Sihward...wurdon þær ofslægene*, 'but his son Osbarn and his sister's son Sihward were killed there'. They are the only two names singled out among the many dead. In the complicated provisions of the reeve Abba's will, made in the first half of the ninth century, if Abba does not have a child the land is to go to the heir of his brothers. The word is *ærfeweard*, which could be used of a son or a daughter or, presumably, of grandchildren. If they have no such heir the land is to go to Freoðomund, and we have not the faintest idea who he is or what his relationship is to the testator. If Freoðomund should have died the land goes to *minra swæstarsuna swelcum se hit geðian wile and him gifeðe bið*, 'such of my sisters' sons as shall wish to have it and to whom it is granted'. The distinction between *ærfeweard* in one clause and *sunu* in another is possibly that the sisters have already given birth to sons, but it is not yet certain whether the brothers will have children or of what sex. Abba probably made this will fairly early, because a good deal of it depends on the proviso of whether or not he has a child himself. *Bearn*, 'child', obviously means either son or daughter. The will is a good example of the words 'sister's son' being used purely descriptively, without any of the emotional overtones which Tacitus implies should be accorded them, and Abba's completely free choice indicates that he prefers his brothers' descendants to inherit. Such matters were much more likely to be decided by degrees of affection within the family than any priorities imposed by clan tradition.

The will of Æðelgifu is, as usual, interesting. She tells us that she was left property by her husband with full right to grant or bequeath it where she wished. Nevertheless, after her husband's death there were those among his kin who were prepared to dispute the widow's inheritance, and Eadhelm, her husband's sister's son, evidently took from her the estate at Standon by force. An appeal to the king by Æðelgifu was successful and her nephew returned the land to her *on his unþonc*, 'against his wishes'. Her husband's kin do not seem to feature among her legatees, but since we do not know the relationship of most of them to the testatrix this is conjecture based on negative evidence. Her husband's daughter – clearly not her own – receives a small bequest of land, 'if she is still alive'. Otherwise the legatees that can be identified by relationship are Æðelgifu's own family. A major legatee is Leofwine, her sister's son. Another sister's son Wulfmær and a sister's daughter Ælfgifu both receive the same legacy of five mancuses, the girl receiving in addition some clothes and furnishings. But Æðelgifu's problems are not only with her husband's family. Her 'kinswoman' Leofrun gets a fairly substantial bequest including the land at Thrupp, which she has only on condition of a promise to lay aside all anger and not to ask for anything more. But in the event of her not being willing to do this the land still goes to her family, being divided instead among her children.

One minor detail that stands out is the extent to which churchmen take note for the welfare of their sisters and their sisters' children. The will of Bishop Theodred of London leaves estates to Osgot his sister's son, and Offa his sister's son, and Offa's brother, whose name is omitted. Bishop Ælfsige leaves land to a sister and an unidentified kinswoman. A charter from Oswald Bishop of Worcester gives three hides of land to Ælfhild 'for the love of God and for the kinship between us' for her lifetime and after her death to two successive heirs. Another area in which such family feeling repeatedly manifests itself is in the manumission of slaves. Most wills that include manumission clauses tend to free people by family, but it is also possible for slaves to acquire enough money to buy their own freedom, and such transactions are recorded in a number of surviving monastic documents. Men buy freedom for themselves, their wives and their children, and the witnesses to their newly acquired status are carefully noted. In an Exeter record a woman Ediþ bought the freedom of herself and her offspring for twenty-four pence. A man buys the freedom of Leoflæd his 'kinswoman'; another that of his brother's daughter.

One of the most interesting things to emerge from a study of the Anglo-Saxon documents relating to family is the feeling of companionableness among kin as distinct from any imposition of paternal or fraternal authority. We are accustomed in the poetry to such compounds as *winemæg*, 'friend-kin', but we usually find it in contexts where it is used of a group of retainers and has masculine

29 Illustration of the episode in Genesis where Tamar gives birth to twins.

connotations. But we have several records of agreements where it is clear that a number of the family, men and women, have settled down with complete amity to work out reasonable divisions of inheritance. One such begins: 'This is the agreement between Ealhburg and Eadweald', and is from the early ninth century. Eadweald is apparently due to inherit from Ealhburg but there are conditions that she requires him to observe. It may have been the same Eadweald who made an agreement with Cyneðryð widow of Æðelmod. This one is particularly interesting in that it works out a rationale for the inheritance where there is no obvious direct heir:

Nis Eðelmode enig meghond neor ðes cynnes ðanne Eadwald his modar his broðar dohtar; mest cyn ðet he ðet lond hebbe and his beorn yfter him.

'There is no kin closer to Æðelmod than Eadweald whose mother was Æðelmod's niece [brother's daughter]. It is most fair that he should have the land, and his children after him.'

It is not only in wills and charters that we get this sense of friendship between kin, including brothers and sisters, nephews and nieces, but also men and women more remotely related. Æðelweard, who wrote a Latin chronicle early in the eleventh century in the time of King Æðelræd, was a member of the secular nobility. He claims descent from King Æthelwulf (King Ælfred's father) and at the beginning of his *Chronicle* tells us a good deal about the recent family history of the West-Saxon royal house. It is actually one of the documents that tells us most clearly about the power-political games that King Ælfred's descendants played, establishing Continental alliances through daughters and sisters. But Æðelweard's interest is in the relationship between himself and his *consobrina Mathilda* to whom his book is addressed. I suppose *consobrina* is the word an Anglo-Saxon would come up with if he was trying to think of a Latin equivalent for *mæg*, 'kinswoman'. The relationship is fairly remote. Mathilda is the great-great-granddaughter of King Ælfred, and the connection between the writer Æðelweard and his *consobrina* is that they are both descended from Ælfred's father.

At the time when Æðelweard was writing Mathilda was probably abbess of Essen in Germany. Æðelweard opens his *Chronicle* with an account of the correspondence between them, addressing her as *carissima*, and mentioning the delight her letter has given him. At the beginning of Books II and III she is not named, but is again addressed as *carissima*. In Book IV she is *carissima soror*, and the author in apologising for the length of the work, says that as he has written out of love for her so may she read in love for himself, and he asks that she shall not be too severe a judge. In the main body of Book IV she is again addressed lovingly by name, and the author says that he dedicates this work to her out of family affection. We do not even know if they had met. But the terms mark no small degree of affection and respect for a kinswoman both remote geographically, and remote on the family tree.

## FURTHER READING

Some editions of laws and wills have already been cited after chapters 2 and 3 above, but other wills including Ælfred's are published by HARMER in *English Historical Documents*. Text and translation of Æðelweard's *Chronicle* are by CAMPBELL. *Gísla saga* is translated by JOHNSTON. An early but useful work is PHILLPOTTS, *Kindred and Clan*, and some articles on kinship in this period will be found in the bibliography under LANCASTER, LOYN and HOLT.

# 5. Manor and Court

In the Domesday survey of land-holding there is an Anglo-Saxon woman named as having held numerous estates in the time of Edward the Confessor. She is called by the Norman scribes Eddiva, spelt in various ways. She is almost always referred to as *pulchra*, 'the beautiful', sometimes as *dives*, 'the rich'. Her cognomen occasionally is in a Latinised spelling of its English form *faira*, 'the fair'. Eddiva represents Old English Eadgifu so we may call her Eadgifu the Fair. There have been scholarly attempts to identify her with some character of political significance named in later chronicles, possibly the mistress, less probably the wife, of Earl Harold son of Godwine who fell in 1066. Yet we are told so little in chronicles that the material on which to base identification remains elusive. It is only from the Domesday material that we get real evidence of her wealth and power. She held land in Buckinghamshire, Hertfordshire, Cambridgeshire, Essex and Suffolk, probably also in Lincolnshire and Yorkshire. Her lands have been calculated as amounting to 230 hides, more than 27,000 acres. I list a few of the Cambridgeshire entries:

Exning:...Eadgifu the Fair held this manor, and in this manor were 7 freemen, Eadgifu's men....
Fulbourn:...Young Godwine, Eadgifu the Fair's man, held this manor.
Cherry Hinton:...Eadgifu the Fair held this manor. 8 freemen were there....
Teversham:...2 freemen, Eadgifu's men, held it....
In the same village...5 men of Eadgifu's held this land....
Horseheath:...Eadgifu held this land. 2 freemen, her men, were there.
In the same village...Godwine, Eadgifu's man, held this land....
Babraham: Alric the priest held this land under Eadgifu....

The list could be continued indefinitely. Many of her under-tenants are named: 'Godmann Eadgifu's man held this land'; 'Ealdræd held this land under Eadgifu'. Their rights and hers are spelt out with the usual care, whether they had the right to sell the tenancy or not, or to withdraw from her service, and in which places and circumstances she retained jurisdiction. Among her Cambridgeshire under-tenants four are women. Godgifu held an estate in Croydon of something less than one hide and had freedom to withdraw. Leofgifu held about thirty acres of land in the same village and sixty in Arrington. She too 'could withdraw'. Leofflæd, who had forty acres in Balsham, 'could not withdraw'. Sægifu, who held land in Whaddon, 'could grant to whom she would'. A dramatic incident is narrated in Hertfordshire Domesday. In the description of an estate in Watton it is said:

Godwine held this land from St Peter's Church, Westminster; he could not sell but after his death it was to return to the Church. But his wife turned with this land to Eadgifu the Fair, by force, and held it in the lifetime and after the death of King Edward [uxor eius cum hac terre uertit se per uim ad Eddeuam pulchram. et tenebat eam die qua rex Eadwardus fuit vivus et mortuus].

What factional interests are represented here, and what support Eadgifu the Fair was mustering cannot be determined. After 1066 we hear no more of her fate than we have learned of her life. If she lived or stayed in England after the Conquest she was evidently, like most pre-Conquest magnates, deprived of all her lands.

She is by no means the only powerful woman we know of from the Anglo-Saxon period, but we are sometimes a little better informed at the very least about their family connections. We know, for example, virtually nothing about Queen Cyneðryð, wife of the eighth-century Offa of Mercia, that can be counted as historical fact, but at least we know her role in a historical context. She became in late legend a stereotype figure of the evil woman and was accused in a number of hagiographical writings and Norman chronicles of instigating the murder of Æðelbert of East Anglia, king and saint. The *Anglo-Saxon Chronicle*, which is the nearest we can get to a contemporary statement, says without accusation or embellishment: 'In this year [792] Offa king of the Mercians had king Æðelbert beheaded'. But there are four facts that tell us something about Cyneðryð: she was a queen of Mercia; Alcuin refers to her *pietas*, her 'piety', in a letter to her son; she was the only queen in the whole of Anglo-Saxon history to have had coins struck in her name; and she was either known widely enough or feared enough for legends to cluster round her. I am not sure that we should dismiss Alcuin's use of the word *pietas* as simple courtesy – there were after all other graceful words he might have chosen if that one seemed less than accurate, and indeed if she were in her lifetime to have acquired any reputation for crime the word would have been an insult and a mockery. Her name on the coins is very

30 Coin of Cyneðryð.

real evidence of power and authority, and it is a common folk-tale pattern that women of secular power are held to have misused it either directly or by influence.

The assumption that the influence and advice of women is malign rather than benevolent, however, is not made by early writers of charters, many of which note the occasions when the grant is not merely from a king but from king and queen jointly, or from the king at his queen's request. Ine of Wessex in 725 granting land to Glastonbury gives it *cum coniuge Æthelburge*, 'with my wife Æðelburg'. A few years later his successor Æðelheard, leaving land to the same foundation, does so *simulque regina Fridogiþa*, 'in conjunction with the queen Friðugyð', and Friðugyð attested the charter. But when we come to look for any other evidence of the activities of these early queens of Wessex we have in the *Anglo-Saxon Chronicle* one sentence only on each of them. In 722 apparently 'Queen Æðelburg destroyed Taunton which Ine had built'. In 737 Queen Friðugyð journeyed to Rome. The second of these is a commonplace enough comment on leading men and women in the church or state. The first is one on which we should have liked some more information. As it stands it is merely another indication of the power that could be in the hands of a royal woman, and we have no idea of the political angle. There is no obvious element of judgement in the chronicler's comment.

There is only one royal lady in Anglo-Saxon England whose career as ruler we can look at a little more closely, and that is the famous Æðelflæd, Lady of the Mercians, daughter of King Ælfred of Wessex. Her title corresponds exactly to that of her husband. She was *hlæfdige Myrcena*, as he was *hlaford Myrcena*, 'Lord of the Mercians'. It is clear that he was ill for some time before his death and that she took over the real power in Mercia well before he died in 911. For the next seven years until her own death in 918 she was one of the most powerful figures in England. The basic West-Saxon text of the *Anglo-Saxon Chronicle* plays down her role, but a text incorporated into the *Chronicle* known as the *Mercian Register* gives us a competent survey of Æðelflæd's achievements. In 910 she began her policy of fortress-building and by 915 she had built ten. Not all the places are now identifiable; some that are include Bridgnorth, Tamworth, Stafford and Warwick. The *Register* does not imply that she sat at home sending men out to do the work. The annal for 914 for example reads:

In this year by the grace of God Æðelflæd, Lady of the Mercians, went with all the Mercians to Tamworth, and built the fortress there in the early summer, and before the beginning of August, the one at Stafford.

In the west she had problems with the Welsh against whom she sent a punitive expedition after the killing of Abbot Ecgbeorht in 916. In 917 and 918 she turned her attention against the Vikings, winning Derby and district back from them, and subsequently gaining control of Leicester without a fight. The Vikings in

York promised her allegiance. In between the accounts of these political manoeuvres we get glimpses of a person. When she won Derby she lost four of her *þegnas*, and the *Register* comments that 'they were dear to her'.

Æðelflæd was, in her policy of fortress-building and her strategy against the Vikings, acting in collaboration with her brother Edward the Elder, who was carrying out a similar programme in Wessex. This makes it the more surprising that the official West-Saxon version of the *Chronicle* should have given her so little recognition. In addition to her support of Edward she was, at any rate according to Irish sources, occupied in fighting against Norwegian immigrants in the north-west also, and making alliances with Britons, Picts and Scots against them. It has been pointed out that her high reputation outside Mercia and Wessex is signalled by the fact that Welsh and Irish sources record her death, and the *Annals of Ulster* which do not note the deaths of Ælfred and Edward, Kings of Wessex, do note that of Æðelflæd, *famosissima regina Saxonum*: 'most famous queen of the English'. William of Malmesbury, one of our more reliable post-Conquest historians, also has much to say in her praise: she *viros domesticos protegeret, alienos terreret*, 'protected her own men and terrified aliens'. Indeed there is no reason why she should not have absorbed her father's theories on kingship. William's comments sound like a paraphrase of King Ælfred's approving words on former rulers in England who had been successful both in protecting their own territory and in extending their dominions.

William of Malmesbury was not the only post-Conquest historian to admire Æðelflæd's achievements. Henry of Huntingdon, writing in the twelfth century, derives a good deal of his pre-Conquest material from the *Anglo-Saxon Chronicle* but does not always get it right. Thus he thinks that Æðelflæd was daughter not wife of Æðelræd. He is nevertheless so impressed with her record that it calls from him a tribute in verse beginning *O Elfleda potens* and mistakenly calling her *virgo*, 'virgin'. The verse dwells mainly, as indeed William of Malmesbury does, on the paradox of her feminine nature and masculine achievements. Both use the word *virago*, which had not then acquired any contemptuous overtones. But it is of some interest that this 'paradox' seems to strike the post-Conquest writers much more forcibly than it does any of Æðelflæd's contemporaries. We do not note any particular expressions of astonishment in the *Mercian Register*.

Æðelflæd has not left many charters. There are two from herself and her husband to ecclesiastical establishments. Another in a later manuscript describes a gift of land from Æðelflæd *domina Merciorum* to *meo fideli amico Alchelme*, 'my loyal friend'. Her only other authenticated charter grants land to Eadric *minister*, evidently one of her *þegnas*. An interesting charter from Bishop Wærferð and the community at Worcester dated 904 gives land to Æðelflæd and her husband, referring to them equally in the phrase *syllað and gewritað Æðelrede and Æðelflæde heora hlafordum*, 'give and grant by charter to Æðelræd and Æðelflæd their lords'. Their daughter is also named here: 'If Ælfwynn survives them it shall...remain uncontested so long as she lives; and after the death of the three of them it shall be given back without dispute to the lord of the church for the souls of the three of them'.

It is a pity not to know more about Ælfwynn. She appears to be a witness to two charters, which is unusual for a woman who was neither queen, queen-mother nor abbess. She would have been a grown woman at the time of her mother's death – possibly as old as thirty. We would expect her to have succeeded Æðelflæd as *hlæfdige Myrcena*, and it seems that for a brief period of about six months she did so. After that her uncle Edward, King of Wessex, took action and the wording of the *Mercian Register* implies that he aroused resentment. Æðelflæd died before midsummer. Three weeks before Christmas 'the daughter of Æðelræd Lord of the Mercians was deprived of all rule in Mercia and taken into Wessex. She was called Ælfwynn'. We hear no more of her and Edward died a few years later in 924. His son Æðelstan, much extolled by the *Anglo-Saxon Chronicle* and by later historians, succeeded in Wessex, and the *Mercian Register* tells us that he was chosen by the Mercians also as king. If William of Malmesbury's information is accurate he had actually been brought up among them at the court of his father's sister Æðelflæd *hlæfdige*. She could have taught him much.

The peaceable and peace-time activities of queens and princesses inevitably get little attention in chronicles centering on power-struggles. We have charters from them recording gifts of land and estates, usually to ecclesiastical foundations, very rarely to individuals. Æðelswið, who was a sister to King Ælfred and queen of the Mercians before her niece Æðelflæd became their lady, is one of the few who gave land to a *minister* or *þegn* in her own name, though she is also joint-donor with her husband in two other charters. On all charters she is styled *regina*, 'queen', on one of them 'queen of the Mercians', on another, more largely *regina Anglorum*, 'queen of the English'. She and her husband Burgræd jointly grant

31, 32 The rings of Æðelswið (*left*) and Eawyn (*above*)

land to Bishop Alwine, and to an otherwise unidentified character Wulflaf. She attests charters where she is not named as one of the givers, and similarly her husband attests her charter in which she personally grants land to the *þegn* Cuðwulf who is described as *fidelissimus*, 'most loyal'. Land and estates were doubtless the most cherished rewards for service, but they were not the only things within the queen's gift. That women were ring-givers in reality as well as in heroic poetry is indicated by the survival of a superb gold finger-ring with Æðelswið's name on it. On it she is styled 'Queen Æðelswið', EAÐELSVIÐ REGNA. The ring is too large for the female hand, and unless it was designed deliberately in order to slide over gloves or arthritic knuckles, its size suggests it was intended for the male hand, and the name on it intended to record giver not owner. The text is somewhat awkwardly fitted in and was almost certainly not part of the original design. Other pieces of jewellery with names on often do make it clear that the name is that of the owner. One woman's ring from roughly the same period as Æðelswið's though of unknown provenance has an unmistakeable ownership formula: *Eawen mie ah*, 'Eawyn owns me'.

That queens were not merely owners and givers of estates and rings but were personally concerned in the control of estates and their revenues is indicated by several surviving documents. Edith, widow of Edward the Confessor, sends a letter in which her main concern appears to be a gift of land, but which ends plaintively, 'and I ask also from you a just judgement on Wudumann, to whom I entrusted my horses, and who has withheld from me for six years my rent both in honey and in cash'. Queen Eadgifu, third wife of Edward the Elder and sister-in-law of the Lady of the Mercians, had considerable trouble over her estate at Cooling, and eventually donated it to Christ Church. The account of its previous history is full of significant detail. She inherited the estate from her father, and held its title-deed. A man called Goda had previously occupied the place temporarily in return for a loan to Eadgifu's father, and he continues to claim his right to it, doubtless believing that possession was nine-tenths of the law. Eadgifu's assertion that her father had paid the debt had to be ratified by formal oath. Some time later Goda forfeited all his estates, which King Edward then handed over to Eadgifu. She said that she would not repay Goda as he had deserved, and restored his lands to him, 'but she refused to give back the title-deeds until she knew how loyally he would behave towards her with respect to the lands'.

There are, of course, far fewer charters from men and women of lower rank than from kings or queens, and the ones that survive on the whole deal with bequests to ecclesiastical foundations. Even so it is remarkable how many of them are by husband and wife jointly, and it is I think even more remarkable how often the grants of kings to laymen are to husband and wife jointly. We would not expect there to be very many records of gifts by individual women other than royalty, but these too occur. References in these documents to land sold by women, given away by women, inherited by women or in some other way under their control make it clear that they moved in the world of landed property with as much assurance and as full rights as the men of their family. For example in 736 Æðelbald King of the Mercians gave land to Cynebeorht and whoever he wished to choose for his heir. The same king granted a charter to Cyneburh and whoever she should choose for her heir. They were almost certainly grants for ecclesiastical foundations, but the parallel in confirming the right of deciding who was to be the successor is important. Edmund the priest apparently could not grant to Ely land which had been his wife's gift to him without her consent. At any rate the consent is formally noted. But the most interesting range of evidence is found in the wills of both Anglo-Saxon men and women.

Of the Old English wills that survive over a quarter are by women, and there are several more by husband and wife jointly. But in addition to the vernacular documents there are summaries of bequests in various monastic cartularies or chronicles, and the ones that survive are undoubtedly only a fraction of the number that were made. The absence of a will is in fact catered for by the laws of Cnut. His law number 70 specifies that if a man dies intestate (the Old English word is *cwydeleas*, 'silent') his property is to be divided justly between his widow, his children and his close kin. Earlier in the laws of Æðelbert, number 78 specified that a woman who had borne her husband a child was entitled to inherit half his goods on his death. The wills, however, are an excellent range of evidence for the rights of women not only to inherit (as already seen), but also to dispose of estates and of goods according to their own wishes. All the wills left by women include bequests of substantial amounts of land.

Throughout the Anglo-Saxon period the divisions of property within a family must have varied enormously according to time, place, and personal preference. The women who inherit under Wynflæd's will of around 950 are most carefully specified. She leaves estates to her son and grandson, but the first major legatee named is her daughter Æðelflæd, whose name keeps recurring. Æðelflæd receives the personal jewellery, 'the estate at Ebbesborne and the title-deed as a perpetual inheritance to dispose of as she pleases'. Eadmær, almost certainly Wynflæd's son, is also granted estates but is more in the position of a trustee since their subsequent disposal is laid down with great care. 'If Æðelflæd survive [Eadmær] she is to succeed to the estate at Faccombe...If it is God's will that Eadwold be old enough in his father's lifetime, then I ask Eadmær to relinquish to him one of two estates...and after his lifetime, both'. We have no idea what the status or relationship to Wynflæd is of the women Ceolðryð, Ceolwyn, Eadburg, Cynelufu, etc., but they do not receive negligible bequests. These are in movable goods, not in land. Ceolðryð gets a mancus of gold and some valuable clothing; Cynelufu gets 'her share of the untamed horses'. The daughter Æðelflæd is, however, clearly the favoured legatee. She gets 'everything which is un-bequeathed, books and such small things'.

33 A detail from Æðelgifu's will.

We may detect a slightly astringent note in the late tenth-century will of Ælfgifu. It seems obvious from the wording of her bequests that she had no children. It has been conjectured that she was the wife whom Archbishop Odo divorced from King Eadwig because of their kinship but there is no evidence. What is certain is that there is no actual mention of a husband in the phrases where one would expect it. She left to Bishop Æðelwold an estate and asked him to pray *for minae modor an for me*, 'for my mother and for me'. Widows normally ask for prayers for their husband's soul and their own. Almost all Ælfgifu's bequests are either to members of the royal family or to the church except for a small group, apparently her brothers and sisters. What lies behind the wording: 'And to my sister Ælfwaru I grant all that I have lent her; and to my brother's wife Æðelflæd the headband which I have lent her' can only be conjectured.

In Wynflæd's will her daughter Æðelflæd was clearly a favourite, but it would be quite improper to imply that women in general in their wills indulged in any unfair sexual discrimination. There are, of course, equal bequests to male kinsmen, and there is careful and considerate provision for male dependants, both free and unfree. The will of that Æðelflæd who was the second wife of King Edmund contains some of the most succinct provisions. The first section simply makes gifts to her *hlaford*, which must here mean 'king' not 'husband', though in other wills the phrase 'royal lord' sometimes occurs. The second section disposes of estates. Seventeen full estates are specified. The final section deals with smaller bequests of land to various servants such as her reeve and her priests.

And to my reeve Ecgwine I grant the four hides at Hadham...And I grant to my servant [*cniht*] Brihtwold two hides in Donyland...And I grant to Ælfwold my priest two hides in Donyland...And I grant to Æðelmær my priest two hides...And I wish that half my men in every village be freed for my soul.

It may be thought that a royal will is in some ways distinguished from the wills of minor aristocracy, but there is no less assurance in the wills of Leofgifu and of Æðelgifu, both of them clearly women of considerable wealth, and both of them now completely unidentifiable. The main difference between their wills and that of the queen Æðelflæd is that far more of the minor dependants and minor legacies are specified alongside the major ones. Leofgifu grants land to two of her stewards, and her reeve Godric at Waldingfield gets thirty acres. Æðelric, the 'house priest', *hirdprest*, gets an estate at Lawford. Leofgifu also asks that all her *men* should be free *on hirde and on tune*, 'in the household and in the village'. Both here and in other wills *men* must be used generically for men and women, but for really detailed manumission clauses we must look at Æðelgifu's will of around 1000. It is clear that Æðelgifu is no absentee landlord, for she knows her dependants on every estate, their occupations and their family relationships. On the estate at Munden 'Boga and all his family are to be freed, and Winsige and his wife, and Mann and his wife, and Dufe the Old and Æðelðryð'. At Standon the manumissions include Wulfstan 'and his two sons and his stepdaughter'. Other statements specify adults as remaining in service but 'their children are to be freed'. She frees also those in the following occupations: two of her swineherds, Wulfric the huntsman, Mann her goldsmith, an unnamed shepherd, a fuller and, surprisingly, a priest. Many of the wills of both men and women specify bequests to priests, but this is the only indication that a priest could actually be unfree. The other occupational descriptions in Æðelgifu's will are not in any way unusual, though we might note in passing that her fuller was male not female. Most men and women of equivalent rank and wealth would have their own goldsmith, free or unfree. Grimbald, one of Eadgifu the Fair's men, who held land from her in Cambridgeshire (without right to grant or sell) is named as her *aurifaber*, 'goldsmith', and a Gospel-book from Thorney Abbey, Cambridgeshire, has an eleventh-century inscription noting Wulfwine Eadgifu's goldsmith as the donor of two ounces of gold, formerly decorating the binding of the book. Whether Eadgifu the Fair employed two goldsmiths, or we have here two women of the same name is not certain. Location and date make Eadgifu the Fair a possible contender.

Many of the entries in the opening leaves of books in monastic libraries record manumissions by women. The clearest example of a woman's charity is in a Durham manuscript.

[Geatflæd] has given freedom for the love of God and the need of her soul to Ecceard the smith and to Ælstan and his wife, and to all their children, born and unborn, and to Arkil and to Cole and to Ecgferð Aldhun's daughter, and to all those people whom she took for their food in the evil days.

The phrase *þa men þe heo nam heora heafod for hyra mete* is literally something like 'those people from whom she accepted their heads for their food' which indicates on their part a choice of servitude against famine, but a manumission is not a will, and these people did not have to wait for their owner's death for the return of their freedom. Another manumission, this time from Exeter, tells us that *Ælfgyfu gode* bought a family – man and wife and their children – from someone else for twelve mancuses in order to set them free. I am inclined to think that *gode* here is not a proper name but an appellation 'the good'.

It is to be expected that where women had control of estates and inheritance they would become involved in lawsuits as well as in simple land transactions. There are a number of documents which make casually clear a woman's right to sell or exchange land, and the record of a lawsuit between a woman called Wynflæd and a man called Leofwine is instructive. In the first place it is said that Wynflæd's possession of two estates was a matter of exchange: 'Ælfric gave Wynflæd the estates at Hagbourne and at Bradfield in return for the estate at Datchet'. Wynflæd is required to prove ownership of these estates and she does so with the support of many people, named and unnamed. These include a remarkable number of women: 'and the abbess Eadgifu and the abbess Leofrun and Æðelhild and Eadgifu of Lewknor and her sister and her daughter and Ælfgifu and her daughter, and Wulfwyn and Æðelgifu and Ælfwaru and Ælfgifu and Æðelflæd...' Of the twenty-four people named altogether there are eleven men and thirteen women. The text continues *and menig god þegen and god wif þe we ealle atellan ne magon*, 'and many reliable *þegnas* and women, though we cannot now recount them all'. Wynflæd achieves possession of her estate but it is agreed that she should restore to Leofwine all his father's gold and silver. There is some slight ambiguity about how far she carried out this provision, and indeed it is never clear to us what the relationship was between her claim and Leofwine's. In this instance it appears that the matter was settled fairly amicably, but it was not unknown for women to take unlawful and aggressive action. A document basically concerned with the crimes of a man called Wulfbold begins by describing his attack on his stepmother's estates. The king required him to restore what he had stolen, but Wulfbold took no notice and continued a career of crime until his death. The writer, with a fine cumulative sense of outrage, continues: 'After he was dead, over and above all this, his widow went with her child and killed Eadmær the king's *þegn*...' However not all women, apparently, were as competent as might be wished in the handling of their estates. A charter of Æðelræd's refers to a *matrona* named Leoftæt (or Leoflæd) who forfeited estates in Warwickshire *suis ineptiis*. It would be interesting to know what follies or what unfitness was the cause.

A vast range of evidence for women in relation to the land is to be found in place-names, but it is not all evidence of the same kind and needs to be sifted with care. In charter boundaries there are many examples of topographical features, natural and artificial, linked with a woman's name though we cannot necessarily establish the nature of the connection. The Ælflæd who gave her name to *Ælflæde brycg*, the Burghild whose name is concealed in Buckle Street, the Eadburg of Aberford (Eadburg's ford) and the Æðelflæd whose name occurs in the phrase *Æðelflæde stig* in a 956 Worcestershire charter boundary, were probably responsible for the building or upkeep of the bridge, ford or road in question, but this cannot be established conclusively. It would be delightful but unscholarly to assume that this Æðelflæd was the Lady of the Mercians, or to speculate that the original manuscript reading *sige*, 'victory', later altered to *stige*, 'way', was a proper commemorative form. On the other hand though we know nothing about the Ælfgifu whose name is found in Alvechurch, 'Ælfgifu's church', we may reasonably take it for granted that she had it built or perhaps restored. There is a good deal of supportive evidence for women in such a role. We may note in this connection the will of Siflæd:

and min kirke be fre. And Wlmer prest singe þerate. and his bearntem so longe. so he þen to þen hode. and fre leswe into þere kirke.

'And my church is to be free, and Wulfmær the priest is to sing there, and his descendants so long as they are ordained. There is to be free meadow for the church.'

A charming note in the agreement drawn up between Osulf and his wife Leofrun with Bury St Edmunds requiring that four priests shall sing twelve masses each week, insists that the choice of two priests shall rest with Abbot Leofstan and with Leofrun. Osulf, it seems, leaves such matters to his wife's judgement.

Crofts, cottages, fields, woods and streams linked with female personal names abound, and again it is hard to know quite what the links imply. In the case of cottage and field, land-holding is a reasonable proposition; in the case of a wood, the woman may simply have had rights of collecting fuel. On the other hand, where the name is combined with the standard word for a settlement *tun*, we may assume that the woman who gave her name to a *tun* was an estate-holder of some significance. Not all the *tunas* to which women gave their names now survive. There are a number recorded in Anglo-Saxon charter boundaries which have subsequently been lost, an unidentified *Cyneburginctun* in a West-Midland charter of 840, for example, but Domesday records thirty or more place-names of this type. Others which are not in Domesday turn up in later documents and since it is highly improbable that formations of this kind could have been made after the Conquest, we are entitled to infer that the Eadburg whose name gave us Edburton, Sussex (twelfth-century form *Eadburgeton*) was herself an Anglo-Saxon woman. Certainly there are enough names of this kind fully to support the evidence of wills, charters and Domesday records of pre-Conquest holdings, showing that it was by no means abnormal for a woman to be the lord/lady in charge of an estate. What they tell us in addition to this is that she may have been of sufficient importance or charisma for her name to be permanently associated with it. A random selection from a number of counties shows us Darlton in Nottinghamshire containing the name Deorlufu, Wollaton in Devon derived from Wulfgifu, Elton in Welford, Berkshire, from Æðelflæd, Chilverton in Kent from Ceolwaru and so on.

It has also been pointed out that the extent to which women's names occur in compounds with Old English *leah*, 'glade' or 'clearing' (e.g. Audley in Staffordshire), shows the extent to which women were responsible for the exploitation of land for agriculture. Where female names occur with *burh* it has been suggested that *burh* should be interpreted as 'religious foundation' but it is more probable that it had here its normal meaning of 'fortified manor house'. Any woman who was in charge of an estate would automatically have normal *þegn's* duties as described in *Rectitudines: fyrdfæreld, and burhbote and brycgeweorc*, 'military service, and fortress-repair, and upkeep of bridges', unless her charter made specific concessions. King Edgar granted land at Overton to that *dilectissima femine Ælflæde* free of all secular dues except for military service and fortress work. Manorial status involved manorial responsibilities regardless of the sex of the land-holder. Thus Bibury, Gloucestershire, probably Beage's *burh*, is likely to have been named after the woman Beage to whom an estate there was leased in the eighth century. Other names of this type are Queniborough, Leicestershire; Bucklebury, Berkshire; Alderbury, Wiltshire, named respectively after the otherwise unknown women Cwene, Burghild and Æðelwaru. It is obvious that the combination of women's names with elements implying land-holding and manorial status (*tun* and *burh*), with land-clearance (*leah*), with church, road and bridge-building or repair (*cyrice*, *stræt*, *ford*, *brycg*), suggests a reasonable range of administrative responsibilities. Of course the personal names of men in similar formations occur more often, but it is significant that women's names appear as frequently as they do.

In the time that such women were able to take off from the practical side of running their estates we may note to what extent they were concerned with education and literacy. This was of course not a range of interest that was confined to women. King Ælfred in the letter to his bishops accompanying his translation of *Cura Pastoralis* expressed his own view: 'all the young people who are now in England, free-born, who have the aptitude to apply themselves, should be set to learning...until they can fully understand how to read English writing'. The word *geoguð*, 'youth', which I have translated 'young people' is sometimes translated 'young men', but there is not a scrap of evidence for assuming such discrimination, and it is clear that among Ælfred's own children education was not confined to his sons. Nor since, according to his biographer, it was his mother who first introduced him to the delights of reading English poetry, is he likely to have thought of literacy as a male prerogative.

It is difficult in this early period to be quite clear what we mean by 'literacy'. It is sometimes taken to mean competence in Latin rather than the vernacular, and certainly since letters between royalty were likely to be written in Latin it is of some interest whether kings and queens were able to read and write these themselves, or needed to employ a competent Latinist. Ælfred assumes that competence in the written vernacular is not unusual, and his statement is

34 A detail from the text of *The Husband's Message* from the *Exeter Book*, including the lines:

> Remembering the former vow of the two of you
> I put together the runes...confirming the oath...'

important since this is an area where it is remarkably hard to gather evidence. We have also to take into account the extent to which runic literacy prevailed among a people whose formal education would be unlikely to include this skill. Finally, it is worth remembering that the teaching of religion may have included more learning by rote than actual studying of text, especially in secular households.

There are two or three texts which suggest that runes might be used to pass private messages between men and women. The poems Riddle 60 from the *Exeter Book* and *The Husband's Message* are sometimes thought of as two sections of one poem, sometimes as two distinct compositions. In either case the two sections (or poems) refer to personal communication. In the second the message is to a woman, a prince's daughter, and in runes. In the first the object, probably to be interpreted as a rune-stave, says that it is a great wonder how it can be fashioned by the point of a knife and a man's ingenuity to speak words 'mouthless' over the mead-bench, carrying a message for 'the two of us alone'. In Riddle 91 a piece of wood refers to itself as *wifes sond*, 'a woman's message'. It is even possible that the woman's duty described in the *Exeter* gnomic verse as *healdan rune* referred to handing on this range of knowledge. Too little material survives in secular contexts for us to check this, and in any case it would be a possibility only in the earlier period of Anglo-Saxon culture. In the later period from which we have evidence of literacy it tends to be literacy in the Roman alphabet, though probably the English language.

I find it difficult to believe that women owned or gave away inscribed jewellery

35 Sutton, Isle of Ely,
brooch. The ownership
formula is inscribed on the
back.

without themselves being able to read the inscriptions, but it is of course possible
that formulae and individual words or names were known, without this implying
greater competence. The ring referred to above with the formula EAÐELSVIÐ
REGNA is a case in point. REGNA must be an error for *regina* and whether this
mattered to donor or recipient we cannot tell. Even those otherwise illiterate in
Latin would know what it was supposed to mean. On the other hand, rings and
brooches with more complex inscriptions are unlikely to have been made for
people who could not have the fun of reading them. The Sutton, Isle of Ely,
brooch has two inscriptions, one of them in Old English, which may be read
as verse:

> Ædvwen me ag:    age hyo Drihten.
> Drihten hine awerie    ðe me hire ætferie,
> bvton hyo me selle    hire agenes willes.

'Ædwen owns me, may the Lord own her. May the Lord curse him who takes me from
her, unless she gives me by her own choice.'

Wynflæd left in her will books to her daughter Æðelflæd, which is one of the
few indications we have that private households might have had small libraries.
Most other people who bequeathed books are ecclesiastics, but one book which
we know to have been given by a woman to the abbey of Horton in Dorsetshire
was a copy of that learned work beloved of King Ælfred and Queen Elizabeth
I, Boethius's *De Consolatione Philosophiae* (Consolation of Philosophy). Horton
was founded about 1050, and the manuscript itself is eleventh century. The first

page records that the book was the gift of Ælfgyð. Æðelgifu mentions not 'books', but 'a book', in her will, and since she left it to St Alban's we may feel fairly sure it was a religious one. Æðelgifu also makes the interesting provision that three of the women in her employment are to be freed on the condition that they sing four psalters every week for a month after her death and a psalter every week for a year. Whether these unfree girls had been taught to chant the psalters by rote or to read them, this specification suggests that they had received a fairly intensive religious education, and Æðelgifu's wording implies that she was personally concerned with it.

It has been said that in the Middle Ages though men in the religious orders tended to be more learned than women, the contrary was true in secular life. It is a generalisation which would be difficult to support from Anglo-Saxon evidence. One difficulty in dealing with the purely secular material is that the existence of a will or a charter does not tell us how widely it was read – whether for example there would be more than one person in a household who could control the contents or decipher a letter arriving from queen or king. Nor do the abilities to read and write necessarily go together, and women who could read documents may still have had trained scribes to write them. Nevertheless, the sheer bulk of the material suggests a fair number of people who could understand it. A charter is, after all, not magic. It is no use being able to say 'I have a charter that gives me the right to this land' unless one can also point out where it specifies the boundaries or other details. It must have been in the interests of land-holders, both men and women, not to have to rely too much on other people for such important information, but there is very little support for dividing the sexes here into the literate and the less literate, and we can point to a fair amount of evidence for the literacy in some degree of both men and women. The three sisters Beornwyn, Ælflæd and Walenburg who received a charter from Egbert, King of the West-Saxons, confirming their joint inheritance, needed it because the original charter had been lost. The new charter specifies that their inheritance was to be shared between them in equal proportions, but added a note that at some stage Beornwyn took Dartington in Devon for her share of the family possessions, whereupon Ælflæd took land elsewhere *in dominium peculiare*, 'for her personal property'. The implications of the document must be on the one hand that the sisters knew the exact contents of the old charter (including boundaries) for the new one to be drawn up, and that it was worth their while having a record made of a private arrangement between themselves. Neither husbands nor heirs are mentioned.

Two of the queens in the late Anglo-Saxon period appear to have had some claims to learning, not merely literacy. The *Encomium Emmae* is a work written for Ælfgifu-Emma the wife of Æðelræd and later of Cnut. We may assume she commissioned it, but whether she did or not, such a book would be a poor sort of compliment to a woman who could not read it. Edith, wife of Edward the

36 Queen Ælfgifu-Emma graciously accepts the gift of a book, *Encomium Emmae Reginae*, written in her praise.

Confessor, is commended by post-Conquest writers for her learning, and she is one of the few Anglo-Saxon queens whose letters are preserved. They are public letters, presumably dictated by her rather than actually written, but they show her regular use of the written word as a form of communication.

Another letter is one from Queen Ælfðryð wife of King Edgar showing a woman of rank in a different role. There is in Old English only one occurrence of the word *þingestre*, which means something like 'female advocate' and it is used of the Virgin Mary in a sentence where Mary is asked to intercede for humanity: *þæt heo beo milde mundbore & bliþe þingestre*, 'may she be a generous protector and a gracious advocate'. It is incidentally also the only occurrence of the feminine form *mundbore*. Yet neither of these words could have been invented only to be used of Mary, they must have already been part of Old English vocabulary. We have already had plenty of evidence for women in the role of *mundbore*, 'protector', but *þingestre* is slightly more problematic. It cannot refer to any public or professional status, but it obviously can refer to a role that

37 (*top*) Types of jewellery worn by women: (*left*) Chessell Down brooch (from the Isle of Wight; (*centre*) Faversham pendant (Kent); (*right*) Sarre brooch and necklace (Kent).

38 (*above*) Types of jewellery worn by men: (*top left and centre*) Taplow clasps; (*bottom left*) Taplow buckle (Buckinghamshire); (*bottom right*) Faversham buckle; (*top right*) Faversham clasp (Kent).

39 The headbands of these women are coloured yellow in the manuscript and perhaps represent the type of gold band mentioned in the wills.

women of power could be asked to assume. The letter of Ælfðryð tells us:

Wulfgyð rode to me at Combe, looking for me. And I then, because she was kin to me...obtained from Bishop Æðelwold that they [Wulfgyð and her husband] might enjoy the land for their lifetime...And with great difficulty we two brought matters to this conclusion.

The will of Brihtric and Ælfswið contains a clause leaving to the queen a ring worth thirty mancuses of gold and a stallion *to foresprǣce þæt se cwyde standan moste*, 'for her advocacy that the will may stand'. It is fairly obvious that women would not have been asked to assume this role unless they were expected to be effective, and it is also obvious that such requests were open and formal, not a private matter of special pleading.

So far we have been concerned mostly with responsibility and administration, and not with any visual impression of the Anglo-Saxon aristocratic woman. The picture given to us by the poetry depends on a fairly narrow range of status words, like *freolic*, 'noble', which are emotive rather than descriptive. Women are commended for their wisdom. A few words refer to their appearance. A favourite epithet of the poet who describes Judith in the poem of that name is *wundenlocc* but I am not sure whether that refers to curled or plaited hair, and most manuscript illustrations show women with their heads covered. The only other words that give us any visual impression are the ones referring to jewellery, and these are not particularly informative. A queen or princess is *beaghroden*, 'wearing rings', and since we do not know whether a *beag* is a finger-ring, an arm-ring or a neck-ring unless there is something else in the context to tell us, even *beaghroden* is not as helpful as it might be. In the early period we can get a good deal of information from pagan furnished graves in which women are buried with their jewellery, and the impressive contents of some women's graves show us not only the extent of their wealth, but also a good deal about their range and type of personal possessions. In this early period the distinctive item is the necklace and pendant. Both sexes wore brooches, rings and ornamented belt-buckles. Brooches in any case were needed to fasten clothing together, but certain types of brooches were worn only by women. But the Anglo-Saxon period covers several centuries and fashions change. From the later period our sources are less precise. Instead of grave-goods with their clear and distinctive patterns of information, there are odd finds of single items. Wills sometimes specify rings or brooches as part of a bequest. Wynflæd leaves to her daughter Æðelflæd *hyre agrafenan beah and hyre mentelpreon*. The ring which is 'engraved' perhaps had an inscription; the *mentelpreon* must be a brooch for fastening a cloak. Many wills of men and women leave rings of considerable value to their kin of either sex, to their lord, or to a religious foundation, which suggests that on the whole these were thought of in terms of strict cash value rather than sentiment. We may suspect here that *beag* usually means 'arm-ring' but we cannot be sure. The three items which recur in bequests to women are rings, brooches, and 'bands', probably gold headbands. It is, I think, on the whole, surprising that so little is mentioned. Æðelgifu, who has her own goldsmith, only includes one headband and one brooch in her bequests, though there are other things such as silver cups, which are doubtless her smith's work. Both Æðelgifu and Wynflæd go into greater detail in describing bequests of clothing, spending as much time in determining who is to have which *cyrtel* as Bishop Theodred does in allocating chasubles. But for the actual appearance of women we are inevitably dependent on manuscript illustrations, which are stylised, tend to be of religious women, and may in any case be copies from foreign source material not from life.

FURTHER READING

Many of the primary sources used in this chapter have been cited already in earlier reading lists, e.g. editions and translations of wills, laws and charters, of Domesday, and of the *Anglo-Saxon Chronicle*. Letters are usually quoted from HARMER, *Anglo-Saxon Writs*. On Æðelflæd, Lady of the Mercians, see specifically WAINWRIGHT, on the place-name evidence see STENTON's article, and GELLING, *Signposts to the Past*. For texts on jewellery, runic, see PAGE, *An Introduction to English Runes*; non-runic, OKASHA, *Hand-List of Anglo-Saxon non-runic inscriptions*. For literacy in general see WORMALD's article, 'The uses of literacy in Anglo-Saxon England and its neighbours'.

40 Choir of virgins: all with crowns and haloes; three also hold books.

# 6. The Religious Life

Bede tells us in his *Ecclesiastical History* that the first woman in the Northumbrian kingdom to take the vows and habit of a nun was Heiu, who founded a monastery at Hartlepool. I say 'monastery' advisedly since many of these early foundations were double houses, monastery and nunnery side by side, always in Anglo-Saxon England ruled by an abbess. Towards the end of the period the monk Ælfric in his Old English version of the *Life of St Edmund* wrote: 'The English race is not deprived of God's saints when in England lie buried such holy ones as this saintly king, and the blessed Cuðberht, and Saint Æðelðryð in Ely, and her sister also'. Between Bede and Ælfric there is much evidence for the development of the Christian religious life in England and the part played in it by women.

The study of saints' lives in some areas and periods can be a dreary one, when we find the same visions, the same miracles, the same martyrdoms repeated over and over again so that all we recognise is the pattern of the story, and we do not find any reality in the person about whom the story is told. But in Anglo-Saxon history many of the men and women who are described as saints come across to us as real people, some admirable, some exasperating, depending on our twentieth-century reactions to their temperaments and qualities. In addition to the biographies there are other, more revealing ranges of evidence, in surviving correspondence, in charter and law.

From the time that Christianity came to England men and women shared equally, not only in conversion to the new faith, but in the learning that accompanied it. When Hild was persuaded by Bishop Aidan not to go to a monastery abroad but to assist in building the monastic tradition in her home country of Northumbria she made both Hartlepool and later Whitby into places of serious Christian education. 'She compelled those under her direction to devote time to the study of the holy scriptures' to such good effect that five men from her monastery subsequently became bishops. Men and women engaged in the Christian monastic life wrote letters to each other in the Latin of their new literacy. Aldhelm addressed his prose *De Virginitate* to the abbess Hildelið and her nuns in the monastery of Barking. Aldhelm's Latin is notoriously difficult and complex, but his work was evidently in use as a regular text-book in the Anglo-Saxon period for both men and women. Early manuscripts of it contain not only the Latin text but also translations of the difficult words either into Old

41 The nuns of Barking
eager to receive a copy of
Aldhelm's *De virginitate*. The
text shows him as offering it
with more deference than the
illustration implies.

English or into a more readily comprehensible Latin. Eighth-century letter-writers, such as the nun Leoba, show themselves much influenced by his style and vocabulary. Aldhelm certainly takes it for granted that the nuns for whom his book was written can cope with his convoluted syntax and abstruse vocabulary, and in fact asks them to let him know whether the style of his work is 'pleasing to [their] intelligence'. It is significant to note that there is no hint whatsoever of the patronising tone concerning the inferior abilities and status of women that characterises the early Middle English *Ancrene Wisse*, 'A Guide for Anchoresses'. The *Ancrene Wisse*, one of our few post-Conquest religious texts to be written in English rather than Latin, is so written out of deference to female ignorance. A good deal of the work is devoted to making sure that women, even women with a religious vocation, shall know their place in a masculine hierarchy and society. Aldhelm, on the other hand, thanks the nuns of Barking with courtesy for their letters to him, admiring their 'extremely rich verbal eloquence' and hopes that they will continue to send him such letters.

From the complex opening pages of Aldhelm's work we are able to put together some idea of the scholarly activities on which the nuns of Barking were engaged. He speaks of their remarkable mental disposition 'roaming widely through the flowering fields of scripture...now scrutinising with careful application the hidden mysteries of the ancient laws...now exploring wisely the fourfold text of [the Gospels]...now duly rummaging through the old stories of the historians and the entries of chroniclers...now sagaciously inquiring into the rules of the grammarians and the teachers of experts on...the rules of metrics...' It sounds a serious enough programme of study, and there is not the hint of an indication that it would differ in range, weight or depth according to the sex of the student. The manner in which Aldhelm and other male ecclesiastics in this early period write to nuns and abbesses is rarely that of instructor to pupil, it is that of brother to sister, and this is as true of the tone of the letters as it is of the formal words of greeting. Men and women were constantly engaged in the practical problems of the spread of the new faith, the supply of books in particular. Boniface, spreading the Christian gospel in the still heathen parts of Germany, writes continually to his contacts in England for additions to his library.

Among the women with whom Boniface exchanged letters the most notable are Leoba, Eadburg and Bucge. Leoba and Bucge are hypocoristic forms of full proper names. Bucge is referred to in one letter as *Haeaburg cognomento Bugge*, so clearly the shortened form was based on the second element. Leoba is derived from the full name Leobgyð. Both forms of her name are used, but her biographer in particular delights in the shortened version and its significance 'the loved one'.

The first letter, from Bucge and her mother Eangyð jointly, apologises for writing *rustico stilo et inpolito sermone*, 'in rustic style and unpolished language', and, though this modesty is a literary convention, it would seem unlikely from the letter itself that they had much time to devote to study. They have, they write, little leisure for the concern of their own souls and their own sins, when they have the much more difficult and serious problem of being in charge of those men and women of various ages, talents and customs entrusted to them. Discord is common among men, but the devil particularly delights in sowing discord in monastic communities, and this too has to be dealt with. The community is troubled by poverty and has not enough land to support it. There are political troubles, and they have virtually no kin living who can give them any help. The letter conjures up a very vivid picture of the administrative problems of the community itself and its precarious existence in the world at large. Both Eangyð and later Bucge develop a strong desire to get away from it and hope to gain peace from these concerns by a pilgrimage to Rome.

Eangyð evidently dies before she can undertake such a pilgrimage. Bucge consults Boniface on the problems involved. His reply is full of good sense, but he also makes it clear that he would consider it presumption on his part to appear to dictate to her in any way. He fully recognises her need for peace of mind, and attempts to weigh up the pros and cons of various courses of action. There

42 The Virtues laying violent hands on *Discordia* who has appeared by stealth in their midst. A drawing from Prudentius' *Psychomachia*.

are practical problems involved in the timing, because of the threats of the Saracens against Rome. He has gone to the trouble of writing to an English woman in Rome, 'our sister Wihtburg', and sums up the situation, carefully leaving Bucge to make her own decision: 'Make the necessary preparations for the journey, wait for word from her [i.e. from Wihtburg on the Saracen problem] and afterwards do what God's grace shall inspire you to do'. His final paragraph is moving in its simple requests and reassurances. He asks her to pray for him since he is troubled both in mind and body, and ends: 'Rest assured that our long friendship shall never fail. Farewell in Christ'.

Other sources make it clear that Bucge achieved both her pilgrimage and her return home. After her return she once more got involved in the political scene. A letter from Æðelbert of Kent to Boniface written in the mid-eighth century mentions having consulted with *venerabilis abbatissa* Bucge when she returned from Rome and took up again the rule of her monastery. She is one of the many people to whom Boniface wrote for books, and the correspondence both of Bucge and Eadburg suggests that copying of manuscripts was done in their scriptoria. Bucge apologises in one of her letters for having failed to send him a martyrology. It is perhaps a matter of obtaining it rather than having it copied that is the difficulty. A letter of Boniface to Eadburg, abbess of Minster in Thanet, is more explicit. It is written about 735 to his 'dearest sister who has brought light and consolation to an exile in Germany by sending him gifts of spiritual books'. He asks that she will 'continue the good work . . . by copying out for me in gold the epistles of my lord St Peter, that a reverence and love of the holy scriptures may be impressed on the minds of the heathens to whom I preach'. He himself provides her with the gold. It is interesting that among the dozens of requests for books which he sent constantly to all his English contacts, the request for a really finely executed piece of work goes to Eadburg's scriptorium.

We do not have a lot of evidence for the productions of these scriptoria nor for the contents of their libraries. Cuðswið, a seventh-century abbess, probably of Inkberrow near Worcester, owned an Italian manuscript of Jerome's commentary on Ecclesiastes, as an inscription makes clear: *Cuthsuuithae. boec. thaerae abbatissan*, 'a book of the abbess Cuðswið'. The library of Hild, or at any rate of her successor at Whitby, contained enough material for the author of the *Life of Gregory* to put his work together from a number of sources, drawing not only on the scriptures but on the works of Gregory, Jerome and Augustine, and others which we cannot now identify. The works of Aldhelm were probably there also, since the one letter we have from the pen of the abbess Ælflæd who succeeded Hild suggests his influence. Excavations on the site have recovered among other things the bronze styli that would have been used in the scriptorium. When Hild discovered the poetic gift of Cædmon, a lay-brother or servant working on the monastic estate, with her usual perspicuity she instantly realised the potential

43 The eighth-century *Codex aureus* shows the kind of lettering in gold that Boniface asks for.

of this as a teaching medium, and had her monks learn from him the English poetry in praise of God which he composed. We do not have certain evidence that it was written down, but it seems a reasonable possibility. The ninth-century Anglo-Saxon who translated Bede's Latin account of the story assumed that this was so, and tells us that Cædmon's teachers 'wrote and learned at his mouth'.

We may assume that both monks and nuns were involved in the composing and the copying of manuscripts, but in most cases it is now impossible to identify whether the author or scribe of any product from an Anglo-Saxon scriptorium was male or female. Although we know the names of some male authors, we certainly cannot tell whether those early and lost lives of Hild of Whitby or Æðelburg of Barking were by monks or nuns. The only major works that can with certainty be attributed in this early period to a female author are the lives of Willibald and of his brother Wynnebald composed by an English nun at the monastery of Heidenheim, who must have been one of the helpers summoned by the Boniface mission. Willibald, who was a West Saxon, travelled widely, making a pilgrimage not only to Rome but to the Holy Land, and it is clear that the nun who recorded his memories shared his intellectual curiosity. It is not only places of religious interest that she writes about, but also natural phenomena such as volcanic eruptions. She also had control of cryptography, another skill which delighted these early explorers of the uses of literacy. She signs herself by cipher, and the revealed text gives her name as *Hugeburc*, in normalised Old English Hygeburg. We may compare the epigraphical range of the commissioners and carvers of the stone at Hackness, one of Hild's foundations, which contains texts in the Latin alphabet, two forms of the runic alphabet and a further cryptic script resembling ogam.

The eagerness with which some of the nuns pursued learning also comes over clearly enough in the Bonifacian correspondence and the life of Leoba. Aldhelm's *De Virginitate* made it clear that the nuns to whom he addressed it studied the rules of Latin metre, and he, of course, also wrote poems for women, and his own *De Metris*. Leoba includes in her first letter to Boniface four lines of Latin poetry of her own composition, explaining with diffidence that this is not because she thinks herself a great poet, but having been taught how to do it she enjoys experimenting with the form. Another nun of the period, Berhtgyð, who, according to a late but fairly reliable version of the *Life of Boniface*, came to Germany with Leoba and the rest and was extremely learned, *valde erudita in liberali scientia*, also leaves us some of her poems. Berhtgyð's letters to her brother reveal intense loneliness and a sense of isolation and in two of them she breaks into verse, sometimes repeating the sense of the prose. When she writes a line such as *Have, care crucicola salutata a sorore*, 'dear servant of the cross receive the greetings of your sister', she betrays, as elsewhere, her dependence on the vocabulary of Aldhelm, and the implication both of her verse and of Leoba's is that they had both been brought up on Aldhelm's work. Leoba says that she was taught the art by her *magistra* Eadburg. It is sometimes assumed that this was the learned abbess of Minster, but the name is a common Old English one, and Leoba's biographer does not associate her with that foundation. It is, however, clear that Eadburg was teaching Leoba from Aldhelm, since her four lines are fairly derivative, and must be based on a close acquaintance with his writings.

Both the tone and the date of the letter suggest that Leoba was little more than a girl when she wrote it. We have no other letters from her hand, but ten years later we have a letter from Boniface to Leoba and Tecla and Cynehild complaining of his difficulties and lamenting that when he dies he will leave no spiritual sons and daughters in his place. Whether this or another was the letter that prompted Leoba to go out to Germany cannot be known. Her biographer Rudolf of Fulda tells us that Boniface sent for Leoba, and that on her arrival he placed her as abbess over the nuns at Bischofsheim. Rudolf does not refer to any correspondence between Leoba and Boniface, simply saying that her 'reputation for learning and holiness had spread far and wide, and her praise was on everyone's lips'. But Leoba and Boniface were related and it is likely that in the interval between her first childish letter to him in which she asks that she may regard him as her brother, and her taking up the role of abbess in Germany, their correspondence had developed to a point where Boniface knew more of his young kinswoman than simply her general reputation.

Rudolf's biography of her is not a very exciting or even competent piece of work, but through it we obtain some insights into Leoba's qualities of mind and character. Her love of scholarship clearly stayed with her throughout her life.

For, since she had been trained from infancy in the rudiments of grammar and the study of the other liberal arts, she tried by constant reflection to attain a perfect knowledge of divine things so that through the combination of her reading with her quick intelligence, by natural gifts and hard work, she became extremely learned. She read with attention all the books of the Old and New Testaments and learned by heart all the commandments of God. To these she added by way of completion the writings of the church Fathers, the decrees of the Councils and the whole of ecclesiastical law.

What is particularly attractive about the description is the way in which Leoba clearly combined her personal desire for study with calm administrative good sense. In a period when monastic zeal so easily led to over-indulgence in asceticism Leoba 'took care not to go to excess in...spiritual exercises' nor permitted those in her charge to do so. 'She said that lack of sleep dulled the mind, especially for study.' Similarly the miracles that are told of her suggest something more like competence and efficiency in coping with disaster and hysteria. The reality of her learning is brought home to us more by anecdote than repeated assertions. Her biographer tells us that she enjoyed being read to, but however sleepy she appeared to be she always detected errors in the reading.

Sometimes the novices deliberately made mistakes to see if she would observe, but found it impossible to do this unnoticed.

The affection in which such women were held comes across to us with remarkable freshness and clarity. Bede, a somewhat austere writer, brings Hild of Whitby alive for us when he says that 'all who knew her called her mother'. Boniface writing to his 'most dear sister' Bucge or Eadburg, thanking them for their gifts and prayers and support, or Boniface arranging that the bones of his kinswoman Leoba shall be buried near his own, so that 'they who had served God in their lifetime with equal sincerity and zeal should await together the day of Resurrection', continually makes us aware of a loving comradeship and community. Lul, Deneheard and Burgheard jointly send a breathlessly affectionate and deferential letter to the abbess Cyneburg, letting her know of their safe arrival in Germany, hoping she will overlook the *rusticitas* of their Latin and write some comforting words back to them. The gifts, too, are not without a certain charm and poignancy. Bucge, who had not managed to get a copy of the martyrology for Boniface, nevertheless sent him 'fifty shillings and an altar-cloth, because I was unable to get for you a more precious gift'. Lul and the others sent to abbess Cyneburg portions of incense, pepper and cinnamon. The quantities are small but sent 'with full affection'. Spices were valuable commodities and appear as gifts fairly often. Lul sent to Eadburg cinnamon and storax (a fragrant gum-resin, presumably for use in incense) but also, perhaps as a tribute to her scholarship, a silver stylus. Eadburg herself sent Boniface not only books but clothing. But over and over again on both sides of the correspondence the need expressed is for books and, scarcely less, for letters.

That Boniface and his mission received many of the books they asked for is implied by the surviving Anglo-Saxon manuscripts in Continental libraries. It is only recently, however, that we have realised that Anglo-Saxon textiles also survive abroad. The abbey of Aldeneik in Luxembourg, which was visited by Boniface, contained among its treasures, a reliquary which apparently reuses Anglo-Saxon metalwork, as well as two church vestments, a chasuble and probably a veil. They are described on labels attached to them as *casula* and *velamen*, and the first may at one time have been an altar-cloth. The materials include woven silk and embroidered strips with elaborate patterns in gold thread. There are also four monograms in embroidered fabric, though it is not certain what the combination of letters is that they intend to represent. The embroidered strips and the monograms are Anglo-Saxon work of the late eighth century, and the woven textile, which shows the figure of King David, is either of Anglo-Saxon origin or based on an Anglo-Saxon design. Whether Eadburg's gift of an altar-cloth was similarly sophisticated we cannot know, but these textiles give us a very good idea of the high-quality work that was being produced in English communities in the eighth century. They are too late to have been taken out or sent by the

44 Part of an Anglo-Saxon textile from Aldeneik.

Boniface mission itself, but provide excellent evidence for the continuing contact between English and Continental religious communities.

In the world at large it is evident that the advice of women like Leoba and Bucge and Hild was regularly sought. Bede says of Hild that her wisdom was such that she was consulted not only by the ordinary people, but by kings and noblemen. Leoba, according to her biographer, liked the Frankish court little, but Queen Hiltigard loved her, 'the nobles received her, the bishops welcomed her with joy. Because of her wide knowledge of the scriptures and her wisdom in counsel they often discussed spiritual matters and ecclesiastical discipline with her'. But our main knowledge of them is within their own communities, and even more within the general community of all those who were striving for the establishment and spread of Christian thought in newly converted or still pagan areas.

There are some very pretty poems composed in the sixth century by Venantius Fortunatus for the Frankish queen and saint Radegund after she had retired to the foundation she established at Poitiers. *O regina potens, aurum cui et purpura vile est* ('Great queen to whom gold and purple are nothing') is the opening of one poem which the poet apparently sent to Radegund accompanied by a gift of spring flowers, the purple violets and golden crocus. I do not know of anything as graceful as this in the Anglo-Saxon tradition, but both Bede and Aldhelm tried

45 How the tenth century envisaged the virgin saint Æðelðryð of Ely: *Imago sanctae Æþelðryþæ Abbatissae ac Perpetuae Virginis.*

their hand at poems in praise of women. Bede sounds faintly diffident about
including his hymn in praise of the virgin saint Æðelðryð in his *Ecclesiastical
History*. He composed it, he tells us, many years earlier, and defends its inclusion
on the grounds that in holy scripture 'many songs are inserted into the history'.
It is both a poem in praise of virginity in general and a celebration of the
Anglo-Saxon Æðelðryð of Ely in particular. It tells us nothing factual about her
that Bede's prose account has not said already, but the mood that moved Bede
to write it 'many years ago' is clearly the same one of national pride that later
moves Ælfric to thank God that the English nation too has its own saints. 'A
splendid virgin blesses our age also, the splendid Æðelðryð shines for us.'
Aldhelm's poem for Bucge is rather more interesting from our point of view,
because of its factual information.

The woman who is the subject of Aldhelm's poem is not the same as the Bucge
of the Bonifacian correspondence. She is the daughter of Centwine, who was
King of Wessex, 676–85. Aldhelm's poem is in praise of the church that Bucge
had built, and this therefore, in all the magnificence that Aldhelm describes, must
have been standing and functioning before the date of Aldhelm's death in 709.
Similar churches were doubtless going up on monastic sites all over Britain, and
we have descriptions of some of them. Bede gives us a fairly full account of
Benedict's church at Monkwearmouth built in 674, and Benedict spent much
of his time rushing off to the Continent to obtain splendid equipment and
furnishings for it. Bede also refers to Wilfrid's church at Ripon, 'clothed in gold
and purple', and Wilfrid's biography gives us more detailed descriptions. But
to learn of a woman who commissioned the splendid church that is revealed in
Aldhelm's poem gives us a quite different slant on the ambitions and activities
of nuns and abbesses from the picture we have gained of, for example, the calm
and scholarly Leoba. Aldhelm's account is probably based on direct personal
knowledge. The opening lines of the poem are straightforward enough:

> Hoc templum Bugge pulchro molimine structum
> Nobilis erexit Centvvini filia regis...

'Bucge, the high-born daughter of King Centwine, erected this church as a glorious
achievement...'

Aldhelm's description allows us to visualise the church. It was dedicated to the
Virgin Mary, the light of the sun illuminated it through windows of glass, the
altars were covered with gold-embroidered cloths, there was a golden chalice and
silver paten, the cross gleamed with gold, silver and jewels, and there was
fragrance from incense-burners. Bede told us that Benedict had to send to Gaul
for glassmakers, since the craft was unknown in England. We are not told how
Bucge obtained these valued craftsmen.

Aldhelm, as well as giving us the smell of the incense and the gleam of light
and gold gives us the music, the voices of throngs of brothers and sisters rising

in worship, in hymns and psalms and responses. He also writes of the ten-stringed
lyre, which is of course an echo of the thirty-second psalm, but presumably
indicates that stringed instruments were a normal musical accompaniment to
worship. It is clear from the mention of brothers and sisters that this too was
a double monastery of monks and nuns, and their sharing of worship is reflected
also in the line

Et lector lectrixve volumina sacra revolvant

'and readers, man and woman, open the sacred volumes'.

Bucge and her church are also commemorated in an epitaph, unlikely to be
by Aldhelm, though the author probably knew Aldhelm's poem. It tells us only
a little more than we learn from Aldhelm himself – only that she lies under a
marble slab after ruling her monastery for thirty-four years – but it is a rare
achievement in this period that is commemorated in two extant poems. Another
church we know of, commissioned by a woman, also aroused awe and admiration.
Bucge's contemporary Seaxburg seems, unlike her sister St Æðelðryð of Ely,
to have preferred the reputation of a church-builder to that of a virgin. She was
the wife of Eorcenbert of Kent, mother of two Kentish kings, and subsequently
retired to a nunnery to be abbess of Ely after Æðelðryð's death. An eleventh-
century text preserves the record that she established a monastery dedicated to
the Virgin Mary on the island of Sheppey, and that her son Hloðhere gave her
a grant of land for its maintenance. Another eleventh-century manuscript vividly
reproduces the tradition of her church-building in the words:

Ða gelicode ðære halgan cwene Seaxburge þæt heo ðær binnan for myrhðe and for mærðe
hyre ðær mynster getimbrode; and gestaðelode swa geo men cwædon þæt ðrittegum
gearum ne gestilde næfre stefen cearciendes wænes ne ceoriendes wales.

'Then it pleased the saintly queen Seaxburg that she would there [in the island of
Sheppey] build a minster for delight and for glory; and she had it built, as men used
to tell, so that for thirty years there never stilled the sound of groaning wagon nor
complaining slave.'

This manuscript says also not that Hloðhere gave her the land but that 'she
bought from him his share of that land for the free use of the minster'. But
whereas we cannot recover the precise details of the land transaction, the thirty
years of groaning wagons sounds remarkably like a genuine and cherished
tradition. One is also mildly impressed by Seaxburg's resourcefulness in locating
a white marble sarcophagus for her saintly sister's translation – a story that is
told to us by Bede.

After the Norman Conquest there was something of a fashion for writing
professional hagiography and almost all the early women who had acquired the
status of saint acquired also a more or less fictional biography to go with it.
Place-names tend to reflect not so much the saint herself as her foundation, and

are often late evidence also. Osgyð, of whom we know little that is fact rather than legend, founded a convent at Chich in Essex. The present place-name St Osyth did not replace Chich till the twelfth or thirteenth century. Church dedications also are difficult evidence to handle, since it is often impossible to ascertain whether they represent pre-Conquest cults or Norman revival of them. There are other ranges of evidence to look at which tell us slightly more. In the *Liber Vitae Ecclesiae Dunelmensis*, an early ninth-century manuscript which came to Durham from Lindisfarne, there are lists of names of those who should be remembered at the altar. The second section of this list is devoted to women and contains 198 names of queens and abbesses. Queens who did not after their husbands' deaths retire to take charge of a monastery may have benefited foundations in other ways, for example with gifts of estates. It is difficult to know quite on what basis to analyse the names. We would expect them to be Northumbrian-based and it is certainly possible to equate some of the names on the list with ones we know from other sources. The Christian site at Hartlepool has two elegant carved stones with the women's names Hildiðryð and Hildigyð in runic letters. Both these names occur in the *Liber Vitae* list. The stone at Hackness, a place where Hild developed a separate cell from the Whitby monastery, commemorates *Œdilburga beata*. This, too, is a name in the

46 The *Hildigyð* name-stone from Hartlepool.

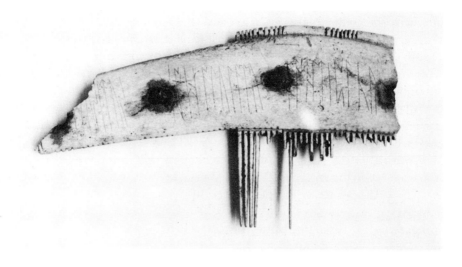

47 The Whitby comb, with runic text partly Latin, partly Old English asking 'My God, God Almighty, help Cy...'

Lindisfarne list. The great cross at Bewcastle in Cumberland has the woman's name Cyniburg on it. A Cyniburg occurs in the list also. But these equations are facile. Certainly most of the great names which we know from other sources, including many mentioned by Bede, are in the list, but so are very many other names we know from no other sources, and many names also occurring several times over. To the compiler it may have been clear whom he was commemorating in each part of the list. To us the impression is of sheer quantity and also – an emotion that would have been familiar to the Anglo-Saxons – the awareness of transience, not only of life, but even of reputation, where all good deeds on earth have been reduced in human memory to an unidentifiable name in a list: *edgyth*, *uerngyth*, *tidburg*, *ecgburg*, and so on through the other 194.

There are fragments of memorial stones surviving at Whitby containing the elements of feminine personal names, but so much is damaged there is little profit in trying to assemble the material to give us a few names of those who lived there before it was all raided and burned. A comb, found not on the monastic site itself, nevertheless has a Christian text suggesting its association with it, but the name is not complete and we cannot even be sure of the sex of the owner. Such small finds with names are rare enough, and even when names are recorded further identification is not usually possible. We do not know who the nun was whose decorated seal-die was found at Wallingford. It belongs to the end of the Anglo-Saxon period and the text reads: *Sigillvm Godgyðe monache deo date*, 'the seal of Godgyð, a nun given to God'. We do however find in charters evidence for land being given to individual named nuns as well as to major foundations. In the mid-tenth century, for example, King Edmund grants land to the nun Ælfðryð, and a rather larger amount to the nun Wynflæd, where it is said that this is partly restitution of land granted by his predecessors, and partly a new grant. It looks as if Wynflæd had been obliged to make a case out to get some of this land returned to her. Far more of these later charters concern grants to new foundations, to the nuns at for example Wilton or Shaftesbury. The early charters which give land for the founding of a monastery tend to be to an individual and to be specific about the purpose of the donation. Simple grant charters at the beginning of the period read very pleasantly:

1. I, Noðhelm, king of the South Saxons...will gladly give to you, my sister Noðgyð, some portion of land for the founding of a monastery on it and the building of a church which may be devoted to the divine praises.

2. I, Æðelmod...grant for the relief of my soul, to you, Beorngyð, venerable abbess, and to Folcburg, and through you to your monastery, 20 hides by the river Cherwell...that you may hold it by right and your authority, as much as you may claim for your monastery.

Those are both seventh-century grants. Later matters became more complicated. By the eighth century a synod is attempting to sort out the control, ownership and inheritance rights of Bucge's monastery in Gloucestershire. In the late eighth century the synod of Clovesho is similarly sorting out a dispute over the monastery at Cookham, which ends in a financial arrangement between Archbishop Æðelheard and Abbess Cyneðryð. Large estates are involved and the finances are clearly complex.

Administration and alienation of property were not the only worries of those in charge. The earliest laws have references to the rights of the church, but not the rights or duties of women in religious orders. The first clear reference is in the matter of a foreigner being killed. Among the laws of Ine number 23 makes the provision that if anyone kills a foreigner (which presumably means from other regions of England as well as abroad) his *wergild* is to be paid partly to the king, partly to the man's relatives. If he has no kin the *wergild* is divided between the king and the person who took the man under his protection. Then the third clause specifies that if the protector *abbod sie oððe abbodesse*, 'is either an abbot or an abbess' they have the same rights to half the *wergild* as a secular person does. This law belongs to the end of the seventh century, the period in which the great double foundations in charge of abbesses were being constructed. It is the first clear statement in the laws of a woman's right to receive *wergild* for those under her protection.

Ælfred's law number 8 has several interesting provisions. One is for the payment of compensation if anyone remove a nun from a nunnery without 'permission of king or bishop'. The fine for this is set at 120 shillings, half to the king and half to the bishop or to *þære cirican hlaforde, ðe ðone munuc age,* 'the lord of the church in whose charge the nun is'. What is particularly interesting is that the masculine forms are used (*hlaford* and *munuc*) where the second must refer to the nun, and the first the 'lord' would in all probability be the abbess. The rest of this law is mainly concerned with the inheritance problems, and obviously relates to nuns who willingly stayed away from their nunneries. 'If she lives longer than he who took her away' she shall not inherit, and neither shall her child inherit. Their *wergild* rights are not infringed, but the payment of such *wergild* is not allowed to benefit the lapsed nun or her kin. 'If her child is killed the part of the *wergild* due to the mother's side is to be paid to the king'. The initial fine of 120 shillings is best seen in comparison with a similar provision for a man who leaves one district and lord and goes into the service of another, without the knowledge of the lord whom he has left: 'If he does this without the knowledge [of his lord] he who takes him into his service is to pay a fine of 120 shillings'.

We have already looked at the provisions of Ælfred's laws for sexual assaults on women, where they specified in detail the fines for different degrees of harassment. The law for sexual assault on nuns does not repeat the details, it simply doubles the fines: 'If anyone takes hold of a nun with sexual intent and without her permission, either by her dress or by her breast, he is to pay compensation at twice the amount we have established for seculars'. These early laws are useful and specific. The later ones have a tendency to become contaminated by the language of homily. It adds little to our knowledge of the function or status of the religious orders within society that among Æðelræd's ordinances one demands 'that abbots and abbesses order their lives properly' and that monks and nuns should live according to the rule and pray zealously for all Christian people. One provision in the eleventh-century *Law of the Northumbrian Priests* suggests, like King Ælfred's, a rational division of responsibility: 'If anyone lies with a nun both of them (*ge he ge heo*) are to pay their *wergild*'. The *Penitential of Theodore* prescribes seven years' penance for the consecrated virgin who commits fornication.

That not everyone who became a nun had a natural aptitude for the life of poverty and chastity was to be expected, and whereas the laws make provision for the infringement of the rules of chastity, the infringements of the rules of poverty tend to be mentioned in more informal circumstances. Every historian quotes Bede's tale of the double monastery at Coldingham under the abbess Æbbe where the inhabitants filled the cells designed for reading and praying with 'feasting, drinking and talking' instead; where the women wove themselves elaborate garments, and where divine vengeance came in the form of fire that burned the entire monastery to ashes. It is worth noting that of all the great double monasteries of the period it is the only one of which scandal is related, but Aldhelm also is concerned with the pleasure that consecrated men and women

48 *Sobrietas*, Sobriety and her followers rejecting the spoils of battle, from the Corpus manuscript of Prudentius' *Psychomachia*. The text describes the spoils as feminine knick-knacks – 'a hair-pin...a brooch, a veil...a coronet, a necklace' – but the illustrator clearly envisages them as drinking-cups and horns.

take in worldly finery. 'This sort of glamorization for either sex consists in fine linen shirts, in scarlet or blue tunics, in necklines and sleeves embroidered with silk; their shoes are trimmed with red-dyed leather; the hair of their forelocks and the curls at their temples are crimped with a curling iron; dark-grey veils for the head give way to bright and coloured head-dresses which are sewn with interlaces of ribbons and hang down as far as the ankles. Fingernails are sharpened after the manner of falcons or hawks...' I am not perfectly sure at what point the description ceases to be relevant to 'either sex' and concentrates on women, but such attacks were commonly directed at both men and women in religious orders. Ælfric in a later century specifies priests who wear rings and elaborate clothing. It is, however, a particular pleasure to note the reply that St Edith of Wilton is reported to have given on such an occasion. It is even possible that since she herself lived in the late tenth century the story told by her post-Conquest biographer preserves a genuine anecdote. Edith was apparently accustomed to dress more richly than was common to nuns or abbesses and

49 The seal of Edith of Wilton.

Bishop Æðelwold of Winchester took it upon himself to rebuke her, pointing out that Christ takes no delight in external appearances, it is the heart he asks for. 'Quite so, Father, and I have given my heart.' William of Malmesbury has a slightly different version of the story, including a disparaging reference by Edith to the Bishop's 'ragged furs'. According to William, the Bishop blushed and was silenced.

St Edith belongs to the second major phase of Anglo-Saxon religious life. The first phase, which we have looked at in some detail, is centred on the seventh and eighth centuries, the first centuries of serious Christian development. How much of the subsequent decline was a falling away from the first fine but not careless rapture, and how far we should blame the Viking raiders, is not at all clear. King Ælfred thought even before the churches were raided and burned the enthusiasm for learning and the knowledge of Latin had disappeared. We cannot tell how far he was generalising, and since, especially in the north, the Vikings did raid and burn, and whole libraries such as that of Whitby were entirely lost to us, we cannot distinguish speculation from fact in Ælfred's lament. From his reign onwards we have a new and well-documented surge of interest culminating in the tenth-century monastic reform under Dunstan and Æðelwold. Ælfred himself towards the end of the ninth century founded the nunnery at Shaftesbury and placed his daughter Æðelgifu there as abbess. There are subsequent major grants to Shaftesbury's nuns from King Æðelstan in 932, again in 935, from Eadwig in 956; confirmation of land from Edgar in 966 and a grant from Æðelræd in 1001.

Ælfred's wife Ealhswið is associated with the foundation of Nunnaminster, St Mary's Abbey, Winchester. A manuscript of the eighth or ninth century, the *Libellus Precorum*, 'little book of prayers', has a ninth-century addition in Old English specifying the land owned by Ealhswið at Winchester: *þæs hagan gemære þe Ealhswið hæfð æt wintanceastre*. The book is thought to have been originally Ealhswið's own, subsequently Nunnaminster's, though firm evidence is lacking. Continued female ownership is however indicated by the tenth-century addition *ora pro me peccatrice*, where the conventional formula 'pray for me, a sinner' gives the grammatically feminine form of the noun. Subsequent royal grants to Nunnaminster include three estates and thirty pounds from King Eadred and one estate and a silver bowl worth five pounds from the prince Æðelstan, son of Æðelræd. The most interesting charter, however, is one in which King Edgar endeavours to sort out the property and boundaries of the three religious houses in Winchester, which suggests perhaps some history of quarrelling. Two mills are granted to Nunnaminster 'for the sake of peace and concord'.

The tenth-century monastic reform is documented in the text *Regularis Concordia*. This quite specifically places King Edgar as guardian of the rule in monasteries and his queen as guardian and protector of the nunneries, so that no scandal should arise. The double houses have vanished, and the new communities are either monasteries or nunneries. Most of what we know about them is through the charters. It is clear that the nunneries were supported by grants from queens and other powerful women but it is by no means clear that they ever became the centres of culture and learning that their forerunners had been. This is not, however, to single them out for comment, for there is similarly no great tradition of learning and Latinity from the monasteries, which were reproached at the time because the monks lived like noblemen, delighting in gold and silver and fine clothes, and have been reproached by recent writers for their insularity and ignorance. The strengths of the tenth and eleventh centuries lay in other areas, and though we have a good deal of evidence for the part played by women outside the nunneries, we no longer have the range of evidence for their activities within them that we had for the earlier period. On the whole women are now granting estates to nunneries, rather than seeking land where they may found them. Ælfðryð, it is true, founded the nunneries of Amesbury and Wherwell, but was popularly supposed by her contemporaries to be doing so in expiation for murdering Edward King and Martyr, her stepson. It is a very different world from the seventh- and eighth-century one of the nuns of Barking, of Hild and Leoba, of Bucge and Eadburg. If power-politics were always a part of monastic life, they at least never showed themselves quite so blatantly in the early period as they do in the injunction of one document of the monastic reform: 'We also instruct abbesses... that none of them shall presume senselessly to give

God's estates either to their kinsmen or to secular great persons, neither for money nor for flattery'. We have virtually no evidence of the quality of life within these nunneries, and where literacy in the Latin tongue had declined disastrously among monk and priest, it is perhaps not to be expected that it thrived exceptionally among nuns. Pastoral advice was written in English rather than Latin out of deference not to the incompetence of women but the incompetence of bishops, and the equality of sexes which flourished in the eighth century in learning and in literacy, was replaced in the tenth century by equality in ignorance.

## FURTHER READING

Some major texts used in this chapter have already been noted. For Bede, see COLGRAVE's edition, for Aldhelm see EHWALD for text, LAPIDGE for translation. LAPIDGE also has an article giving the text of the epitaph of Bucge, 'Some remnants of Bede's lost Liber Epigrammatum'. The Boniface correspondence is edited by TANGL, translated in TALBOT's *The Anglo-Saxon Missionaries in Germany*. Some of it is also in WHITELOCK, *English Historical Documents*. The *Life* of Leoba is also translated by TALBOT. Useful articles are MEYER, 'Women and the Tenth Century Monastic Reform', NICHOLSON, 'Feminae Gloriosae: women in the age of Bede'. Indispensable is LEVISON, *England and the Continent in the Eighth Century*. The Anglo-Saxon embroideries from Aldeneik will be published by Mildred BUDNY and Dominic TWEDDLE.

# 7. Viking Women in Britain

The writing of a chapter on Viking women in Britain poses more acutely than other chapters problems of what source material is available and what sources it is proper to use. The Viking Age covers a number of centuries, and in mainland Scandinavia the dates may be differently defined from those in England. The term 'Viking' itself tends to be used of the inhabitants of a number of countries. Even in Britain the term is used to cover different periods of Viking invasion and settlement from the eighth century to the eleventh, and what is true of the Danelaw after the early invasions is not necessarily true of the Viking kingdom of York in the tenth century. Norse settlements on the fringes of the British Isles in the Orkneys or the Isle of Man retained or developed different characters from those in Yorkshire, Lincolnshire, or the East Midlands. If, then, it is difficult to generalise about the Vikings and yet more difficult to generalise about Vikings in Britain, it is clearly impossible to generalise about Viking women.

Written sources are to be found in a variety of languages, alphabets, periods and areas. Literature on the Vikings is preserved in Old Norse texts of Scandinavia and Ireland, some of it – such as runic inscriptions or Eddic and skaldic poems – not too distant from the period to which it relates, some of it – such as the Icelandic family sagas – describing the Viking period but remote from it by several centuries. Contemporary Old English literature is on the whole written, as one might expect, from a hostile viewpoint, and Latin chronicles written after the Norman Conquest tend to retain a similar bias. They are, moreover, obviously more concerned with power-politics than domestic matters. Irish material on the Vikings tends to be late and suffers similar, if not more marked, disadvantages.

For my previous chapters concentration on Anglo-Saxon has meant also concentration on England, but this chapter is necessarily different. Much of our evidence for Vikings in this country comes from 'Celtic' rather than 'Anglo-Saxon' districts, and thus where the Anglo-Saxon chapters contain evidence for England only, this chapter necessarily relates to the Viking presence in the whole of the British Isles. It is specifically from such intensive areas of Norse settlement as the Isle of Man that we get concentrated archaeological and runic material, which cannot be paralleled elsewhere in Britain.

My decisions on how to use the available evidence may be summarised as follows: as far as possible I endeavour to use specifically the material relating to Britain, but the archaeological evidence can be interpreted only by close reference to parallel cultural finds in mainland Scandinavia. Scandinavian law-codes I have carefully avoided, since the only laws which we know governed the behaviour of Vikings in Britain are the ones outlined for us in Anglo-Saxon texts. The evidence of Old Norse Viking-Age poetry, wherever composed, I use to throw some light on general attitudes to women and to domestic duties. The evidence of the sagas is very much more difficult, being late and not historically trustworthy, and I draw on this only occasionally for a few references to Viking women in the British Isles, or to general social attitudes which would not be markedly susceptible to rapid change.

Finally, there is the evidence of Norse place-names in Britain, and specifically for England the evidence of landownership at the time of the Norman Conquest afforded by Domesday Book. All of this provides a heterogeneous enough collection of material. Whether any rational or coherent picture of Viking women in Britain can emerge from it remains to be seen.

In the Isle of Man there is a burial mound which is drawn to the attention of twentieth-century tourists by a notice describing it as the grave of a Viking warrior buried with his woman, horse and other livestock. A pagan Viking burial must be earlier than the mid-tenth century, and this one is usually dated to the ninth or early tenth. It is commonly assumed that where there is difficulty in sexing a skeleton, owing to the decayed state of the bones, the grave-goods are a reasonable guide. Where weapons accompany a burial it is probably male, where jewellery and domestic accessories are present it is probably female. Such a rough and ready guide is perhaps not foolproof, but neither is it unreasonable. This Manx burial included most of the grave-goods associated with men: sword, spears, shield, a ring-headed bronze pin which was the normal masculine cloak-fastener, and so on. The body with which these objects were associated was coffined and a mound raised over it. Within this mound was the skeleton of a woman, whose skull had been smashed. She was between twenty and thirty years old.

There is a certain amount of evidence from other sources for the sacrifice of slave women in pagan Viking contexts. Furnished graves commonly hold most of the comforts one might be expected to require in the afterlife. But new light was thrown on this subject by a recent excavation at Gerdrup near Roskilde in Denmark. This is the grave of a woman of the Viking Age which the excavators date to the ninth century. Richly furnished women's graves are known, but this one is not richly furnished. The woman's skeleton is placed carefully with two artefacts resting on it and one beside it; on it are an iron knife and a needlecase; beside it is a spear. The woman is estimated to have been about forty years old. Associated with it is a second skeleton a small distance away, the bones laid out with less care. This is the skeleton of a male between thirty and forty years old.

50 Woman's silk cap from
the Viking site at
Coppergate, York.

His feet have been tied at the ankles and his neck broken. We do not know of
any other burials of Viking-Age women with weapons, but this, as indicated
above, is because the presence of a weapon itself has usually been taken to be
adequate evidence for the sex of the skeleton it accompanies, and we have
therefore no means of knowing if the Gerdrup situation is unique. No parallel
instance in England has been noted so far, but the Gerdrup grave is immensely
important in changing the pattern of assumptions that can be made from
archaeological evidence about the status of women, and though there are several
ways in which it could be interpreted it might even be adduced as a reason for
paying a little more serious attention to the many traditions that survive in Old
Norse literature about warrior-women. *Hervarar saga* is obviously a blend of
much legendary and folk-tale material, but it is interesting that such a tradition
as that of Hervör's role should exist: 'As soon as she could do anything for herself
she trained herself more with bow and shield and sword than with needlework
and embroidery'. The Gerdrup woman does not seem to have thought that the
one precluded the other.

Richly furnished Viking burials of either sex are not found in England, partly perhaps because the settlement was in a Christian country, and partly because local Christian cemeteries were sometimes used, most of which have remained in use as burial grounds. On the edge of the British Isles there is more evidence. A Shetland grave assumed to be Norse and female from the nature and style of the grave-goods contained a pair of oval brooches, a third brooch of trefoil type and a string of beads. Other personal ornaments such as arm-rings are found in women's graves, and occasional implements such as shears or needlecases. There is, perhaps surprisingly, no trace of kitchen utensils, though these are found in mainland Scandinavian women's graves. The pair of oval brooches is particularly common in Norse female burials, and such brooches are described in contemporary poetry as normal wear for a free-born woman. When, therefore, a pair of such brooches was found together with an iron two-edged sword in a grave in Santon, Norfolk, these finds were interpreted as evidence for a double burial of a man and a woman, the sword indicating a male owner, the brooches a female: but after the Gerdrup excavation, other assumptions will also be tenable.

Irish medieval traditions which cannot be relied on for their historical accuracy, nevertheless show that there too legends of strongminded and militant Viking women persisted. There are two references in *The War of the Gædhil with the Gaill* to *Ingen Ruaidh*, 'the red girl', who, we are told, invaded Munster with a fleet of ships in the tenth century. The same text, after speaking of the raids of one Viking warrior, adds: 'Cluiainmicnois [a monastic settlement] was taken by his wife. It was on the altar of the great church she used to give her answers [audiences?]'. The historical accuracy of such statements as these may be open to challenge, but the picture they present of Viking raiders is not one in which women were regarded solely as impedimenta.

The areas settled by Vikings in England are still perhaps most readily shown by the map of place-names with Old Norse elements. Major settlement names in the Viking areas very commonly include a masculine personal name. Feminine name elements are found more in the minor and secondary sites. The woman's name Ragnhildr, for example, occurs in Raventhorpe as the early spellings show. In Domesday Book Raventhorpe, Lincolnshire, is *Rageneltorp*, the Yorkshire one *Ragheneltorp*, both meaning the 'thorpe' of Ragnhildr. Later medieval spellings of field names such as *Renildtoft* and *Ragenildcroft* indicate the same name in the first element.

51 (*opposite above*) The Santon brooches, typical of Viking women's jewellery.

52 (*opposite below*) Jewellery worn by Viking men: the Halton Moor, Yorks., silver neck-ring; the Virginia, Co. Cavan, armring; and the Tundergarth, Dumfriesshire, gold fingerring.

53 The Scandinavian
settlement.

● Parish names of
    Scandinavian origin
— Southern limit of the
    Danelaw
--- Pre-1974 County
    boundaries

Some settlers were perhaps men who married Anglo-Saxon wives and then gave their daughters Scandinavian names, but the preponderance of Scandinavian women's names suggests also a reasonably high number of women emigrating with their families. Chronicles are not likely to tell us much about this, since they record battles rather than settlements, but occasionally the *Anglo-Saxon Chronicle* makes it clear that when the early Danish raiders were moving around southern England they were accompanied by their families. In 892 when Hæsten came up the Thames with eighty ships the chronicler does not specify who was in the ships, but a little later when Hæsten had built a fortification at Benfleet and subsequently gone off raiding, the Anglo-Saxons stormed the fortress 'and took away everything that was in it, both in goods, in women [*in wifum*], and in children'. The women and children included Hæsten's own wife and two sons whose rank ensured that they were brought directly to the king. A little later in the same part of the *Chronicle* we are given the laconic assurance that 'the Danes had placed their women [*wif*], in safety in East Anglia'. We are not told the nationality of these women: some may have come from Scandinavia, others may have been acquired en route. The pattern is likely to be complex and cosmopolitan.

The evidence in the northern areas of England, while not disproving intermarriage with the Anglo-Saxons, suggests in addition family settlement. Female jewellery of a Viking rather than an Anglo-Saxon type presumably was imported on the whole by the actual wearers of it. Old Norse women's names turn up in the north throughout the Middle Ages, as metronymics, in place-names, in charters or on carved stones. The Domesday Book records which tell us something about the holders of land before the Conquest give perhaps the most useful and interesting information. The woman's name Gunnvör is found three times in Yorkshire Domesday material: she held one manor in Cloughton, one in Brigham and one in Rudston. She is perhaps the lady who is commemorated on the carved sundial in Aldbrough in East Yorkshire: 'Ulf ordered this church to be built for himself and for Gunnvör's soul', though it is not necessary to assume their identity. There are also a number of names in the Lincolnshire and Yorkshire charters of men who are sons of women with this Norse name, an *Uchthredus filius Gunware* in the early twelfth century for example. When sons are referred to by metronymic not patronymic this need not imply bastardy. It is certainly more normal for sons' and daughters' names to be linked to that of father rather than mother, but the latter is also quite a common usage in these documents and other sources. It may sometimes simply indicate that an estate had been inherited through the female line. Inga and Þóra are both Norse women's names, and in one document of the thirteenth century a girl called Inga is referred to as *filia Thore* in one section and *filia Gileberti* in another. These are late examples but obviously reflect continuity of practice. Lincolnshire Domesday, for example, refers to a certain *Rolf filius Scheldeuuare*. His mother's name was Old Norse Skjaldvör.

The Domesday material has much else of interest. *Game* (Old Norse Gamall), for example, is reported as holding land in Thoralby 'with his mother and brother'. Here joint tenancy is specified by the relationship. Mostly in the very laconic entries in Yorkshire Domesday I think it is wise to assume that the two names imply two separate landholders, not joint tenants, though there are obviously places where it is tempting to assume, especially in an entry where only one manor is specified, that the names of man and woman linked in the same phrase refer to husband and wife. In Hotham where there was only one manor *Grim* and *Ingrede* (Old Norse Grímr and Ingiríðr) had five hides. On the other hand when we are told that in Raventhorpe there are four manors and five hides held by *Gida*, *Osber*, *Turchil* and *Siward*, and *Gida* (Old Norse Gýða) is the only woman's name of the four, it is to be assumed that these are all independent owners. Gýða also had a manor at Leckonfield.

These were not negligible estates and occasionally women with Norse names are specified as holding land in more than one region. *Sigrede* (Old Norse Sigiríðr) had a hide of land in Sutton and a manor at Watlas. *Turloga* (Þorlaug) held a manor in Sproxton. *Godrida* and *Audvid* (Old Norse Guðríðr and Auðviðr) may have been married and may have held jointly the four hides of land in Grimston, but since two manors are specified we need not assume it. But by far the most significant entry in the Domesday material for Yorkshire concerns the property of a woman named Ása. She had a manor in Scoreby, two and a half hides of land in Hayton, possibly also land in Lowthorpe, though I think that might be another woman of the same name. Her land becomes the subject of a post-Conquest complaint which tells us a good deal about her standing, not to mention the astonishment of the Norman scribe producing the record:

Concerning all the land of Ása they testify that it ought to belong to Robert Malet, because she had her land separate and free from the control of Björnulfr, her husband, even when they were together, so that he could neither make a gift nor sale of it, nor forfeit it; but after their separation she retired with all her land and possessed it as its lady.

It should perhaps be stressed that we are not talking here about any of the great landowners. Domesday Book mentions several countesses, *comitissae*, who held vast numbers of estates, Alfgifu, Godgifu, Judith, etc. These include the Danish Gyða, the wife of Earl Godwine, mother of King Harold. The women with the Old Norse name of Gyða who held smaller amounts of land in Warwickshire, Leicestershire, Yorkshire and Lincolnshire are not identified with her, nor indeed can we be certain that they were of Scandinavian descent, since children would often be named after great ladies by way of fashion or compliment.

It is in fact almost impossible to tell to what extent in the first half of the eleventh century Norse names in England were matters of fashion rather than indicative of descent. The reign of King Cnut made a good deal of impact. In the Danelaw areas specifically it seems not unreasonable to make a general assumption that prevalence of Norse names in a family or an area indicates a Scandinavian strain in the family background, and that Old English names in a family indicate some Anglo-Saxon connection. But outside the Danelaw even such a general assumption cannot be substantiated. In the Warwickshire Domesday the two women's names Old Norse Gyða and Old English Sægyð both occur once only, and they occur in the same entry as joint holders of what was clearly an attractive property of about one thousand acres:

Walton: Gyða and Sægyð held it; they were free. 10 hides. Land for 10 ploughs. In lordship 2 ploughs; 9 slaves: 32 villagers and 3 smallholders with 10 ploughs. 2 mills at 12s; meadow, 8 acres; woodland 4 furlongs long and 2 wide.

In the village of Tabley, Cheshire, there were two manors held by a man and

54 Ælfgifu-Emma, here styled *Ælfgifu regina*, and Cnut presenting an altar cross to New Minster, Winchester.

woman with respectively the Old English name Wulfsige and the Old Norse name Sigríðr; the land seems scarcely enough to support two households:

In the village itself 1 bovate of land and a third part of 1 hide paying tax. Sigríðr and Wulfsige held it as 2 manors; they were free. Land for one plough.

Women with Norse names as well as those married to or related to men with Norse names also figure as benefactors and beneficiaries in eleventh-century wills and charters. Since the Old Norse female name Þorgunnr had no obvious fashionable connections or overtones we may perhaps assume that the Thurgunt who, being old and ill, left to Ramsey Abbey both land and valuables was herself a Scandinavian. Her husband Þorkell appears in one source as 'Turkil the Dane', and the two names together suggest a couple who came over with Cnut. It is proper to report that after his wife's death Turkil carefully carried out the provisions of her will. A nickname is perhaps better evidence of Norse connections than a proper name, and the man with the indubitably Norse name and nickname Thurketel Heyng (Þorkell Hæing) asserts in his will that his wife's part of the property is to be uncontested for ever for her to keep or give away as she chooses. He leaves an estate to his daughter whose Old English name Ælfwynn might imply that her mother was English.

If we turn to the laws dealing with the northern part of the country after the Viking invasions and settlement we find that there are three aspects stressed. One is that in certain matters the laws of the Danelaw may function independently from those of southern England. Edgar's law of 962 says that 'it is my will that there should be in force among the Danes such good laws as they may best decide on'. Unfortunately we do not have records of Scandinavian laws from this period, and it would be improper to use the later laws in mainland Scandinavia or in Iceland as evidence for legal practice among the Viking settlers in Britain. We cannot tell what good laws the Danes decided on at this stage, and later laws, worded with more precision, are not necessarily more lucid. The laws of Cnut distinguish penalties thus: 'If anyone refuse to pay church dues he is to pay *lahslit* [law-breaking?] among the Danes, full fine among the English'. But there are two areas where it is clear that the kings of England, under the guidance of the church, are determined to insist on parity of behaviour and attitudes in all areas under their control. One is the stamping out of all heathen practices and the encouragement of due respect for the sanctities of the church; the other which is directly connected with this is improvement of sexual morality. Sexual licence is seen as linked with heathenism. The laws which develop these themes most fully are the so-called *Canons of Edgar*, the laws of Cnut, and the *Law of the Northumbrian Priests*.

The *Law of the Northumbrian Priests* is an early eleventh-century document, and its attitude may be summed up in section 61: 'We forbid that any man should have more women [*wif*] than one; and she is to be legally betrothed and wedded'. One historian has seen this as evidence that monogamy was not strictly established in Old English society, but it should more properly be considered as evidence for Viking Northumbria. It is true that the church from the beginning attacked the sexual laxity of the Anglo-Saxons, but in the eleventh century these attacks take on a new dimension. It is a new race of pagans that has to be convinced of the evils of the priesthood marrying, the evils of bedding more than one woman, or of marrying within the forbidden degrees of kinship. It is not actually forbidden at this date for clergy to marry, though clerics write very strongly against it. The *Law of the Northumbrian Priests*, however, has a clause not merely against priests marrying, or laymen keeping women, but against priests themselves who, after living with or marrying one woman, abandon her for another: 'If a priest leaves a woman [*cwene* not *wif*] and takes another, he is to be excommunicated'. The statement for the layman is less severe: 'If a man leaves his lawful wife [*riht æwe*] and while she lives, unlawfully takes another wife [*wif*] he may not have God's forgiveness unless he atone for it'. There is the usual problem here of deciding what precise status the words imply, whether *wif* is consistently 'wife' or 'woman', and the legislator himself is attempting clarity of expression. He probably intends *cwene* to imply something less than legal wifely status, and certainly uses *æwe*, 'lawful wife', for added emphasis.

The extent to which these laws were unsuccessful in Viking Northumbria is suggested by the situation outlined in a tract called *De obsessione Dunelmi*, 'The Siege of Durham', preserved in one manuscript and describing pre-Conquest eleventh-century events in the north of England. The point of the account seems

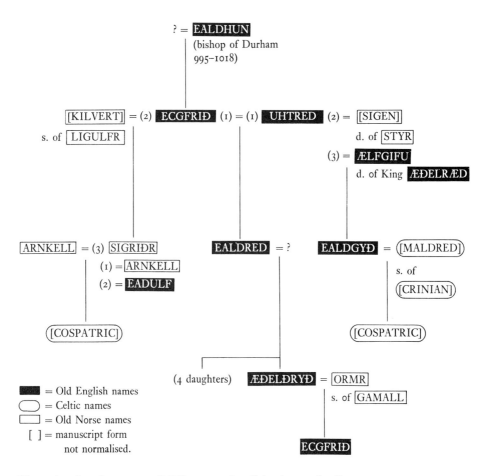

Chart showing the names of different nationalities in one family.

very largely an attempt to sort out an inheritance squabble, resulting from a series of divorces and remarriages among the great men and women of the area, when important estates were changing hands. The main character is called in the Latin text Ecgfrida, and she is the daughter of Ealdhun Bishop of Durham, though we are not told by whom. Ecgfrida must represent an Old English name, perhaps Ecgfrið or Ecgfriðu. She is married to Uhtred, son of Wælðeof, and six estates are given by the Bishop to her husband on her marriage. The text implies that the Bishop's ownership of these estates was by virtue of his office not by personal inheritance. Ecgfrida's subsequent divorce is, apparently, followed by division of these estates, Ecgfrida herself retaining three. Both Ecgfrida and Uhtred remarry and the quarrel over the estates springs up among the descendants. Sigríðr, the daughter of Ecgfrida's second marriage (to a man with Norse name and parentage) marries three times, though we are not told whether this is through death or divorce, and among her descendants is a man with the Celtic and fashionable name Cospatric. A daughter of Uhtred's second marriage marries into a family with some less obviously fashionable Celtic names. But it was evidently a thoroughly cosmopolitan society, a society also in which a bishop could openly acknowledge his daughter and give away episcopal estates on her marriage, a society which followed the Scandinavian practice of providing a dowry with the daughter as well as a *morgengifu* from the husband, a society in which divorce and remarriage was no problem for men or women. Ecgfrida's second marriage apparently did not turn out too happily either, and the last we hear of her is that she entered a nunnery, returned three estates to the church and Bishop, and served God well to the end of her days.

There is a provision in the *Law of the Northumbrian Priests*, as there was in the early law of Æðelbert, for man and wife to separate if they choose, though the ecclesiastical law does not permit remarriage, and insists that if a couple separate they must thereafter live in chastity. But this law must have been a difficult one to enforce in a society which took the right of divorce for granted, and there does seem to be a fair amount of evidence that the earliest Anglo-Saxon settlers did so, and that for Viking-Age men and women all that was basically required was to declare their intention in front of witnesses. An Arab chronicler reporting a visit to Viking territory is quoted as having said: 'A woman stays with her husband as long as it pleases her to do so, and leaves him if it no longer pleases her'. This would not be good evidence on its own. Foreigners may easily have misunderstood a situation, or even been deliberately misled. But in this case the statement corroborates the situation as it regularly appears to us in Icelandic saga. That the threat of divorce could be, for a woman, a powerful sexual and financial weapon comes across clearly in an episode in *Gísla saga*. A man called Þorkell has reason to suspect his wife of infidelity and begins to reproach her. She offers him the choice of keeping quiet about it or: 'I shall call witnesses at once and declare my divorce from you, and I will have my father claim back my marriage-gift and my dowry; and if this is your choice you will never have my bed-company again'. Þorkell chooses the former alternative.

Not many Icelandic family sagas have much to tell us about Viking women in the British Isles. *Orkneyinga saga*, 'The saga of the Orkney Islanders', is the one from which we should obviously expect most information. What we get from it are odd vignettes of characters but scarcely enough information to distinguish the individual from the stereotype. Reasonable freedom of sexual relationships is implied by the constant reference to who was whose mistress, or illegitimate child. Romance colours some poems of Rögnvaldr but they are poems for the exotic Ermingerd of Narbonne, not for any local girl. The only one addressed to his compatriot, a woman called Ragna, was less than complimentary on the subject of her head-dress. Earl Þorfinnr escaped from a burning house 'carrying his wife Ingibjorg in his arms'; Jón *vængr* who made a girl pregnant before disappearing on a Viking expedition was obliged to marry her on his return; it is all an everyday story of Viking folk, as seen by a thirteenth-century Icelander.

Other sagas show their heroes briefly in England or Britain. In *Eiríks saga* Leifr spends a summer in the Hebrides and when he leaves there a woman with the Norse name of Þorgunnr, described as 'well-born', points out to him that she is pregnant by him and would prefer to go back to Greenland with him. Leif's refusal to take her implies that her kin would be more angry about her abduction than her pregnancy. It is implied also that she did not find his gifts of a gold ring, a cloak of Greenland cloth, and a belt with walrus-ivory fittings adequate compensation.

It is clear that we cannot take such anecdotes as accurate guides to actual events, only as indications of social attitudes. With some other saga portrayals, notably the one in *Egils saga* of the Viking queen Gunnhildr in York, we are in the world of folk-tale rather than history. But the one saga in which the author's interests focus again and again on women is *Laxdæla saga*, and at least some of the action of *Laxdæla* purports to have taken place in the British Isles.

Some of the women are pure romantic folk-tale as, for example, the beautiful, mute slave-girl Melkorka who turns out to be an Irish princess and manages to preserve through all the vicissitudes of slavery the gold ring that will finally furnish proof of identity. The bedridden old nurse in Ireland who 'needed no crutches' when she came to meet her foster-daughter's handsome son is similarly a stock figure. Yet within such folk-tale patterns moments of insight into something nearer the realities of the Viking world occur. The ambivalent attitude to slavery occurs again when the betrothal of Melkorka's son is in question. The prospective bride reacts angrily at the thought of being married off to the son of a slave. Her father, a well-travelled man, is more impressed by the Irish royal grandfather than the slave status of the mother: 'Don't you know that he is the grandson of the Irish king Myrkjartan? He is of much higher rank through his mother's connections, than on his father's side'. We also get a glimpse here of the sense of unity within the Viking world. Melkorka, born Irish, was found as a slave for sale in the tent of 'Gilli the Russian' at a mainland Scandinavian market. She was bought by an Icelander, and her Icelandic son travels to Ireland to locate his grandfather. There was nothing parochial in such patterns of behaviour, and it is probable that Viking women in England shared in this cosmopolitan confidence. Women in Scandinavia raised rune-stone memorials for their dead who had fallen in distant lands, but Ingerun in eleventh-century Sweden had a rune-stone carved for herself before she set off on pilgrimage: 'she wishes to travel east, and out to Jerusalem'.

Similar confident control is depicted in the *Laxdœla saga* account of *Unnr in djúpúðga*, commonly translated 'Unnr the deep-minded', though a manuscript spelling variant suggests the alternative 'the deeply wealthy'. Unnr was brought up in Norway and married there, but when her father emigrated to Britain and settled in Scotland she and others including her son Þorsteinn came with him. After the death of her father and son in hostilities with the Scots she took control of the family and organised their emigration to Iceland. The *Laxdœla* account deserves quoting in full:

Unnr the deep-minded was in Caithness when her son Þorsteinn was killed; when she knew that Þorsteinn was dead and her father also, it seemed to her that she had no future there. She then had a cargo-ship built secretly in a forest, and when the ship was complete she got ready to sail, and had great wealth with her. She took with her all of her kin who were yet living, and it is commonly believed that you would not find another example of a woman who got away in such hostile circumstances with so much money and such a following.

There is not a hint of patronage in this generous expression of admiration. It is a commendation of a different order from the domestic tributes on runic memorials in Scandinavia. The Norwegian girl who was said in the mid-eleventh century to have 'the most skilful fingers in Horðaland' was presumably being praised for her embroidery.

In Britain the highest number of Norse runic inscriptions is found in the Isle of Man, where we have something approaching thirty. Most of these are laconic, recording little about the characters involved other than their relationship. Among them a number of texts record stones raised for women. One of the stones at Kirk Andreas records that Sandulfr the Black raised this cross for his wife Arinbjörg. Another Manx inscription gives us genealogical information about the wife for whom the cross was raised, but the text recording the husband's name is lost. The legible portion tells us the memorial was for his wife, Astríðr daughter of Oddr. All the names in these two inscriptions are Norse, but there are two other texts in Old Norse runes and language put up for wives with Celtic names. In one of them, indeed, the man who commissioned it had a Celtic name also. Another stone was put up by a man for Fríðr his mother, yet another by a father

55, 56 Memorial cross for
Arinbjörg commissioned by
her husband, with a detail of
the runes along the edge.

for his daughter. One with a difficult and ambiguous inscription is perhaps for
a foster-mother. The proportion of women's names may have been higher, since
damaged texts have sometimes lost the name of the person commemorated, but
it still seems reasonably high. What has been called 'the oldest runic memorial
in the Norse settlements over in the west' is the cross at Kilbar, Barra, in the
Outer Hebrides, assigned to the tenth century. It commemorates a woman with
the Norse name Þorgerðr. She may have been the daughter of the man who
commissioned it, but too much of the text is lost to be sure of this. It is, however,
clear that in the areas of Britain where runic monuments were put up by the
Vikings, some care was taken to ensure that the valued women of the family had
their proper memorial stones.

The domestic duties of such women would vary according to status. It is not,
I think, possible to tell in a slave economy the extent to which household chores
were clearly divided between male and female slave. Free-born women in the
pagan period are buried with a particular type and range of grave-goods which
so often include apparatus connected with clothing the family (weaving-swords,

spindle-whorls and needlecases) that we must assume this to have been one of their major areas of activity. General responsibility for feeding the family seems also to have been the woman's. An Old Norse poem *Rígsþula*, probably of the tenth century, describes women of three different classes and the manner in which they serve food to a guest, and this presumably would vary little whether these Viking women were offering hospitality in Bergen, York or Dublin. Some stanzas may have been displaced in the text but the general pattern is clear. The first woman puts out bread, 'heavy and thick and swollen with husks', broth, and boiled veal. She and her descendants typify the class of slaves, girls with muddy feet and sunburned arms. We do not know what the second woman offered her guest since there is a gap at this point. She and her descendants are the free-born, the farmers and craftsmen. The women are legally married and holders of keys. The poet devotes two whole stanzas to the excellent meal served by the third woman. She covers the table with a white embroidered linen cloth. She places on it white loaves of wheat, silver table-ware, roasted fowl and wine. Her descendants are the aristocracy. Her son is called Jarl, 'earl', and marries a bride who is blonde, slender-fingered and wise.

The class-consciousness represented in these three divisions comes out most clearly in the stanzas describing the names of the descendants. From the first woman are descended women described by such unimaginative nick-names as 'Fat-legs', 'Snub-nose', 'Rag-wearer'. From the second come 'The Fair', 'The Wise', 'The Slender', 'The Graceful'. The corresponding list is missing in the third section, and it is possible that this second list ought more appropriately to belong there. But either way it is clear that the second two classes, the free-born and the aristocracy, are described with admiration and respect, and that the slave class is described with distaste and ridicule.

Whether the women of the upper classes were much concerned with the actual preparation of food or not, it is certain that they were responsible for the serving of drink. As in the Anglo-Saxon heroic poetry, women are always depicted as pourers of wine or beer or mead at feasting. In the Viking-Age poetry known as skaldic verse people and objects are referred to by elaborate and artificial metaphors known as kennings. Thus a ship might be 'an elk of the waves', a man might be a 'tree of battle'. Names of gods and goddesses are regular features of kennings for men and women. The association of woman with the serving or preparation of drink is demonstrated in the repeated kennings which make use of this connection. She is *víns Vór*, 'goddess of wine'; *öls eik*, 'tree of ale'; *öl-Nanna*, 'goddess of ale'; *Hörn horna*, 'goddess of drinking horns', and a host of other appellations of the same type. Even the valkyries are represented in this domestic fashion in a poem commissioned by the Viking woman who was for a time queen in York, Gunnhildr the wife of Eiríkr Bloodaxe. Eiríkr was killed in 954, and the poem commemorating him, composed shortly afterwards, begins with a speech purporting to be by the god Óðinn: 'I told the Valkyries to get

57 Typical Swedish pendant in the form of a woman offering a drinking horn, possibly representing a valkyrie welcoming the dead to Valhöll.

up, to strew the benches [i.e. with cushions], to wash out the drinking vessels and to serve wine for the coming of a prince'. It would appear to represent Eiríkr arriving in Valhöll greeted in the style to which he was accustomed in York. Many carvings and amulets show the Viking woman carrying a drinking horn. Most of the amulets are silver and Swedish, but two carvings in northern England also have this motif. The Gosforth (Cumbria) cross has the typical details of this portrayal, the hair-style, the trailing dress, and the drinking-horn itself. A recent interpretation suggests that this woman is deliberately included on the cross as a symbol of the converted heathen. In the church at Sockburn-on-Tees a carved stone shows a warrior with a shield being offered a horn by a woman, in the same manner as on the picture stones in Gotland (Sweden). The only case I know of in Old Norse literature where a man serves alcohol is in the poem *Völundarkviða* where Völundr offers strong drink to Böðvildr – 'he knew more than she did' – as a prelude to rape.

More attractive pictures of the relationship between the sexes are offered by the love poetry of the Viking Age. There are a number of poems recorded, mostly in Icelandic sources. In mainland Scandinavia the composing or at any rate the circulating of love poetry was considered by the woman's kin to be a slur on the family's honour and in Iceland it could be punished by the lesser outlawry. We have no means of knowing what the situation was in England, and certainly English law has nothing to say on the matter. But some Vikings in Britain were poets. Magnús Bareleg, King of Norway, refused to return home to the women of Norway because, as he says in a love poem, his heart is in Dublin:

Hvat skulum heimför kvitta?
Hugr's minn í Dyflinni.
Enn til Kaupangs kvinna
Kemk eigi austr í hausti.
Unik þvít eigi synjar
Ingjan gamans þinga.
Oerska veldr þvít írskum
Annk betr an mér svanna.

Why chatter of going home?
My heart is in Dublin.
I shall not come east in the autumn
Any more to the women of Kaupangr.
I stay because Irish Ingjan
Does not deny me love's battle.
I am young and I love an Irish girl
Better than myself.

He presumably tells us the nationality of his love by calling her *ingjan*, an Irish, not a Norse, word for 'girl'. The poet Kormákr loves an Icelandic girl, but being a seasoned traveller, he is able to assess her worth in cosmopolitan terms: she is worth the land of the English and the soil of the Irish: *verð er Engla jarðar / . . . ok Íra grundar.*

We are not told of any love poetry composed by Vikings for Anglo-Saxon women. One sour-tempered chronicler with access to a northern source, now lost, writing a couple of hundred years afterwards, claimed that the success of Vikings with English women was due to the fact that they bathed on Saturdays, combed their hair and wore fine clothing. Their motive, he claims, was to seduce women and 'obtain the daughters of noblemen as their mistresses'. A connection between dress and morals is fairly typical of the outbursts of enraged Anglo-Saxons. A letter in Old English by an unknown author rebuked the writer's brother Edward for 'dressing in the Danish fashion with bared neck and blinded eyes'. He calls it a 'shameful manner of dress'. And if little of the Viking love poetry survives composed either for women of their own nationality in Britain or for the local girls they met and married, there is also comparatively little to tell us about the reciprocal feelings of Viking women in any part of their world. One pleasant, ribald anonymous verse preserved in two sagas reminds us a little of the tone of the Old English riddles. Ingólfr, we are told, was the most handsome man in the north country.

> All the girls wanted to have Ingólfr –
> those who were grown-up – what a pity I'm still too young.
> 'I too', said the old woman, 'intend to have Ingólfr –
> So long as two teeth in my gums still chatter together.'

Most of our sources on Vikings in Britain show them in pagan and secular contexts whether in such frivolities as their love-lives or such serious matters as the acquisition of wealth and power. As they came under the influence of their Christian environment it becomes more difficult to distinguish their behaviour and practices from those of the host country. There are no full and detailed records of the transition period, nor much information in the literature on how

Viking men and women here reacted to conversion. Some scattered items provide scraps of evidence such as the runic crosses of the Isle of Man, and the sundial at Aldbrough with its Norse inscription for the soul of a woman with a Norse name.

In so far as the wills of those with Old Norse names survive it is usually because they are leaving land to monastic foundations, as we saw earlier with Þorgunnr. There is also a charter recording the donations of Gyða, the Danish mother of King Harold, to the foundation of St Óláfr at Exeter. Óláfr was the Norwegian king and martyr killed in battle in the year 1030. His cult rapidly put him at the forefront of Scandinavian royal saints, and was noticeably vigorous in England. The converted Vikings in Britain thus had their own saint, and Gyða's donation shows a proper and interesting mixture of Christian zeal and national consciousness. *Orkneyinga saga*, 'The saga of the Orkney Islanders', has much to tell us of Magnús, another Norse saint, and only a little to say about his wife, not even giving us her name. But local record apparently preserved a name for the lady, and gave her saintly status equal to her husband's. When William of Worcester in the fifteenth century made notes about the Orkneys in his *Itinerarium* he had learned not only of the shrine of Magnús, but also that 'Saint Ingarth, queen and countess, wife of Saint Magnus lies likewise in the island of Egilsay'. Ingarth clearly represents Old Norse Ingigerðr, and she may perhaps be noted here as the only Viking woman in the British Isles who is reported to have reached sainthood.

## FURTHER READING

Isle of Man archaeology has been published by WILSON, runes in a series of articles by PAGE. There are so many books out now on Vikings in general and even on Vikings in England, that selection is difficult. The reader will find some of them in the bibliography under BAILEY, GRAHAM-CAMPBELL, LOYN, WILSON. Much useful analysis of place-names is by FELLOWS-JENSEN, especially *Scandinavian Personal Names in Lincolnshire and Yorkshire*. Translations of the sagas are readily available in Penguin and Everyman editions, and are cited in the bibliography under FELL, JOHNSTON, JONES, LAING, PRESS, and PÁLSSON. The Gerdrup burial is discussed in an article by Tom CHRISTENSEN. The Durham family tangles are dealt with by HART in *The Early Charters of Northern England*. Most of the longer poems are in any text or translation of Eddic poetry. AUDEN AND TAYLOR's *Norse Poems* is accessible and easy reading.

# 8. After 1066
# The Factual Evidence

Post-Conquest England saw nearly all the native aristocracy and gentry dis-possessed by 'Norman' settlers, who for a generation or two remained somewhat apart. In matters of family structure, land-tenure and inheritance the newcomers observed legal and social customs partly at variance with those prevailing in pre-Conquest days. To regulate these customs they established within little more than a century a formidable bureaucracy, of which many products survive. Yet, for all the documentation, women of the twelfth and thirteenth centuries are only intermittently visible to historians, because the matters with which extant records mostly deal are ones, like land-holding and politics, in which women had a limited share: a negative finding significant in itself.

When a medieval theorist divided society into three orders – those who fight, those who till the earth, and those who pray – he explicitly omitted women, noting their role simply as 'to marry and to serve' the fighters and the workers. Throughout the Middle Ages and beyond marriage was a central theme of women's lives, but no personal diaries survive to tell of it, nor any truly private, vernacular letters from earlier than the fifteenth century. Some shreds of personal testimony exist. The early fifteenth-century *Book of Margery Kempe* depicts, from her point of view and as an incident in her spiritual odyssey, a marriage which produced fourteen children. The church-court records of matrimonial causes, which begin in the early thirteenth century and are voluminous by the late fourteenth, sometimes seem, despite their Latinised form, to catch the voices of the parties and their witnesses; but for the most part these remain unpublished.

On the other hand, accessible evidence abounds for the place of marriage in socio-economic and moral-theological structures: civil and canon laws alike expound women's role in society, showing also what individuals could expect from life. Laws often encapsulate the ethos of the community whose conduct they regulate. For twelfth-century England the problem is that sometimes the codes conflicted (as they had in earlier times begun to do) with canon law prohibiting what civil and customary law allowed or even prescribed. As to which code more nearly reflected current attitudes, the best clue lies perhaps in the term 'customary': whereas canon law rested on ideal concepts of behaviour, twelfth-century Anglo-Norman civil law codified traditional customs. Certainly canon law was in the long run to influence social morality; but for the twelfth century civil law seems best to represent current attitudes to marriage and to women's role in society.

Post-Conquest society was based upon, indeed obsessed with, land-tenure. How this coloured the view taken of marriage by the twelfth-century Anglo-Norman or English aristocracy is clear from one administrative document: the *Rotuli de dominabus et pueris et puellis* compiled in 1185. Translating the title as 'A Register of Rich Widows and of Orphaned Heirs and Heiresses' gives an inkling of its content: it lists widows 'in the king's gift' and orphans 'in wardship', giving brief accounts of their family circumstances but detailed ones of their property, down to the last pig. Because all land belonged ultimately to the king, to be granted by him according to military or political expediency, familial inheritance – male primogeniture being the preferred Norman custom – suffered constraints, with heirs obliged to seek and to pay for royal approval of their succession. If a baron died before his heir was of age the lands reverted meanwhile to the Crown, the widow and under-age children being taken into the wardship of the king, who saw to the arranging of marriages for them: the position of the 'widows and orphans' in our *Register*. That was simply a special case of the regular royal control of nobles' marriages, including any that a baron might in his lifetime plan for a daughter or other kinswoman, because of the way that marriage affected land-holding. In this system based (at least theoretically) on 'military' tenure, a woman land-holder was an anomaly. Because military duties could (as when a male land-holder was aged or disabled) be vicariously performed or commuted for a money-payment, a female could, in the absence of a male heir, inherit her family's land, but her rights in respect of it remained circumscribed. When an heiress married (not 'if': no woman of property was likely to be left single) her husband acquired for as long as the marriage lasted full control of her properties and, if he fathered a live child, retained it all his life. A widow's remarriage likewise conveyed all her holdings, including the 'dower' due from her late husband's estate, to her new one. A union contracted without prior royal approval incurred a fine, and might entail forfeiture of the lands. A register of heiresses and of propertied widows could thus assist royal clerks charged with collecting the fees due either from would-be suitors or, alternatively, from ladies anxious to keep their freedom. That fees and fines were in fact exacted is proved by surviving account-rolls. The system gave widows of an age to assert themselves and with money to hand fair freedom of choice, for their orphaned children as well as for themselves. But the fees were substantial and accordingly resented; a main freedom laid down in Magna Carta was that thenceforth no widow wishing to remain single should have to suffer financial penalty.

Young girls' wishes were another matter. Children of both sexes, whether orphaned or not, were married off at the tenderest ages: the *Register* notes one 'widow' as aged ten and her brother's 'wife', aged five, as already living in her mother-in-law's household. Rank and riches were no protection – rather the reverse. Heiresses' marriages, with their tenurial consequences, were saleable commodities, to be purchased by the highest bidder or granted by the king, as favour or reward, to a courtier or a captain. Thus, in the late 1180s Henry II rewarded William the Marshal, a landless younger son of minor nobility, with the hand of the orphan heiress of the great Clare family, such a match being what William needed to add wealth and rank (the earldom of Pembroke) to his personal distinction. Nowhere are the girl's feelings mentioned, even though it was she who, as a middle-aged widow, commissioned William's extant verse-biography; her acquiescence in a marriage to a man twice her age was seemingly taken for granted by all parties, herself included. Not all girls did manage to acquiesce in their arranged marriages. The future St Christina of Markyate (of burgess, not baronial, stock) refused, despite threats and thrashings, to accept the husband her parents had chosen; she ran away dressed as a boy, to take refuge with an anchoress; how her life unfolded we shall see later.

A twelfth-century girl's reactions to an arranged marriage may have been different from a modern one's. Hard though it is to interpret in human terms stories preserved only in quasi-official documents, some episodes seem significant. About 1162 the fifty-year-old Aubrey de Vere, earl of Oxford – still childless after two marriages (one swiftly annulled, the other ended by early death) – married a twelve-year-old bride called Agnes, only to repudiate her less than a year later on the pretext of her alleged previous betrothal to his brother Geoffrey; the true motive more probably lay in the disgrace recently incurred by her father, a former royal constable. Protesting that she had never known of any such betrothal, far less consented to it, Agnes appealed for validation of her marriage to the Bishop of London and then to the Pope. To hinder her prosecution of the case, the earl kept her in custody so close as to prevent her even from attending church. In 1172 the Pope pronounced the marriage valid and commanded the earl thenceforth to treat the countess as his wife before God, threatening eternal punishment of any dereliction. The couple had several offspring, including an heir to the earldom. Widowed in her forties, Agnes paid a large fee not to be obliged to remarry (*pro pace habenda de se maritanda*). Uncomfortable though the marriage seems, her anxiety to maintain it is understandable: committed since the age of three to the de Vere family and since humiliated by the disgrace of her own, she can have seen little future elsewhere. Most women of this time must have envisaged marriage as a job, a distasteful one possibly, but for all that essential to any tolerable way of life.

So far we have focused on the nobility, whose lives are reflected in the records most readily accessible. The middling strata of society observed like customs. Among the 'under-tenants' or 'knightly class' usages were similar to those of the nobility, with this difference, that the rights of wardship and of marriage control over under-tenants were exercised not by the Crown but by their immediate lords, the barons. As for the urban society, at this time beginning to develop, the more prosperous burgesses (those whose lives are most open to our scrutiny) evidently took much the same view of marriage as did nobles and gentry, arranging alliances for economic advantage. At all events, such urban 'patriciates' as have been studied – the London one, for instance – had their leading families linked in complex webs of intermarriage hardly likely to have resulted from a free play of fancy. In one respect burgesses were freer than nobility or gentry, being exempt from the 'incidents' (fees and fines) accompanying feudal tenure. Borough customs sometimes explicitly provide that citizens shall freely 'give their daughters in marriage'. The limitation of such 'freedom' is clear: so much was 'giving in marriage' deemed to be not the parents' prerogative but their duty that municipal charities, such as the London 'court of orphanage', were set up for freemen's orphans, not only to manage their business affairs but also to arrange marriages for them.

Given this regulation of marriage choice among the upper ranks of society, scant freedom might be expected among the peasantry. Rural society was divided by ranks and its customs, unlike those of nobility and gentry, varied from manor to manor. Free farmers enjoyed liberties analogous to those of burgesses: rights, that is, for parents to arrange their children's marriages without payment or need for outside approval. For villeins matters were different. The customs ruling their lives (hence the term, 'customary tenant'), although varying in detail, followed certain general principles. In the harshest view villeins formed part of a manor's livestock, and could be conveyed along with their land from one lord to another. For a villein girl to marry away from the lordship of her birth robbed the lord not only of her work but also of any villein children she might produce, and therefore she had to seek the lord's approval of any proposed marriage and pay for this a fee called 'merchet', liability for which was proof of servile status. This was not mere form: cases are recorded where women who had married without leave were taken back to their original homes. On widows, too, custom could bear hard. Sometimes a widow succeeded automatically to her late husband's holding. In other cases a lord, deeming only an adult male equal to working the land and performing adequately the labour services due from it, might force a widow lacking a grown son either to remarry or else to move out; the lord himself might choose the prospective husband, who was for his part liable to be fined if (as some did) he refused the match despite the land that went with it. When the dead man left an adult male heir then the widow was entitled to claim from him (often her own eldest son) her 'free bench', that is, a right to shelter and maintenance for as long as she continued in 'chaste widowhood'; for, unlike a noblewoman with her dower, on remarriage (or if detected in fornication) a peasant widow forfeited her rights. Another difference lay in average ages of marriage: unlike a daughter of the great and rich, who might be married off at twelve, a peasant girl had to wait, perhaps until well into her twenties, for a suitable holding to be available for the founding of a new household. Peasant customs thus varied in detail rather than principle from those of nobility, gentry and bourgeoisie. Women's own freedom of choice could hardly have been more circumscribed than among the nobles, for whom it was regularly subordinated to questions of land, money and rank. Comparative poverty did not necessarily mean – except in terms of material comfort – a more restricted life. By the time church-court records appear promises and vows were being freely exchanged between couples clearly obeying their own wishes, not those of parents or of lords. How often peasant girls took lovers is shown by the frequently recorded fines for births of bastards; church-court records tell of couples seen lying, in unambiguous postures, under hedges. On those manors where custom prescribed that a female serf's bastard child should not follow her condition but be free, such births might occasionally have represented deliberate choice of a route to freedom.

Customs and civil laws regulating conduct on mainly economic principles had long been experiencing the rivalry of the differently orientated canon law, which, in contrast, neither varied from realm to realm nor was tailored to rank, but arrogated to itself a universality based upon divine sanction. Already in the pre-Conquest period influence from this system had begun to introduce new rigour to English legislation about marriage and sexual morality: a process now accelerated and intensified by the late eleventh-century Gregorian Reforms. All enforcement of marriage laws and of morals was in time to be taken over by the church courts; and, by dint of thus presiding over public behaviour, canon law eventually succeeded in modifying private expectations. During the twelfth century its relationships with civil custom were still being worked out.

The canon law of marriage rested on a particular concept of woman's basic nature. Despite Christian protestations that all human souls were equal, anti-feminist attitudes inherited from Græco-Roman society had early come to dominate the Church. Excluded from every priestly office, women found themselves enjoined to public silence. These restrictions the churchmen justified by reference to the Bible, especially as interpreted by the Fathers of the Church. *Genesis* was held to show Eve, and all her daughters with her, as essentially inferior to Adam, having been created after him, from one of his ribs, and explicitly as a 'help' to him, not as an equal partner. It depicted her as readier than Adam to succumb to temptation and therefore, unless strictly disciplined, a moral danger to him; as instigator of the Fall, she had justly (it was claimed) been set under Adam's authority. Such a view of women, as inferior to men in morals and in intellect, underlay the Pauline pronouncements on marriage:

> Wives, submit yourselves unto your own husbands, as unto the Lord. For the husband is head of the wife, even as Christ is head of the Church...Husbands, love your wives, even as Christ also loved the Church...Let everyone of you in particular so love his

58 Initial from a manuscript of the *Song of Songs*. An allegorical illustration of the verse, 'Let him kiss with the kiss of his mouth'; Christ and Ecclesia embrace.

wife even as himself; and the wife see that she reverence [*timeat*] her husband. (*Ephesians*, v. 22–33; cf. I *Corinthians* vi.)

During the twelfth-century renewal of theology and of canon law such notions – earlier elaborated by the Fathers, in particular Tertullian, Augustine, Ambrose and Jerome – were studied and commented on anew. In degrees of anti-feminist bias the reinterpretations varied marginally, with some venturing to suggest that Mary's part in the Incarnation counterbalanced the harm that Eve had wrought. The Fall none the less continued to dominate theological concepts of woman, and hence of marriage, while the horror of the flesh felt by so many male clerics inspired condemnations of sexuality and consequent restrictions upon the role of women.

Despite such unpromising premisses, twelfth-century canon law did somewhat temper Anglo-Norman marriage customs, and this, by a paradox, partly because of its theological basis. To the pragmatism of feudal custom canon law opposed an ideal, allegorised concept; the Pauline view of marriage as figuring Christ's relationship with His Church had generated an ideal of the spiritual love – to be as little as possible contaminated by fleshly passions – that ought to subsist between spouses. Hence the injunctions laid upon Aubrey de Vere to 'love his wife as his own self'. Canon lawyers came to demand as a precondition for a valid marriage full and free consent from both parties. Any contract made under duress or between children below years of discretion was void, whilst any freely made between competent parties was binding, even though clandestine and even though opposed by parent, guardian or overlord (the Church's authority did not, however, extend over related questions of property and inheritance). Some flexibility remained, so that child marriages, for instance, might still be countenanced if necessary 'for peace'. Safeguards for self-determination in any case remained imperfect: the age of valid consent was set for girls at twelve, and at this time when parents might freely thrash their adolescent children (as did the mother of the future St Christina) interpretations of 'duress' were not always generous to the victim. That apart, awareness of economic dependency must have dissuaded many a girl from questioning parental plans. In the long run, nevertheless, canonical insistence on freely given mutual consent did modify secular views of marriage.

For all that, canon law was not a liberalising force. Theology alleged women to be essentially inferior to men and in need of constant male tutelage (Gratian saw servitude as their proper condition). The tighter the grip of canon law grew on secular affairs, the further women's already limited rights were eroded, always under pretext of affording their weakness a necessary protection. Without her husband's consent no married woman could now – by contrast with pre-Conquest custom – make a valid will; in practice a husband would often allow his dying wife to make bequests of her personal chattels and even of such lands as might fall to her portion, but that in no way mitigated the code's essential harshness. A woman's own consent was needed before her husband could alienate matrimonial property acquired through her right, an act which might reduce provision for her widowhood; but how 'free' such consent sometimes was may be doubted (in other contexts the law regularly assumed a wife to be subject to 'duress').

Although the law-codes, canon and civil, combine to reveal not only the practical constraints within which women (and men) had to live their lives but also something of the social climate shaping expectations, what form average expectations took remains uncertain. Individual reactions varied: whereas the future St Christina, rather than accept the decent enough young man her parents proposed, fled to a hermitage, the young countess of Oxford strove to validate her union with the elderly, callous Aubrey de Vere. In all ranks of life, it may be surmised, many a girl saw her arranged marriage not as an exercise in parental tyranny, but as a means of social promotion, enabling her to become at very least mistress of her own household and probably in time a matriarch. Even child-betrothal might, for all the Church's strictures against it, have had its good side, for children raised in the same nursery could have learnt mutual tolerance, comradeship even. An arranged marriage, besides, offers less scope for dis-appointment than one of inclination.

That remains surmise, for lack of private papers prevents access to personal feelings. As for literary treatments of love and marriage, fictional ones are reserved for the following chapter; those not avowedly fictional need assessment by special criteria. The author of *Holy Maidenhood*, when depicting a wife as her husband's victim, tormented so cruelly she would rather be dead, was both propagandising for the virgin life and reworking commonplaces going back to antiquity. Even chronicles and biographies are not above suspicion, being almost all compiled by monks and clerics frankly intent on drawing from their materials the maximum of edification. When Orderic Vitalis pictures the wives whom the Conqueror's barons had left in Normandy as 'burning with lust' and summoning their husbands to return forthwith, else they would find themselves other mates, can his account be taken at face-value? Men who complied, he says, lost their chances of rich pickings in the newly conquered lands; so was he (himself a cloister-monk since boyhood) seizing a chance to animadvert on the temporal disadvantages of lust rather than recording a real episode? With the private behaviour, let alone sentiments, of their subjects inaccessible to them, chroniclers and biographers necessarily eked their material out with conventional motifs; and marriage had become tangled with theological idealisations. Bishop Turgot's *Life of St Margaret of Scotland* depicts the saint's husband, the warlike King Malcolm, as fondling and kissing for love of her the devotional books which he himself could not read. The monk Eadmer of Canterbury represents as a love-match the political marriage between Henry 1 and one of St Margaret's daughters, Edith, later known as Matilda: although Henry had, Eadmer says, 'fallen in love' with the Scottish princess, rumours of her having taken the veil 'set tongues wagging and held back the two from embracing one another as they desired'. Monastic chroniclers seemingly found a calculated contracting of marriage for worldly advantage even less admissible than fleshly lusts.

Yet, conventionalised and idealised though twelfth-century literature may have been, its currency was fact. Marie de France's *Lays* antedate the *Register of Widows and Heiresses*. Wives given in marriage as tokens of land-transfer and maidens knowing themselves destined for a like fate heard not only preachers commending a spiritual love like Christ's for His Church but also minstrels singing of earthlier loves between women like themselves and men (not quite) like their husbands. Did they listen with envy, or with an ironical twitch of an eyebrow? Illicit affairs were not unknown. Although royalty is never typical, its well-publicised adventures illustrate some possible freedoms. Henry 1, for instance, acknowledged over a score of bastards, by a dozen or so mistresses; the offspring grew up to enjoy appropriate ranks and make advantageous marriages. Nor were the mothers social outcasts. One, another Edith, from a pre-Conquest line of Cumbrian magnates, married into the d'Oilly family of Oxford; another, a Welsh princess, married the Norman grandfather of Gerald of Wales; yet another, a Beaumont, married Gilbert de Clare, first earl of Pembroke. Similar freedoms appear also among people of modest to middling condition, such as the Londoners shown in a late thirteenth-century breach-of-promise case as frequenting, sometimes in couples, a public bath-house with beds, near the Tower.

One small, anomalous group of early twelfth-century women consisted of priests' 'wives'. Clerical marriage, often combined with heredity of benefice, had long been current throughout Western Europe; and so in the early twelfth century it partly remained. Records datable soon after 1100 show priests and their wives admitted jointly to confraternity with Thorney Abbey – a house famed for its austere morals. The hermit Wulfric of Haselbury numbered among his closest friends the married priest Brihtric, whose son succeeded to his benefice. A better-known inheritor of clerical office was the annalist Henry, nowadays surnamed 'of Huntingdon' from the archdeaconry which he held for some forty-five years, having in about 1110 succeeded his father Nicholas in this and in a Lincoln canonry; Henry in his turn fathered a son, Adam. Even the ascetic Cistercian abbot Ailred of Rievaulx was descended from a line of hereditary priests of Hexham. This very paragraph, having on the surface little to do with 'women', illustrates their near invisibility in many records; for instance, Henry of Huntingdon's family history implies, but never names, at least two respectable 'wives' of archdeacons (one of whom may have been the unnamed 'archdeacon's wife' admitted to confraternity with Thorney Abbey in the 1120s).

Such women were, however, becoming less secure. The Gregorian Reforms strengthened demands for clerical celibacy; council after council commanded clergy living in concubinage to repudiate their women forthwith or else surrender their benefices. Commentator after commentator noted, and usually deplored, widespread indifference to these exhortations. Such partnerships, perhaps contracted with less of an eye than most to worldly advantage, may have been closer than most. Rural priests like Brihtric lived much like the peasants they served and had at least as great a need of a second pair of hands about the small-holding. Obeying the directives would, besides, have left many women and children destitute. No woman's comments on the subject survive. Henry of Huntingdon's do: doubly involved, as family man and as archdeacon charged with enforcing church discipline, he took a line opposite to those of the monastic chroniclers. Prohibiting marriage would, he asserted, simply promote vice; and under 1125 he related, almost with glee, that the Papal legate inveighing against clerical marriage had himself been caught with a whore. Prelatical authority in these matters was often undermined by the bishops' own laxity. The first bishop whom Henry served, Robert Bloet of Lincoln, had a son who became dean in his father's diocese. Roger of Salisbury, chief minister of the realm as well as bishop, made little secret of his relationship with Matilda of Ramsbury; one of their sons, another Roger, became royal chancellor, and Matilda's own standing is clear from her being entrusted during the Anarchy with command of one of the Bishop's castles. As for Rannulf Flambard ('the Firebrand'), Bishop of Durham, he had several sons by an aunt of Christina of Markyate's.

Outside religion marriage was the normal state; for women especially a single life outside the cloister was little esteemed. Feudal and familial pressures towards marriage must have been further reinforced by economic ones, because staying even temporarily single required either property (a magnet to fortune-hunters) or else a livelihood, and for that opportunities were limited.

Widows enjoyed greatest freedom. With a marriage-portion of her own, plus a third of her late husband's property, a widowed noblewoman needed only to pay her overlord the requisite fee for self-determination (sometimes backed by a vow of chastity) – not even that after Magna Carta had taken effect. A widow whose husband had held on burgess-tenure might also be well placed: town surveys regularly mention widows holding large properties and assessed for tax at high rates. A merchant's widow might continue the trade on her own account, and even take her husband's place as member of his gild; the ordinances of the London weavers explicitly laid down that, provided she did not marry out of the craft, a member's widow could continue to work one of her husband's looms. As already noted, a peasant woman likewise had her 'free bench'.

Few girls – except perhaps those born to landless squatters – can in the long run have fallen outside the twin net of marriage/nunnery. For villein girls, however, the need to delay marriage until a holding became available sometimes impelled those whose families could not meanwhile support them to seek a living elsewhere. It was for women in this position that jobs were most plentiful. As manorial labour-services were more and more often commuted for money-rents, so demand grew, especially at harvest-times, for hired field-workers of both sexes (often footloose people who got a name for petty crime). A thirteenth-century treatise on farm-management points out that a woman can be engaged to look after poultry and such 'for less money than a man would ask'. Skill and a sense of responsibility could take a woman to be head dairymaid: just as in the Old English text *Rectitudines* the cheesemaker is the only female specialist on the farm, so medieval treatises assume that the dairy, and the dairy only, will be overseen by a woman. Manorial records note licences given to villein girls to leave their villages to seek work. Among these must have been many of the servants that all households of any pretension, in town and country alike, employed. Especially important were nurses and nursemaids, among whose duties the encyclopaedist Bartholomew the Englishman includes that of thoroughly chewing the young child's food. At higher points on the social scale, living as underling in a superior's household must have been the main resort for an ill-provided woman. A girl of gentle birth might become a noblewoman's lady-in-waiting: in the mid-twelfth century the widowed Alice de Clermont, a tenant-in-chief, had in her train an under-tenant's daughter, Mabel of Coton, who witnessed some of her mistress's charters and was admitted with her to confraternity with Thorney Abbey. A more colourful figure is the matron – perhaps a promoted ex-wetnurse – attendant upon one of Henry I's mistresses, depicted by Gerald of Wales as rounding in pithy English on the priest whose intercessions had failed to bring about her lady's (illegitimate) pregnancy.

From the twelfth century onwards developing urban life offered women, married or single, more varied opportunities. Just what occupations they could follow is a tricky question. Occupational surnames must, for both sexes, be treated with reserve, because by 1200 (and for some families earlier) a father's surname might be (but was not invariably) transferred to children of either sex. For women the question is complicated by a tendency (but at this date little more) for them to be known under their husbands' surnames. Names plainly transferred to women from men, whether fathers or husbands, include those like *Edith the Chaplain, Margaret Bullman, Emma Shipman*, and so on. As time passes less and less weight can be placed on surnames: thus a London tax-roll of 1292 lists a *Leticia la aylere*, literally, 'the garlic-dealer', but parallel records not only show her as widow of Luke Garlicmonger but also reveal that Luke in fact dealt in cured fish. To a limited extent specifically feminine terms – seldom, it seems, turned into family-names – can be informative. True, by the Middle English period, and in Northern dialects especially, some of the old feminines in *-stere* had, as noted in an earlier chapter, come to be applied to both sexes, and certain of them, including *baxter* ('baker'), *brewster* and *maltster*, *dexter* and *litster* ('dyer'), and *webster*, were now mainly applied to men; and many of these do soon figure as family-names. Some of these forms did, however, keep mainly

59 A misericord from
Ludlow, showing an ale-wife.

feminine connotations, among them *spinster* and the analogous *silkthrowster*, together with rarer forms like *quernster* ('one who uses a hand-mill'), *ropester*, *soapster*, *hopster* ('dancer') and *songster*. When suffixed to a woman's first name these probably did indicate her own trade, because in England there is little evidence for any conventional feminising of family-names. Less ambiguous are the compounds in *-wife/-woman* (far fewer than those in *-man*), such as *candlewife, featherwife, fishwife, flaxwife, silkwife/-woman, bowerwoman* ('house-maid'), *chapwoman* ('trader'), *cheesewoman*, and the like. The best indications of all, mostly, for our purposes, very late, come from terms added after family-names, as with *Matilda Baker, girdlester* (1377), and those showing spouses as following different trades, as with *John Baron, tailor, and his wife Anneys, embroidress* (1425).

Many townswomen lived, often humbly, by their own hands, like the washerwomen noted in the Domesday description of Bury St Edmunds and the unnamed early twelfth-century one renting a property near Winchester's city ditch. A mid-century schedule of the royal household shows the washerwoman as the only female office-holder (hers is the only pay unspecified); in King John's time this functionary was called Florence. In many towns, though not in London, women so dominated the brewing trade – the one in which Margery Kempe made a commercial venture – that local ordinances regulating it were drafted, quite exceptionally, in the feminine; for offences against the assize of ale women were frequently brought to court. Urban life enhanced opportunities for saleswoman-ship (in London the retailing of bread, for instance, was mainly done by women known as breadmongsters or regratresses) and for trades, in catering as well as

60 A misericord from St Andrew's Church, Norton, Suffolk, showing a woman carding wool.

in cloth-working and needlecraft, that needed skill rather than strength. Spinning was, in town and country alike, so specifically and universally women's work that medieval knockabout farce allotted the distaff a role like that more recently given to the rolling-pin. The fifteenth century saw the London silk-trade wholly in women's dextrous hands. The currency of terms such as *hopster* and *songster* implies that some women worked as entertainers – dancers, acrobats, singers, and perhaps instrumentalists as well; a woman minstrel is recorded in Stratford-upon-Avon, and about 1300 a *saltatrix* or acrobatic dancer called Maud Makejoy performed several times before the royal court. Sometimes such performers are depicted in manuscript marginalia; but these vignettes may represent jest, fantasy or allegory rather than realistic record. As for prostitution, although presumably an ever-present possibility, in the ports and the greater market-towns especially, it barely seems to be mentioned in surviving records dating from before the fourteenth century. Casual references include that to the Papal legate of 1125 caught with a whore; the 'gorgeous girls' who earlier, 'with their back hair let down', entertained Bishop Rannulf Flambard and his monks must have belonged in a like category. A woman witness in a church-court case was deemed unreliable because 'a witch, a thief and a whore'. Whether or not the thirteenth-century girls who accompanied men to London bath-houses were necessarily prostitutes is unclear. At all events, bath-houses got a bad name, and by the later Middle Ages the municipality was frankly regulating the river-traffic to and from 'The Stews' in Southwark.

Some wives, as we have seen, followed trades distinct from those of their husbands. Despite legal restrictions attendant on her 'protected' status, a married woman could trade independently; often, it seems, this status inconvenienced husband more than wife, to judge by the bye-laws which all-male corporations often drew up to exempt men from sharing in debts or penalties that their wives might incur. Some merchant-gilds admitted women – mainly widows, but on occasion daughters inheriting their fathers' businesses – as members in their own right. In some crafts, and notably in the London silk-trade, women functioned *de facto* as 'masters', taking on girl apprentices; the indentures, although for form's sake joining in the husband's name, show the wife's skill as that to be taught. By the later Middle Ages women figured among the entrepreneurs of international trade.

For women disinclined for trade or service virtually the sole alternative to marriage was the cloister. Scope there was limited in comparison with men's. Women's sanctity, it has been observed, was everywhere less readily acknowledged than men's; for whatsoever reason religious houses for women attracted less generous patronage than did those for men. Despite the high esteem for female virginity practical provision was inadequate for the numbers of those anxious to preserve it. The monastic Rules were drafted specifically for men, not just in the grammatical sense but also in assuming male styles of dress, male dietetic needs and male capacities for heavy work. By the early twelfth century this lack of provision for women's religious vocations was acutely felt. The old Benedictine nunneries were not only smaller and fewer than the men's houses (amounting to about a dozen, beside the forty or more of the latter) but were confined to southern England, mainly to Wessex, and were aristocratic in their recruitment; in 1066 there was not one nunnery north of the Trent. So when at this time all of Europe was swept by a spiritual fervour in which women, Englishwomen included, fully shared, existing nunneries could not provide for all the new vocations. There were fundamental reasons why women's religious vocations were more likely than men's to be frustrated. Men's yearnings for a more austere religious life were in the early twelfth century being met by several new Orders, and by the Cistercian Order in particular; but because of their proud austerity these Orders for almost a century set their faces against admitting women (so-called 'Cistercian nunneries' of this period were unofficial, unrecognised by the Order). A main stumbling-block was the ban on female ordination, and even on women's playing the most subsidiary liturgical role: whereas men could form a self-sufficient community, women could never do so, because they were compelled by this ban to rely for all the sacraments, confession included, on male chaplains. Every nunnery, therefore, made demands on the same Order's male religious, who feared and often openly repudiated possible moral dangers to themselves.

Nevertheless, the most remarkable of all attempts to provide for women's vocations came from a man: St Gilbert of Sempringham, founder of the only purely English religious order in all history. Having set up a school for children of both sexes, he became distressed to observe among young women who had been his pupils vocations for which they could find no outlet. So he established beside his church at Sempringham a cloister where these women could live as nuns, with lay-sisters to carry out the mundane chores. To do the heavy work on the associated lands lay-brothers were recruited: so too were learned canons to serve as chaplains. In Lincolnshire and Yorkshire there were soon nine mixed houses, in which perilous contacts between the sexes were minimised by systems of walls and of hatches through which food, and also clothes for washing and mending, could be passed (the lay-sisters did everybody's chores, not only those of the choir-nuns).

Other initiatives came from women themselves, among them the already noted Christina of Markyate, born in the late 1090s into a prosperous family of burgesses at Huntingdon. Although some episodes in her extant *Life* – the prophetic dove's visit to the mother before Christina's birth, the child's precocious piety and vow of chastity, her flight from a forced marriage – smack of hagiographical commonplace, her achievement was real enough. Around her hermitage at Markyate there grew up a community of women which by 1145 had been recognised as a priory dependent on St Albans Abbey; it survived until

61 A miniature from a psalter formerly belonging to Shaftesbury Abbey, one of the richest among English nunneries. A nun kneels in supplication.

the Dissolution. The magnificent manuscript known as the St Albans Psalter (now at Hildesheim) is believed to have been compiled for Christina before 1123. As told in the *Life*, her personal story turns on conflict between sexuality and asceticism. The chastity she had vowed was threatened first by lewd advances from Rannulf Flambard, who before becoming a bishop had fathered a family on one of her aunts, and then by the lawful ones of the husband chosen by her parents. For a time she found peace as a disciple of the fatherly hermit Roger; but after his death she became passionately involved with a priest appointed as her guardian. When prioress of Markyate, she formed a deep friendship with Abbot Geoffrey of St Albans, for whom on occasion she made warm underwear.

Many women had flocked to join Christina in what had originally been a hermitage at Markyate. Others preferred, as she herself had done at first, a more truly solitary life, among them some great ladies: Loretta, the widowed Countess of Leicester, lived for nearly fifty years as a recluse just outside Canterbury; her sister Annora also retired to a hermitage at Iffley. Another recluse was a sister of the Cistercian Abbot Ailred of Rievaulx, who wrote for her a Latin handbook. An even more famous manual of the kind, based partly upon Ailred's, was the English one known as *Ancrene Wisse*, dating from about 1230 and now believed to have been compiled by an Austin canon of Wigmore for a neighbouring cell of anchoresses; possibly, but not certainly, the writer's own sisters. Be that as it may, the tone of this manual, as also of Ailred's, is that of an authoritative instructor, not of a brother or an equal.

Not every nun was fired by devotion. Some resorted to the cloister for lack of an earthly bridegroom, some because widowed, some (especially in the aftermath of the Conquest) to seek refuge from a war-torn countryside. The lax tone of some twelfth-century houses, women's and men's alike, can be inferred from repeated conciliar fulminations against rich attire and forbidden furs and, for women, against jewellery and elaborate coiffures. Some were as children placed in nunneries by their families. For, despite the new canonical prohibitions of committing to religion any child, boy or girl, too young to give an informed consent, during the twelfth century the old practice of oblation partly continued – as well it might in an age countenancing child-marriage. A signal instance of the problems that could arise occurred during the later twelfth century in the Gilbertine double house at Watton in Yorkshire. A girl's 'impudent' eye caught that of a brother. When their clandestine affair and her consequent pregnancy could no longer be concealed, the other nuns thrashed the girl and cast her, fettered, into a cell. The young man fled, but was decoyed and captured by his former brethren, then delivered to the nuns, who forced the girl to mutilate him with her own hands (in itself castration was then a conventional enough punishment for many offences). The guilty nun, now fully contrite, was reconciled with her sisters through a miracle by which angel-midwives spirited away her newborn child, struck off her fetters and restored her to virginity. Such a story, related with great rhetorical display by Ailred of Rievaulx, helps to explain the dread so many monks felt of any association with nuns.

In everyday social life women freely shared. The *Life of St Christina*, for instance, shows the future saint as often (albeit unwillingly) participating, together with her mother, in public as well as private feasts and drinking-parties; one episode depicts the maiden as ceremonially serving drink in the style of fictional heroines in Old English literature. Court records, as has been noted, reveal much freedom of morals as well as of manners, and a limited concern with premarital chastity.

In official life, by contrast, women figured little. Those in control of property had the same powers as men of making grants by charter, and had their personal seals. But, because a wife's property passed wholly into her husband's care, virtually the only women land-holders or taxpayers were widows, and records dealing with such matters usually show them as amounting to under 10 per cent of the total. A married woman could not act independently to sell, give away or bequeath her 'own' property. Although women could, and did, witness charters, their surviving attestations are rare, except for those of male grantors' wives and, less often, those of the attendants of female grantors. Even women of independent standing played little overt part in public affairs: female tenants-in-chief did not figure at royal councils, nor abbesses at ecclesiastical ones (by this time all nuns were subject to rules of enclosure far stricter than were ever imposed upon monks); 'sisters' of merchant- or craft-gilds did not become officials, still less have any voice in local government. It went without saying that no woman was eligible to serve as knight of the shire, or on a criminal or civil jury. In the twelfth century no woman could appear in a criminal court as plaintiff, let alone witness, except concerning her husband's murder or her own rape. In order to bring a charge of rape the victim had to raise an immediate hue and cry, exhibiting at once to a law-officer torn garments and bodily injuries; even so, such charges were commonly dismissed. Confraternity-lists – in theory admitting all on equal terms – named women more seldom than men, often specifying them simply in relation to male heads of family-groups. On the other hand, an English ecclesiastical court could and sometimes did, somewhat uncanonically, convoke a jury of seven 'honest matrons' to examine a man accused of impotence.

Women's marginal position in society was reflected and reinforced by limited access to schooling. Medieval education ranged among men from total illiteracy to subtle multilingual and philosophical accomplishment. Among women too accomplishment varied but normally, it seems, remained lower than that of corresponding men: thus, a canonisation-process of about 1300, in which witnesses used the most 'learned' language they knew, shows some male clerics testifying in Latin but not one woman and, among laypeople of each social rank, more men than women competent in French.

Debarred as they were from the developing universities, which catered mainly for aspiring clergy, medieval women can have had small chance of reaching the highest levels of literacy. For nuns, the strict enclosure now imposed upon them must have hindered access to learning; so too would the reluctance of the male religious, the chief scholars of the age, to meddle further than the liturgy demanded with their sisters' affairs. Evidence as to nuns' attainments is hard to come by, and harder to assess. A 'mortuary-roll' of 1122–3 circulated among Norman and English religious houses contains several sections representing English nunneries, with Wilton offering verses and Shaftesbury some fairly ornate lettering but other houses making only plain and conventional Latin entries. What this means is uncertain: by no means all men's houses displayed resplendent literacy or calligraphy and, besides, nunneries might sometimes have entrusted such duties to their chaplains (of whom the Wilton entry names

62 Part of a monastic commemorative roll compiled in the early 1120s. This entry, representing the great nunnery at Wilton, includes the names of several chaplains.

several). As for books, nunneries, because in general poorer than the men's houses, might *a priori* be assumed to have had less lavish libraries. To attach great weight to comparison between the books surviving from their libraries and those from the men's might be unwise, in so far as conditions of survival might have differed. For what it is worth, such comparison strengthens impressions of women's lesser learning, for the nuns' books are not only fewer but consist mainly of psalters, together with a little hagiography in one or other vernacular. A few Latin texts survive, mainly of the twelfth century; and one Barking liturgical manual of about 1400 is almost wholly in Latin, with French translations given of one or two sections only. Often, however, and increasingly in the later Middle Ages, documents of whatever kind addressed to nuns were couched in one or other vernacular. The author of *Ancrene Wisse* assumed the anchoresses for whom he was writing, and whom he evidently knew well, to read regularly in French as well as in English, but when quoting in Latin he always offered an immediate translation. These women could write, but had to get their confessor's permission before doing so. Ailred of Rievaulx did use Latin – admittedly simpler in style than that of his other works – for the manual he wrote for his anchoress sister, but then she, like he, was a child of a clerical family. As to any literary activity of nuns themselves, little evidence survives (attempts have been made, unconvincingly some may think, to identify Marie de France with an abbess of Shaftesbury). One at least had enough confidence to embark on verse-hagiography in French, together with enough Latin to use works in that language as her sources: the late twelfth-century Clemence of Barking, author of a *Life of St Catherine* and probably also of an anonymous *Life of the Confessor*. Perhaps Barking, with its ancient tradition of learning, may have been better able than some houses to maintain literacy and intellectual activity.

As to laywomen's accomplishments, evidence is even less clear. Some cynics of the time asserted that teaching a girl to write merely enabled her to carry on clandestine correspondence. Against that view would have militated the convenience for merchants and others of having wives who could keep records and accounts. More women, it may be surmised, would have been able to read than could write: for one thing, reading was an aid to religious practice and, for another, until paper became a common commodity, writing-materials cannot have been ever-present. Queens and noblewomen often figure as patrons of literature but, given the custom of oral performance, this need not imply that they themselves could read fluently (at this date, after all, literacy was far from universal among men of such ranks). On the other hand, girls of good birth sent to be educated in nunneries, as many were, would presumably have had the chance to learn reading and perhaps writing as well as morals (then esteemed the most essential element in feminine education), deportment and fine needle-work. The warnings given in *Ancrene Wisse* as well as in Ailred's handbook against an anchoress turning schoolmistress imply that some did take pupils; the leave nevertheless given in the former for one of the handmaids to teach any girl 'who ought not to have to study among boys or men' further implies that some parish schools were, as St Gilbert's had been, open to both sexes. The late thirteenth-century manual compiled by Walter of Bibbesworth to help Lady Dionyse de Munchensy to teach her children French (rather broad 'Anglo-Norman', in fact) implies not only that she could read in two languages, but also that she would do the teaching herself. In the wider sense of education – moral, cultural and social – even illiterate women, nurses and maids as well as mothers, would have been responsible for training young children of both sexes. The expression 'mother-tongue' is no empty one, because mothers and their women helpers have always been instrumental in transmitting language from one generation to the next; the encyclopaedist Bartholomew explicitly includes among the nurse's duties that of teaching her charge to speak. The maintenance of the English language in the face of post-Conquest fashions for French

63 A miscericord showing a dog raiding the cooking-pot, while a woman sits spinning.

probably depended on such women's unrecorded chatter to the children, including those of Anglo-Norman nobles, in their care.

Despite frequent pregnancies, few women can have had large families of children at home: infant mortality was high, in towns especially, and the survivors were early dispersed by marriage or else, according to rank, by apprenticeship or by enlistment as a handmaid or a squire. How large an ordinary medieval household might be is a vexed question. All but the humblest employed servants of both sexes; merchants and craftsmen had living-in apprentices. Most dwellings must have teemed with life; but, for the better-off, congestion would in summer have been eased by the omnipresence, even in towns, of gardens. Among humble folk, the chaotic interpenetration of farm and family is pictured in *Holy Maidenhood* (in one of its few passages so far untraced to any source): returning home, the woman finds her baby screaming, the cat gnawing the bacon and the dog worrying a hide, her loaf scorched, the calf suckling its mother, the cooking-pot boiling over – and her husband in a fury.

For everyone, of whatever rank or sex, who lived before the rise of modern

64 Midwife and patient: a
depiction of the Nativity of
the Virgin, from a
picture-book of New
Testament scenes.

medicine, illness and early death were ever-present spectres. Study of medieval
cemeteries has shown women as having had markedly shorter life-expectancies
than men. This is, of course, an average, based on burials of humble folk, because
the better-off sometimes, as the *Register of Widows* shows, attained ages of
'seventy and upwards'; but it implies widespread poor health. Medieval women's
experience of medical care probably differed from men's. At first sight they might
be thought lucky in being assured, for childbirth and related matters, of help
from their own sex. About the ubiquitous midwives too little is now known. We
may suspect a female freemasonry with private, unwritten traditions (the line
between midwife and white witch seems uncertain), but suspecting is not enough.
At all events, modern scholars who trace the history of contraception in Western
Europe through twelfth-century Latin translations from the Arabic may be losing
sight of some realities of village life (incidentally, surviving treatises, such as they
are, often include recipes for male anaphrodisiacs). Whatever cosy complicities
the midwife system may have allowed between practitioner and client, it had
shortcomings. One late medieval author of a general medical treatise remarked
that, because childbirth was exclusively women's province, he need not dwell
upon its management; the brief advice he then gave to midwives contrasted with

his lengthy disquisitions upon specifically male afflictions. Other treatises ignored obstetrics and gynaecology altogether. The flaw was that such medical training as then existed was, like all higher education, virtually barred to women, who were thus thrown back upon whatever private traditions they may have had. For other reasons, too, medical advances might have benefited female sufferers less than male ones: for, gynaecological problems apart, some women might have been shy of exhibiting their sick bodies to male practitioners. In the early period especially, when a good few physicians were clerks or monks, the reluctance might have been mutual. Public attitudes may be guessed from the coarse crack made in 1114 by Bishops Roger of Salisbury and Robert Bloet (worldly family-men both, not neurotic celibates), when the king proposed for the See of Canterbury Abbot Faritius of Abingdon, a noted physician who had attended the queen, Edith-Matilda of Scotland, in her first confinement: such preferment, they said, would be unseemly for a man who had examined a woman's urine.

A sidelight on female health comes from the records kept at supposedly curative shrines. When listing schools of therapeutic thought, the late medieval author just quoted referred to 'women and fools, who entrust merely to the saints sufferers from ailments of all kinds'. Whether or not women sought professional advice as often as they should have done, they did not, it seems, predominate among the clientele of shrines. Indeed, some shrines, notably St Cuthbert's, excluded female pilgrims. Even where all were admitted on equal terms, analysis of miracles officially recorded shows men as benefiting oftener than women. Discrepancies go further: the women reported as miraculously cured seem to have been, on average, of lower rank than the men and to have come from less far afield (a difference that can hardly, as has been suggested, simply reflect men's greater mobility, which illness would have cancelled out). Social attitudes and usages must have varied between the sexes in ways as yet not understood.

Neither the near invisibility of women in the surviving records nor their various socio-legal handicaps must mislead us into picturing them as personally meek and helpless. Perhaps we should discount the literary and iconographic stereotype of the shrewish wife belabouring her husband, sometimes with a distaff; but purportedly factual sources furnish ample instances of self-assertiveness, even of violence. Women and men shared the same world. We have noted the Watton nuns' ferocity towards their frail sister and how Christina of Markyate's mother thrashed the girl in hopes of extorting a consent to the projected marriage. Thirteenth-and fourteenth-century court records show peasant women as often dishonest, and sometimes bold and violent, with the ratio of female criminality to male supposedly similar to that nowadays taken as 'normal'. As well as women aiding and abetting the crimes of husbands or lovers (receiving stolen goods from relatives was the typical female offence), there were others who with their own hands wielded to effect whatever weapons they found. One Bedfordshire woman slit her sleeping husband's throat with a sickle and then stove his skull in with a billhook 'so that his brains flowed forth'; he had, she said, been seized with a fit of dangerous madness.

Great ladies played their parts in war. One Norman matron, from the Montfort family, was famed for riding armed – for all the world like a Viking 'warrior-maiden' reincarnated – among the knights. At need women commanded castles. In 1075, during the rebellion against the Conqueror led by the Norman earls of Hereford and of Norfolk, the latter's wife (also the former's sister, her marriage having sealed the alliance) captained Norwich castle and held out until granted safe-conduct to Normandy. When Stephen imprisoned Bishop Roger of Salisbury, Roger's mistress, Matilda of Ramsbury, held his castle at Devizes, surrendering it only to save their son Roger, the king's chancellor, from being hanged before its gates. During a rebellion against King John, the elderly Nicola de la Haye, by her own hereditary right castellan of Lincoln, was effective commander there.

Royal women often displayed generalship, among them the two Mauds, granddaughters of St Margaret of Scotland and King Malcolm, whom the Anarchy found on opposite sides. One, Stephen's queen, exhibited when her husband was made prisoner 'a manly steadfastness', sending her forces first to ravage London and then successfully to besiege Winchester. Meanwhile, her cousin and namesake, 'the Empress', daughter of Henry I and of his queen Edith-Matilda, was campaigning against her vigorously. The Empress, despite (perhaps because of) two marriages arranged to further her father's politics – the first, before she was nine, to the German Emperor Henry V; the second, as a widow in her mid-twenties, to Geoffrey of Anjou, some ten years her junior – was wax in no-one's hands. After her father's death her cousin Stephen stole a march and secured for himself the crown which Henry I had intended for her, his only surviving legitimate child. Maud, loyally seconded by her elder (but illegitimate) brother, came to England to claim her rights, and for several years waged war against the usurper; although never herself accepted as queen, she secured the succession for her son, later Henry II. Never is there a hint of her having been self-effacing; rather was it the chroniclers' constant complaint that she was, in contrast with her easy-going cousin Stephen, too high-handed. Perhaps the commentators were measuring her against some stereotype of the 'ideal lady', not against that of the rightful sovereign she was. In Empress Maud the warrior blood of Norman dukes and Scottish kings pulsed no less strongly than in the males of her race.

FURTHER READING

This chapter has been based on central and local administrative records, together with chronicles and biographies. The principal sources are: *Rotuli de Dominabus et Pueris et Puellis*, ed. ROUND; *Councils and Synods*, ed. WHITELOCK ET ALII; *The Laws and Customs of England*, ed. and tr. HALL; *Select Cases from the Ecclesiastical Courts*, ed. ADAMS AND DONAHUE; *Borough Customs*, ed. BATESON; *The Peterborough Chronicle*, ed. CLARK; *The Ecclesiastical History of Orderic Vitalis*, ed. and tr. CHIBNALL; *Henrici Huntendunensis Historia Anglorum*, ed. ARNOLD; *Eadmeri Historia Novorum in Anglia*, ed. RULE (also tr. BOSANQUET); *Willelmi Malmesbiriensis Monachi de Gestis Pontificum Anglorum Libri Quinque*, ed. HAMILTON; *The Historia Novella of William of Malmesbury*, ed. and tr. POTTER; *Gesta Stephani*, ed. and tr. POTTER AND DAVIS; *The Life of St Margaret of Scotland*, in *Pinkerton's Lives of the Scottish Saints*, ed. METCALFE (also tr. METCALFE); *The Life of Christina of Markyate*, ed. and tr. TALBOT; *Aelred de Rievaulx: la vie de recluse*, ed. and tr. DUMONT; *Ancrene Wisse*, ed. TOLKIEN (also tr. SALU); *Hali Meiðhad*, ed. MILLETT.

Secondary sources extensively used include: *Complete Peerage*, ed. C[OKAYNE] ET ALII; *LA FEMME dans les civilisations des x^e–xiii^e siècles*; *LA FEMME* (Recueils Jean Bodin 12); *IL MATRIMONIO nella società altomedievale*; *Medieval Women*, ed. BAKER; *Women in Medieval Society*, ed. STUARD; HOLT, *Magna Carta*; HELMHOLZ, *Marriage Litigation*; SHEEHAN, *The Will in Medieval England*; WILLIAMS, *Medieval London*; THRUPP, *The Merchant Class of Medieval London*; GROSS, *The Gild Merchant*; HALLAM, *Rural England 1066–1348*; HOMANS, *English Villagers of the Thirteenth Century*; RAFTIS, *Warboys* and *Tenure and Mobility*; GRAHAM, *St Gilbert of Sempringham*; LEGGE, *Anglo-Norman in the Cloisters*; LABARGE, *A Baronial Household of the Thirteenth Century*; ROWLAND, *Medieval Woman's Guide to Health*.

# 9. After 1066
# The Literary Image

In the Middle English romance of *King Horn* there is a scene in which the hero arrives in disguise at the court of a king whose daughter, Rymenhild, is secretly betrothed to him. She is about to be married against her will to somebody else and at the bridal feast, following what the poet calls the law of the land, she carries a ceremonial drinking-horn around to the guests. She does not recognise Horn in his grimy garments among the beggars at the end of the hall, and when he rudely accosts her she reproves his base manners, laying aside the horn and offering him instead a large bowl, more suited to his grossness. He refuses it, telling her rather to 'drink to Horn from horn', and with this riddling allusion to his own name the time-honoured ceremony is converted into an intimate exchange as he conveys to her the dangerous knowledge that her lover may not be as far away as she thinks.

The scene provides a useful starting-point for discussing some of the changes that overtake the portrayal of the literary heroine after the Norman Conquest. At first sight Rymenhild's place in the life of the court still seems to be that of the highborn lady of whom we get rare glimpses in Old English epic poetry, where she must be prepared to accept a dynastic marriage and is characteristically seen as a focus of hospitality in a ceremonial, male-centred society. In much the same way Queen Wealhðeow welcomes Beowulf to the hall of Hroðgar, offering the horn and speaking formal words of greeting. To be 'wise in words' is a proper queenly attribute, and later she bestows gifts on him with a speech that touches on the mutual obligations of the heroic way of life, the interdependent duties of high and low. So Rymenhild, while speaking far more sharply in a far less formal poem, reminds the presumptuous beggar of his place, though she does not refuse the guest his due.

Important differences, however, are also suggested. Wealhðeow's words may take us beyond the immediate context of gift-giving but they still deal with matters of general concern and there is nothing confidential or deceptive about them. In *King Horn*, on the other hand, open words and actions also act as a cover for something else, making us aware of a private scene going on inside the public one. They remind us that Rymenhild is troth-plighted to Horn without her father's consent. Moreover, though he is really a king's son Horn's beggarly disguise reflects the apparent social gap that exists between them. When he first arrived at her father's court as an outcast many years before it was Rymenhild who took the initiative in the affair, wooing him with determination in the way that her overwhelming passion as well as her rank demanded. Rymenhild, in other words, has an inner emotional life as well as a public role, and enough freedom of action to make her own choice of a husband, though not enough to escape the match forced on her by her family. The double-edged references to horns emphasise this duality of the woman as both a private person and a public figure, and the public ceremonial encapsulates the private concerns of the two lovers.

Marriage is of central importance for the medieval woman in literature, as well as in life. Post-Conquest literature, however, shows a far greater interest in the emotional aspects, taking the socio-economic ones more for granted. The Old English *Husband's Message* offered a rare glimpse of this more personal approach, and at first sight the situation between Horn and Rymenhild might seem to be a particularised version of what is there expressed more allusively: unlike the speaker in the earlier poem Horn does not yet have the treasures or the mead-joys to support the king's daughter in the manner to which she is entitled, but he can still remind her of the vows she made voluntarily and without regard to her kindred. He will eventually be able to offer her both riches and dignity, for it is worth emphasising that Horn really is her social equal, despite appearances, and is finally restored to his rightful kingdom. Barriers of rank are seldom actually crossed in medieval literary love-affairs, and heroines who seem to love beneath themselves generally end up justified.

It would, however, be wrong to imply that a direct line of continuity links Rymenhild with her queenly forebears in Old English poetry – or indeed with the women of the pre-Conquest historic records, who clearly had a powerful say in the direction of their own lives. Too much time and history lie between. The text of *King Horn* as we have it belongs to the thirteenth century, and although we do not know its ultimate origins there is no doubt that its immediate source was not English at all but a poem written perhaps as much as a century before in Anglo-French. This is characteristic of the post-Conquest literary scene, for with the imposition of a French-speaking ruling class English almost disappears as the written language of a courtly culture, and when it re-emerges, as it is beginning to do by the time of *King Horn*, the literary traditions of the Anglo-Saxons have been largely transmuted and even replaced by those of France. Any traces which *King Horn* seems to preserve of an older, heroic life-style cannot therefore be seen as more than indications that the roots of the story lie somewhere in the general Germanic area, and they must, by 1300, have seemed distinctly archaic. As such they suggest the extent to which English literary fashion was lagging behind French, as well as reminding us of the gaps that can open up between real social customs and poetic fiction, which may preserve details from sources far removed in both time and place.

As the post-Conquest English language gathers strength as a literary medium

French sources become almost the inevitable rule for English poems, and with French material comes also an interest in French manners and literary fashions which have by now taken new directions. Of prime importance here is the development in twelfth-century France of the chivalric romance, replacing the old heroic epic, and it is to this, rather than to no-nonsense Germanic forebears, that Rymenhild's independent spirit should probably be ascribed; for the highborn lady who chooses to take the initiative with a lover who is (apparently) her inferior is a characteristic figure of this new French genre. *King Horn* is one of the earliest examples we have of an attempt to write a romance in English. It therefore demonstrates not merely the vigorous resurgence of English as a literary language, but also the transformation of the old world of epic values into something more socially complex. In particular the role of women changes and a deep and serious interest in the man-to-woman relationship displaces, complements and sometimes conflicts with the more exclusively man-to-man loyalties of the heroic world. In due course a whole new psychological language develops to express a wider and more subtle range of emotions, as love and womanly tenderness emerge as proper subjects for full-scale literary treatment.

There is little trace of this subtlety in *King Horn*, whose language is blunt in the extreme, but the important thing is that Rymenhild acts out of motives of passion – an overwhelming passion which manifests itself in weeping, swooning and the emotional torments which, in more sophisticated literature, are identified as 'love's sickness' (and are, incidentally, indulged in equally by both sexes). This represents an attitude to love quite different from what we see in the Old English elegies. It comes into English through French and is part of the complex phenomenon to which modern critics have given the name 'Courtly Love', though few now would accept this as much more than a blanket term for a great variety of medieval attitudes, concepts and literary fashions. For our purposes it is probably enough to see it as a way of recognising that love is to be taken seriously, that lovers should commit themselves fully to each other and to the experience of love itself, and above all that they should be faithful. It is also very aristocratic: the lower orders could not be regarded as having the sensitivity, or indeed the leisure, for it. The relationship of man and woman was moreover generally presented in matters of love as the opposite of the day-to-day norm, with the role of the woman elevated to a position of total dominion over the man, who is seen as wholly dependent on her 'mercy' for his emotional well-being. Inferiority thus becomes standard for the male lover, whatever his social rank, while the woman becomes a remote, unattainable ideal of beauty and virtue. Lyric poetry in particular presents the adored mistress as a radiant young virgin, typically seen in a fresh spring setting. Emily, heroine of Chaucer's *Knight's Tale*, also presents an icon of this sort, walking alone and untouchable in a May garden, crowned with flowers and singing like an angel for her imprisoned adorers to gaze on from afar.

65 Medieval Calendars like to show a characteristic activity for each month. In this example from the fourteenth-century Queen Mary's Psalter ladies, April and flowers create a single image of spring.

This romantic inversion has sometimes led to the view that love, of this intensely experienced kind, was impossible within marriage where, according to the accepted Pauline pattern, the husband is the head of the wife. Many romances, however, clearly regard marriage as the proper end for a love affair (as it is in *The Knight's Tale*) and are certainly more interested in its emotional than its economic aspects. Extra-marital, if not adulterous, liaisons of course also feature in stories, though it is worth recalling that the real-life dividing-line between the marital and the non-marital union was not always easy to draw in medieval England where a private troth-plight, even one conducted without witnesses, could be accepted as constituting a valid (though possibly illegal) marriage. The vows of Horn and Rymenhild, for instance, could well have been regarded as a valid and unbreakable bond, despite their secrecy.

The vital period when these changes are transforming the literary scene is precisely the one for which we have the fewest texts surviving in English. For a closer look at Rymenhild's real literary forebears we must therefore turn to French – which, in all likelihood, is also what the readers of the time had to do. As it happens, one of the earliest and most accomplished writers of French romance, Marie de France, almost certainly wrote in England in the latter part of the twelfth century. That she was a woman makes her doubly of interest to us, but so much medieval literature is anonymous that we cannot be sure how rare this was. We know almost nothing about her beyond her name and the approximate date of her twelve *Lays* (or short romances) but that too is not unusual.

175

66 At least some ladies learned to write edifying matter. This formalised portrait of Marie de France heads a thirteenth-century text of her translation of Aesop's *Fables*.

Although she writes in French Marie claims to derive her stories from Breton sources, a claim which is often reflected in British names and settings. Thus one of her most sympathetic heroes, Eliduc, falling out of favour with the King of Brittany, crosses the sea and finds a refuge with a local ruler near Exeter, leaving his wife, Guildeluec, to run his Breton estates. This kind of situation can be paralleled in real life, where women often figure as competent administrators in the absence of their husbands, but the last thing we read Marie for is factual information on twelfth-century life: hers is a world deliberately removed from the commonplace, but her refined, magical settings provide a perfect frame for the sensitive portrayal of characters caught up in trying emotional situations.

Our primary interest is in women but Marie is in fact notably fair to both sexes. Eliduc's problems come to a head when his new lord's young daughter, Guilliadun, falls deeply in love with him. Reluctantly he is forced to admit an equal attraction and so finds himself in a quandary of loyalties between wife and beloved. Guilliadun eventually flees with him to Brittany, innocently trusting his integrity, only to discover for the first time that he already has a wife. He leaves her in a secret sanctuary, apparently dead from the hardships of the sea-voyage and her own anguish. Grief-stricken he goes home to Guildeluec but returns to the chapel each day to mourn his love. In due course she is found by Guildeluec, who revives her and at last understands the cause of her husband's agony of mind. Without a second thought she knows at once what she must do and explains to Guilliadun who she is:

I am Eliduc's wife and my heart has been grieving for him. Seeing his grief I had to find out where he went. I followed him, and so I have found you. It is a great joy to me that you are alive, for now I can take you home and restore you to your lover. Then I will give him his freedom and take the veil.

176

This generosity on the part of the wife is as sensitively sketched as the suffering of the husband and the innocent love of the young girl, taken unawares by the strength of her own feelings and torn between the need to reveal them to Eliduc and shame lest he should think her immodest. The initiative has to lie with Guilliadun, just as it does with Rymenhild, socially superior to the distinguished stranger at her father's court, but Guilliadun's reaction is far less blunt. There is a touching hint of worldly wisdom in her awareness that it would be very much to his advantage to marry the heir to her father's kingdom, but she does not put it like that: she simply wants to be his wife, and for Guilliadun no other relationship seems even to be considered.

Guildeluec is not the only woman in Marie's *Lays* who is generous enough actually to give up her man for his own good; nor is Guilliadun the only one who takes the step of running away with her lover. Love, for Marie, means a total commitment to the beloved, overriding all other claims, and her characters are judged according to whether or not they live up to its demands, even to the point of sacrifice. Marriage is not possible for all her lovers though it is often their aim. A frequent impediment is an already existing spouse – more often a husband than a wife, for the situation of the woman entrapped by marriage seems to have a special poignancy for Marie and no husband in her stories shows the generosity of Eliduc's wife. In just one lay (*Le Fresne*) social inequality appears at first to constitute a barrier to marriage, though not to love, but Marie's characters are never sufficiently far apart in upbringing for this to be a common problem: refined loving is only possible between people of equally refined birth. Within this narrow social band, Marie's women are usually equal to their lovers in rank or else above them, echoing their 'courtly' role of wielding emotional dominion over men. On one of the rare occasions when the man outranks the woman, in the lay of *Equitan*, this seems to cause a dilemma acute enough for the heroine to try to put it into words:

Love is of no worth if it is not equal. The love of a poor man who is true and has wit and valour is of greater value and gives greater joy than a prince or king who has no truth in him.

To set character above birth is an excellent ideal, but it is clear that what is really being advocated here is not equality but female superiority: the courtly mistress typically has to condescend to her lover and this heroine at least is not prepared to be condescended to. She goes on to indicate that a woman who loves above her station can never be sure whether she is held by bonds of love or of feudal sovereignty – a tacit acknowledgement perhaps that the worldly power to have and to hold really lies with the man – but her determination to assert her own position marks her out as incapable of the kind of sacrifice for love that is exemplified in *Eliduc*. When she later proves treacherous Marie clearly regards her punishment as fully deserved. The woman is by no means always right.

Within the confines of this aristocratic milieu love should override all barriers, but one inequality which there is no getting over is the age-gap. The lays of *Yonec* and *Guigemar* both tell of young wives married to old husbands. Old age means incapacity and jealousy and both ladies endure a lonely incarceration locked up in towers. The only possible relief is a true lover, who in *Guigemar* simply happens, but in *Yonec* the sad heroine actually indulges in a little romantic speculation:

I have often heard tell that in days gone by things used to come to pass in this land that cheered the melancholy. Knights would find damsels, fair and gentle to their desire, and ladies found lovers, handsome and courteous, worthy and brave, and were blamed for it by none...

Musing thus the heroine conjures up a lover as surely as if she had uttered a charm, but the wishful tone reminds us that Marie's world, for all its human sympathy, is a magical one – a world that even in 1170 belonged to long ago and far away. We may be tempted here to think of young Agnes de Vere, imprisoned in real life by her elderly husband (if for rather different reasons) but the comparison is probably inapt: the 'reality' of these stories lies not in their events but in Marie's attempt to depict the experience of love in its fullness, especially its fullness of suffering and the need for sacrifice it imposes on men and women alike. She may seem to have more to say about the sufferings of women, but she does not claim that they are the only victims.

67 An ivory mirror-case creates a chivalric image of 'Courtly Love': knights besiege a castle of ladies who pelt them with flowers; from the topmost turret Cupid aims his bow.

68 A handmaiden at work with comb and mirror in the margin of the fourteenth-century Luttrell Psalter.

The compass of Marie's romance world is well defined. The capacity for gentle feeling lies with the young and gently born, and it is not easy to find women of a humbler class treated in equal depth. Apart from their heroines Marie's *Lays* supply only the occasional handmaiden or confidante. The latter have an increasingly important role in later romances, especially when it comes to teaching their ladies a little worldly wisdom in the treatment of lovers. Even this, however, is just another way of saying that gentle birth goes with gentle character, and nobility of feeling in the really humbly born is not found within the normal conventions of romance. It is left to the old hag in Chaucer's *Wife of Bath's Tale* to argue powerfully (and some would say incongruously) that 'Christ will we clayme of hym oure gentillesse', which is of course an impeccably Christian position but one which casts the shadow of absolute values over the delicate, self-contained world of romance.

By a happy chance one of the very few important English poems that can plausibly be dated to the twelfth century was written by someone who had read Marie de France, was interested in women and allows us to look a little further down the social scale in his comments on them. *The Owl and the Nightingale* is not a romance but a debate, a genre that was very much commoner in French and Latin than in English. Surviving examples in the former languages cover a wide variety of topics, solemn and less solemn, and one whole group has for its subject the knotty problem of whether a knight or a cleric makes the better lover. With these we shift into the realm of satire spiced with just a touch of the bookish anti-feminism that now grows increasingly common, for from the thirteenth century onwards the susceptible wife who succumbs to the studied charm of a discreet and eloquent cleric becomes something of a cliché. This is a long way from the serious one-to-one fidelity of Marie's knights and ladies, and although the anonymous and witty author of *The Owl and the Nightingale* does not set out to satirise women, he does bring the uncompromising light of Christian morality to bear on certain aspects of sex. Of his two disputants the Nightingale cannot help but be on the side of romantic love but the Owl, whose moral stance is closer to that of the Church, refuses to be blinded by sentimental nonsense. Sex is sex and is neither pretty nor elegant, a fact she demonstrates by means of some pithy descriptions of peasants tumbling each other in the spring (a season she identifies as the time of 'the churls' mad rush', in defiance of a hundred dainty lyrics about love in April). She then goes on to quote one of Marie's *Lays*, which features a nightingale whose sensuous song encourages a married heroine to think about her handsome neighbour, but the Nightingale is quick to deny that she has ever encouraged anyone to lust: she merely sings in the pure cause of love, and if some of her hearers are led by it into illicit unions rather than into holy matrimony that is hardly her fault. Women's flesh is notoriously weak: they simply are not built to resist temptation.

This acceptance of the essentially frail nature of women is a bit of standard dogma which is later turned into a triumphant assertion by the Wife of Bath, but the debate of the Owl and the Nightingale does not end here. The Owl's references to 'churls' have forced the argument out from the romantic shelter of the courtly setting where fornication and adultery can masquerade under the guise of transcendent passion, but even in the cottage, where a spade has to be called a spade, frail woman is still deserving of sympathy. The Nightingale now pleads powerfully on behalf of the 'youngling' who may be swept into sin by the heady strength of first love, but that is just the natural weakness of her age and sex: she can still end up a virtuous and contented wife. A less romantic cause, but one no less just, is that of the abused wife, driven into adultery by a faithless and brutal husband. In a spirit of sheer Christian charity the Owl emerges as her champion, in a passage which echoes the situation of Marie's lonely victims of jealousy, but drops it down the social scale to give us a rare and sympathetic glimpse of the neglected housewife, ill clad and ill fed in a cheerless, tumbledown house:

When her husband comes home she dares not utter a word. He rants and rages like a madman, and that is all he brings home. She can do nothing, say nothing that pleases him and often, when she has done nothing wrong, she gets his fist in her teeth.

If such a wife, uncared for, confined under lock and key, turns elsewhere for comfort, who shall blame her? It is a vivid and moving variant on Marie's romanticised lady in the tower.

This glimpse of the mundane discomforts of marriage brings us to a level of society where, whatever the Nightingale may say, practical considerations simply had to be a part of the bargain. The working man needed a reliable pair of hands to share the load. English romances, often written for a humbler audience than Marie's, sometimes reflect this distinctly uncourtly view. Thus Havelok the

Dane, another dispossessed prince living, like Horn, in reduced circumstances, is appalled when the regent of England, Earl Godrich, forces him to marry the Princess Goldboru whom Havelok knows he cannot possibly support:

> What should I with wif do?
> I ne may her fede ne clothe ne sho...

Havelok has been working as a scullion (for, incidentally, a male cook) and Godrich reckons that marriage to someone as base as this will safely dispose of Goldboru, who stands between him and the throne. This is rough power-politics, with the maiden anything but a prize for the humble lover. Sentiment in fact has almost no place in the story, and Havelok's reaction is simply that of an out-of-work fisherman who can see no earthly use for a princess back home in his Grimsby hovel. But neither he nor Goldboru has the means to resist, and the marriage ceremony is a tightly legal business with the exchange of money counting for more than any exchange of rings:

> Ther weren pennies thicke tolde [counted],
> Mikel plenté, upon the book:
> He his her gave, and she his took.

Outside the genre of romance, satirical literature also shows the practical marriage-bargain at work, with the couple portrayed as partners in crime. Langland's Avarice, in a passage on the Seven Deadly Sins in *Piers Plowman*, far from being a mere intellectual personification is a canny businessman with a finger in several lucrative pies, including drapery. Women are often found in the cloth business and Avarice is ably assisted by his wife though her name, Rose the Retailer, shows her to be, like her husband, a Jill-of-all-trades. Between them they stretch and press and splice the cloth they sell 'till ten yards or twelve tolled out thirteen'. She also waters the ale she deals in – an archetypal dishonest ale-wife. Similar energetic connivance at her husband's guilt is shown by the miller's wife in Chaucer's *Reeve's Tale*, though her daughter, a plain and all-too-susceptible 'youngling', is perfectly ready to give away their secrets, not to mention her maidenhood, to a sympathetic stranger. Mak and Gill in the Towneley *Second Shepherds' Pageant*, hiding a stolen sheep in the cradle, offer another example in a play which also provides a harsh insight into the squalor of domestic life at the level of real poverty, where the only things that come in abundance are babies.

Peasant households occur sometimes in Chaucer, usually in tales that have more in common with fable than with strict social realism, though his old peasant women are generally redoubtable characters who bear out the indications in the historical records that at this level at least a woman was well able to manage on her own. The one in *The Friar's Tale*, for whom a saucepan represents a major investment and twelve pence unthinkable wealth, has her wits very much about her, despite her aching bones. Confronted by a scoundrelly summoner who

69 'Malkyn with a dystaf in hir hand.' This version of the fable of the thieving fox, carved on a misericord at Beverley, Yorkshire, shows a goose rather than Chaucer's Chanticleer.

threatens to drag her off to the Archdeacon's court on a trumped-up charge, she displays a creditable knowledge of her legal rights and ends up with the victory – gained, significantly, by sharp and determined use of her tongue. Another peasant household working somewhat above the limit of absolute poverty is seen in *The Nun's Priest's Tale* where, within a single 'narwe cotage', lived a poor widow, her two daughters, three sows, three cows and a sheep called Molly, not to mention her famous cock, Chaunticleer, and his host of dutiful hens – a satirist's vignette of Man fatally susceptible to the misguided counsel of his womenfolk. At the climax of the story the pursuit of the marauding fox is joined by a whole crowd of dogs, hogs and assorted livestock as well as several men, so perhaps the modest establishment was more prosperous than is implied at the outset, but it is undoubtedly predominantly female. The running mob includes 'Malkyn, with a dystaf in hir hand', caught up in the chase before she had time to put down this indispensable item of female industry.

With Chaucer and Langland we reach the great flowering of medieval English literature which took place in the second half of the fourteenth century and which marks the triumphant coming-of-age of Middle English, the French cultural admixture now permanently absorbed. Chaucer made use of the traditions of both debate and romance but he also, almost alone among English writers, exploited that other once-popular French genre, the fabliau, a kind of story usually marked by a lower-class setting and a cast of standard characters as predictable as anything in romance. A typical set would include – once again – the jealous old husband and young wife, featured in this case strictly for laughs, for where, at the courtly level, the theme of the incarcerated wife is harrowing, at the bourgeois level the cuckolded husband is comic. The lover would almost certainly be a cleric, perhaps a monk or friar.

Most of Chaucer's fabliau women are frail but some play the role more

70 A situation suggestive of the fabliaux though it actually illustrates a Miracle of the Virgin: Mary's compassion for her devotees was boundless, even when they ended up like this.

tastefully than others. *The Shipman's Tale*, for instance, opens a window on a far more sophisticated world than that of the rural mill or cottage, providing a glimpse of the kind of domestic independence which could be achieved at the prosperous middle-class level by the competent and very discreet wife of a busy French merchant. We catch her sometimes about her household duties, with a proper eye to the priorities:

> And forth she gooth as jolif as a pye [magpie],
> And bad the cookes that they sholde hem hye [hurry],
> So that the men myghte dyne, and that anon.

Established domestic routine ensures a regular succession of events into which a well-organised woman can fit both public and private activities without fuss. At the appropriate moment she visits the counting-house to urge her husband, in just the right tone of wifely teasing, to leave 'youre sommes, and youre bookes, and youre thynges' and come to dinner. He is quite unaware that in the meantime the visiting monk, Sir John, has been taking a civilised saunter in the garden to say his office (he too has his 'thynges' to attend to: men always do, to the neglect of their womenfolk) and there he met his hostess – purely by chance of course. The layers of sophisticated game-playing here seem to belong to quite a different social and literary climate from any we have met so far. One is almost reminded of Miss Austen's Charlotte Lucas keeping a weather-eye open for the Reverend Mr Collins:

Miss Lucas perceived him from an upper window as he walked towards the house, and instantly set out to meet him accidentally in the lane. But little had she dared to hope that so much love and eloquence awaited her there.

The parallel may serve to remind us that the social advantages of marriage for a woman were much the same at the beginning of the nineteenth century as at the end of the fourteenth. If it could be based on love so much the better, but if not, the instant rise in status and independence which wifehood brought was clearly worth a little emotional sacrifice. The heroine of *The Shipman's Tale*, to be sure, is negotiating something less respectable and has no intention of endangering her very advantageous marital position, but the Wife of Bath's lengthy *Prologue* provides a detailed picture of marriage as a business deal which, far from ending with the telling of pennies at the church door, continues for the entire course of the partnership, with sexual favours used throughout as bargaining counters. For this highly experienced wife marriage has become a way of life, with the next incumbent carefully earmarked while the current one is still in occupation. This, she reckons, is no more than simple prudence:

> I spak to hym and seyde hym how that he
> If I were wydwe, sholde wedde me.
> For certeinly, I sey for no bobance [boast],
> Yet was I nevere withouten purveiance [provision]
> Of mariage, n'of othere thynges eek.
> I holde a mouses herte nat worth a leek
> That hath but oon hole for to sterte to,
> And if that faille, thanne is al ydo [finished].

As the widow of not one but three rich husbands, the Wife can have little purely economic reason for this well-organized remarriage system, nor is there any excuse for the shattering ruthlessness with which she puts it into effect, making quite sure that she, not he, holds the purse-strings throughout. What she wants is not equality but superiority over her mate – thus providing a satiric, bourgeois comment on the polite, courtly dominion of the lady over her lover which is found higher up the social scale. Even when she marries 'for love, and no richesse', as she claims to have done on the fifth occasion, this does not stop her employing her well-tried blackmail in order to assert her 'sovereignty' in this match as well as the others. Her desiderata are fairly stated at the end of her *Tale*:

> Jhesu Crist us sende
> Housbondes meeke, yonge, and fressh abedde,
> And grace t'overbyde hem that we wedde.

At forty-plus what counts with her now are not money or love but the pleasures of sex, with the advantages of widowhood also clearly understood. Chaucer's most important romantic heroine, Criseyde, was just as fully aware of these and outlined them with only a little less bluntness:

> I am myn owene womman, wel at ese,
> I thank it God, as after myn estat,
> Right yong, and stonde unteyd in lusty leese [pleasant pasture],
> Withouten jalousie or swich debat:
> Shal noon housbonde seyn to me 'chek mat!'

Such independence is not easily surrendered, for love, as we have seen, means total commitment to the needs of another. But already, even as she weighs the pros and cons, she has imprinted on her mind the charismatic image of a young knight on horseback riding past her window, fresh from his triumphs over the besieging Greeks. Even before she gives her heart to Troilus, Criseyde is shown as a woman who needs a man to lean on, turning to her uncle Pandarus for help in her business affairs. It is significant that she later finds Troilus a 'wall of steel' against the world. What the middle-class housewife or the peasant widow accepts as a worthy challenge to her wits, the courtly heroine cannot confront unsupported.

Frailty, in some form or other, might be said to be the name of most of Chaucer's women, whether they are sexually susceptible or just hopelessly at sea in a man's world. The word even fits the Wife of Bath who is, perhaps, the hardest to treat fairly, largely because her enormous gusto so easily seduces us into viewing her as a real person. In fact, as study of Chaucer's sources shows, she is an identikit portrait of the Tyrannical Wife, made up from a multiplicity of parts culled from the standard misogynist works of the time. Dramatically animated by a master's touch, she proves the anti-feminist case to the hilt. Far from denying the second-rate nature of women as compared with men, she rejoices in it and exploits it to the full. Women *are* the weaker sex: they cannot help the way they are, for God in his wisdom made them so. Men had, therefore, better make the best of it. Women certainly will:

> Deceite, wepyng, spynnyng God hath give
> To wommen kyndely [by nature], whil that they may lyve.

A revealing insight into the Wife's triumphant exploitation of woman's God-given frailty occurs when she admits how her beloved fifth husband, Jankyn, could outdo her at her own game of playing hard-to-get. Significantly he was a clerk, and so skilled in the art of persuasion that even though he had beaten her 'on every bone' he could still win her back into his bed. An even franker bit of psychological awareness follows:

> We wommen have, if that I shal not lye,
> In this matere a queynte fantasye;
> Wayte what [whatever] thyng we may nat lightly have,
> Therafter wol we crie al day and crave.
> Forbede us thyng, and that desiren we;
> Presse on us faste, and thanne wol we fle.
> With daunger [reluctance] oute we al oure chaffare [goods];
> Great press at market maketh deere ware.

Wanting the one thing that is out of reach hardly needs comment as a traditional cliché of female nature. Bluebeard's wife had the same problem. So, of course, did Eve.

It is a commonplace in discussion of the portrayal of women in medieval literature that they tend to conform to type. The same might be said of men,

71 Virgo and Virago: the Annunciation is formally portrayed at the foot of this page from the Luttrell Psalter, while a daughter of Eve lurks ominously in the margin.

for medieval writers are not generally interested in the delineation of character as such, but as far as women are concerned the spectrum is neatly defined by the opposing types at either end. At one limit is Eve: frail, seducible, the tempted as well as the temptress; at the other Mary: virginal, maternal, compassionate mediator between fallen man and her divine Son.

So far we have been looking at woman in terms of literary rather than theological types, with particular reference to wife and mistress, but we can now see how the two approaches interrelate. The courtly heroine clearly figures as a kind of secular Mary. In her most virginal aspects she forms the focus of a hundred love lyrics, surrounded by the flowers of spring. So Mary, in a famous

Annunciation lyric, is a 'maiden matchless' waiting in her bower for the arrival
of the 'king of all kings':

> He came all so stille
> To his mother's bower:
> As dew in Aprille
> That fallyth on the flower.

The same images of spring and fruitfulness are applied with equal decorum to
both the divine and the secular mistress, and in each case she is the object not
merely of the awed lover's adoration but also of his heart-felt petitions for the
alleviation of his misery. Here indeed is the lordly lady who truly does have
dominion, but one who manifests her power not in cruelty but in mercy.

Mary also provides her own unique answer to the paradox implicit in the spring
imagery of love-lyrics with their invariable association of purity and fruitfulness.
To her alone was granted the privilege of filling simultaneously two of woman's
most characteristic roles: virgin and mother. As Virgin she is the divine mistress;
as Mother she stands mourning her Son at the foot of the cross, or cradling Him
as an infant in her arms yet knowing already that one day a sword will pierce
her heart (Luke ii.35). For Mary partakes of woman's inevitable suffering even
though, through the miracle of the Virgin Birth, she was spared the childbirth
pains that were the inheritance of every other daughter of Eve since the original
sin in the Garden of Eden.

The image of Eve in literature is more subject to variation than that of Mary:
frailty, as we have seen, wears many faces. Characteristically, woman as Eve is
seducible, especially by persuasive talkers whether clerical or diabolical, and
whether she is ingenuous 'youngling' or susceptible wife or widow. Mostly also
she seems to be middle-class, but that may be because the sympathetic
conventions of romance do not encourage us to look in these moral terms at a
Rymenhild or a Guilliadun. Another aspect of Eve is the virago, a name which
Eve actually bears in the Latin bible of the Middle Ages and which was explained
as 'one who behaves like a man'. That of course is exactly what she is when
we meet her in the guise of the Wife of Bath, domineering, bullying, taking on
the ruling function which ought to belong to the man. Socially speaking, the Wife
of Bath's is also the typical setting in which to find her, making the most of the
independence that could be achieved in running a middle- or lower-class
household. A sad little comment on what it felt like to be on the receiving end
comes from a fifteenth-century lyric:

> If I aske our dame bred,
> She takyth a staf and brekith myn hed,
> And doth me rennen [makes me run] under the bed –
> I dare not seyn [speak] whan she seyth 'Peace!'

If wives and mistresses have tended to dominate the discussion so far it should

72 Woman with her weapon, in a margin of the Luttrell Psalter.

be remembered that this chapter is about literary images, and the interplay of the sexes is generally a favourite subject for literature. The virtuous life of nuns, for instance, does not make for exciting reading, though Langland's portrait of Wrath (another of his Seven Deadly Sins) gives us an acid glimpse of a squabbling convent. The thirteenth-century *Ancrene Wisse*, though not strictly a 'literary' work as such, is nonetheless highly literate and offers a powerful insight into the life of penitential self-discipline to which scores of women must have voluntarily committed themselves for the love of God. The anchoress lived in a kind of seclusion quite different from that of nuns, and the degree of spiritual maturity which could be achieved under these exacting conditions is amply demonstrated in the late fourteenth-century *Revelations* of Julian of Norwich (who, in spite of her name, was a woman). The sanity and scholarly grasp of this book reveal the quality of its writer's mind and stand as a permanent contrast to the standard anti-feminist view of female mentality. But Julian was telling a personal story for the good of her fellow-Christians, not setting out to produce a work of literature, and her book must therefore be taken on its own terms as a personal testament.

Julian, however, reminds us that nuns at least were expected to read and that some read in depth. Learned women are not often taken seriously in literary sources. They had, of course, been forbidden to preach by St Paul (I. Tim. ii. 12) and part of the ironic impact of the Wife of Bath lies in the fact that a sermon is precisely what she delivers, supported by learned authorities at every point – a typical virago, usurping the role of the man. Oddly enough the woman preacher becomes perfectly acceptable if she is a personification. Abstract instructresses often appear in vision literature, to impart wisdom that is clearly regarded as coming from some more-than-earthly region if not actually heaven itself. Lady Philosophy, who appears as the teacher of Boethius in the sixth-century *Consolation of Philosophy*, was an influential exemplar. This kind of personification may well arise simply from the fact that nouns like *philosophia* (and indeed *ecclesia*) are grammatically feminine in Latin. The conflicting strength of the anti-feminist tradition perhaps explains the slightly waspish tone sometimes assumed by these monitory ladies when addressing the fumbling Dreamer in *Piers Plowman*. Dame Study, Scripture and even Holy Church, in their different ways, all put him firmly in his place.

Secular ladies were also expected to be able to read, though for less elevated purposes. A lyric mistress is said to have 'fair true red lips' for reading romances. Chaucer's Criseyde is likewise discovered on one occasion with a group of friends being read to by a 'mayden'. Writing seems to have been a rarer accomplishment, though Marie's *Lays* amply fulfil the fears of those who advised against teaching women this skill as they will only use it to carry on clandestine correspondences. They do, but not always without difficulty. One telling little passage reminds us that writing needs a great deal more equipment than reading, for the heroine has to wait a whole month before she can get hold of the materials to answer a lover's letter. This also indicates the lack of privacy suffered by a wife in her own house. Chaucer's May in *The Merchant's Tale* is, to be sure, exceptionally well supervised, since she is another victim of a jealous husband, though it is not writing letters that causes her problems, only finding somewhere to read them. In the end she has to carry her lover's note to the only room in the house where she knows her husband will not follow her. When she has read it, there is then a handy place for its safe disposal:

> And whan she of this bille hath taken heede,
> She rente it al to cloutes [pieces] atte laste,
> And in the pryvee softely it caste.

Married or marriageable women provide, as we have said, the staple for literature. A role for the single woman hardly seems to exist outside the convent. Once, perhaps, in Chaucer we get a glimpse of one, but it remains unrealised and is, significantly, available only to the pagan Emily. Praying to Diana to release her from the necessity of marrying one or other of her two determined lovers she voices the feminine dilemma with rare poignancy:

> Chaste goddesse, wel wost thow that I
> Desire to ben a mayden al my lyf,
> Ne nevere wol I be no love ne wyf.
> I am, thow wost, yet of thy compaignye,
> A mayde, and love huntynge and venerye [the chase],
> And for to walken in the wodes wilde,
> And noght to ben a wyf and be with childe.

A life of freedom as Diana's votaress might be a practical possibility in Emily's world but the only equivalent in Chaucer's is the confining convent, and the voice of misogynist masculinity asserts itself as soon as Emily is confronted by a fait accompli. Arcite eventually triumphs over Palamon in the tournament that is to decide her fate and Emily is no more able than Criseyde to resist the spectacle of a handsome young man on horseback, flushed with victory and waiting only to lay his heart at her feet – or so Chaucer says:

> He priketh endelong [spurs along] the large place
> Lookynge upward upon this Emelye;
> And she agayn hym caste a freendlich ye [eye]
> (For wommen, as to speken in commune,
> Thei folwen alle the favour of Fortune...)

The heroine must not break the rules. She exists for man and the only kind of writing where rebellion is not only permitted but sanctified is in the unreal world of hagiography. As we have seen in the *Life of Christina of Markyate*, anything is allowed to the aspiring saint: parents can be defied, husbands refused and, in the case of the highly popular St Catherine, a woman can even engage in learned dispute with fifty philosophers and win. The tribulations of female saints sometimes resemble those of secular heroines. St Barbara was incarcerated in a tower by a tyrannical father and is usually depicted with it in pictorial art just as St Catherine is depicted with her wheel. But it is hagiography alone that supplies the really sensational torments: St Juliana, with molten brass poured over her, or St Agnes, stripped naked in a brothel. The literary quality of such stories is often not high, but the number of manuscripts which survive of the

73 Lady with her weapon: part of a sequence of drawings of ladies hunting, from Queen Mary's Psalter.

principal Middle English collection, the thirteenth-century *South English Legendary*, is adequate testimony to their popularity.

Just what needs these tales supplied for their women readers we can only guess but as models of suffering they clearly had value. When the wife in *The Shipman's Tale* describes her married life as a 'legende' she is using a term which was at that time exclusively used of a saint's life – a tale of tribulation patiently endured. A real-life character who seems deliberately to have set out to follow this model is the extraordinary Margery Kempe. This vigorous King's Lynn housewife has left us a spiritual autobiography which, like Julian's *Revelations*, has to be read as a personal document rather than a self-conscious work of literature, but her energetic and flamboyant devotion throws a whole new light on the forms which religious commitment could take at the turn of the fifteenth century. As a failed businesswoman and mother of fourteen she is no patient virgin, and her agonised weepings and 'cryings' in public places, her indefatigable pilgrimages to Rome and Jerusalem, her fearless confrontations with bishops and archbishops who had to be convinced of the genuineness of her self-dedication to God, all suggest a woman determined to emulate in the only way she knew the sufferings of the martyrs of old, though her avowed inspiration was a revered saint of her own day, St Bridget of Sweden.

With Margery Kempe we seem to hover in a strange borderland between fact and fiction. She really lived, and presumably experienced what she says she did, but the model of hagiographic endurance lurks behind her *Book* as surely as that of anti-feminism overshadows the Wife of Bath. In touching contrast to her

agonised outpourings are the occasional scenes in which she records her descent
from the heights of ecstasy to resume her mundane duties as a responsible holder
of the keys, invariable symbol of the medieval housewife's limited but real
domestic authority. Passages like these not only keep us in touch with the
workaday facts that lie behind the hard-fought-for image, they also link her back
through the centuries to those busy Anglo-Saxon forebears with whom this book
has been principally concerned. Here, too, Margery finds space to pay tribute
to a real-life husband, whose tenderness and compassion under extreme
provocation seem a just counterbalance to all the jealous cuckolds of the world
of fiction:

And anon this creature became calmed in her wits and reason, as well as ever she was
before, and prayed her husband as soon as he came to her, that she might have the keys
of the buttery to take her meat and drink as she had done before...[And] her husband
ever having tenderness and compassion for her, commanded that they should deliver to
her the keys; and she took her meat and drink as her bodily strength would serve her,
and knew her friends and her household and all others that came to see how Our Lord
Jesus Christ had wrought his grace in her, so blessed may He be, Who ever is near in
tribulation.

Holder of the keys – or a focus for tribulation? Whatever her role, medieval
English literature has at least a strong tendency to show the woman as a figure
to whom tribulation, whether external or self-generated, was no stranger. Her
sufferings, moreover, are essentially linked to her weakness, which cannot stand
long assaults upon it, especially if the assaults are directed towards her
compassion. This, however, ensures her place in the scheme of salvation as well
as of damnation. As both virgin mistress and Virgin Mother of God, she is the
object of unrelenting importunity. In this situation she cannot help but act in
accordance with the promptings of that weaker flesh which theology assigned
to her – to yield, in other words, in Eve's case to the Devil, for man's undoing,
and in Mary's to the plight of the sinner, so that she herself becomes the suppliant
on his behalf before God. Her weakness is her susceptibility which cannot resist
a true appeal and which compels her to exercise her mercy for, as Chaucer puts
it several times, in contexts more often ironic than serious, 'Pity runneth soon
in gentle heart'.

But if woman is weak in relation to man, man is also weak in relation to God,
and an unexpected transformation of this way of viewing woman is to be found
in certain kinds of Passion poetry in which the poet represents himself as
contemplating the suffering Christ and being moved by Him to a deep response
of personal love. This has the strange effect of putting the poet (whom one
inevitably thinks of as male, though there is no reason why he should be) into
the role normally assigned to the woman in a courtly love-relationship: the viewer
is *she*, subjected to the sight of *Him*, enduring torments on her behalf, unasked,
and pleading only for her love for its alleviation. The language of secular

love-poetry responds again with ease to this situation, even employing a term of everyday endearment, *lemmon*, 'beloved', as an address to Christ:

> Jesu, my lemmon,
> His woundes sore smerte,
> The spere all to his herte
> And thourh his sides gon.

Wooed by the sufferings of Christ for a return of love, it is here proper even for a man to exercise a kind of 'womanly' compassion and succumb to importunity. The 'womanly' nature is now a universal for Everyman, for here popular poetry is embodying that ancient allegory which read the bridal imagery of the *Song of Songs* as God's wooing of man's soul. In this context what better image can there be for the human soul than the womanly one – frail, susceptible and doomed to suffer, yet with the way of security open to it if it will only submit to the abiding protection of the love of God who seeks it with a lover's passion?

## FURTHER READING

There are several anthologies of Middle English metrical romances: *King Horn* and *Havelok the Dane* can be found in those of SANDS or FRENCH AND HALE. The *Lays* of Marie de France are translated by MASON; the original Old French is edited by EWERT. *The Owl and the Nightingale* is edited by STANLEY and translated into modern verse by STONE. Recent editions of *Piers Plowman* are those of SCHMIDT or PEARSALL; a convenient modern prose rendering is by GOODRIDGE. The standard edition of Chaucer is by ROBINSON; there are modern verse translations of *The Canterbury Tales* and of *Troilus and Criseyde* by COGHILL. For a selection of medieval English drama, including the Towneley *Second Shepherds' Pageant*, see CAWLEY. The standard editions of Middle English lyrics are by BROWN and ROBBINS; an attractive anthology with the language partly modernised is by DAVIES. The *Ancrene Wisse* is edited by TOLKIEN and translated, under the title *Ancrene Riwle*, by SALU. Julian of Norwich is translated by WOLTERS, and the fullest edition of her original text is edited by COLLEDGE AND WALSH. The *South English Legendary* is edited by D'EVELYN AND MILL. For Margery Kempe see MEECH AND ALLEN (original text) and BUTLER-BOWDON (modernised). There is an enormous body of criticism of Middle English literature: good recent surveys are those of BREWER, BURROW and PEARSALL. A useful article on Marie de France is by STEVENS. A general survey of medieval women which treats the English literary material sensibly is LUCAS.

# Select Bibliography

INTRODUCTION, CHAPTERS 1–7

ARNOLD-FORSTER, F., *Studies in Church Dedications* 3 vols (London, 1899).

ATTENBOROUGH, F. L., *The Laws of the Earliest English Kings* (Cambridge, 1922).

BAILEY, R. N., *Viking Age Sculpture in Northern England* (London, 1980).

BAKER, D. ed. *Medieval Women. Dedicated and presented to Professor Rosalind M. T. Hill on the Occasion of her Seventieth Birthday* (Oxford, 1978).

BERSU, G. and WILSON, D. M., *Three Viking Graves in the Isle of Man* (London, 1966).

BETHURUM, D. ed. *The Homilies of Wulfstan* (Oxford, 1957).

BLAKE, E. O. ed. *Liber Eliensis* (London, 1962).

BOYLE, J. R., 'Who was Eddeva?' *Transactions of the East Riding Antiquarian Society* 4 (1896) 11–22.

BRADLEY, S. A. J., *Anglo-Saxon Poetry* (London, 1982).

BROOKS, N., GELLING, M. and JOHNSON, D., 'A New Charter of King Edgar', *Anglo-Saxon England* 13 (1984) forthcoming.

BUDNY, M. and TWEDDLE, D., The Maaseik embroideries', *Anglo-Saxon England* 13 (1984) forthcoming.

CAMERON, K., *English Place-Names* (London, 1961).

CAMERON, M. L., 'The sources of medical knowledge in Anglo-Saxon England', *Anglo-Saxon England* 11 (1983), 135–155.

CAMERON, M. L., 'Bald's *Leechbook*: its sources and their use in its compilation', *Anglo-Saxon England* 12 (1983), 153–182.

CAMPBELL, A. ed. *The Chronicle of Ethelweard* (London, 1962).

CHAMBERS, R. W. ed. *Widsith* (Cambridge, 1912).

CHRISTENSEN, T., 'Gerdrup-graven', *Romu* II Arsskrift fra Roskilde Museum (1981), 19–28.

COCKAYNE, O., *Leechdoms, Wortcunning and Starcraft of Early England* Rolls Series 3 vols. (London, 1864–6).

COLGRAVE, B. and MYNORS, R. A. B. ed. and trans. *Bede's Ecclesiastical History of the English People* (Oxford, 1969).

DICKINS, B. and ROSS, A. S. C. eds. *The Dream of the Rood* (London, 1934, reprinted 1956).

DODWELL, C. R. *Anglo-Saxon Art: A New Perspective* (Oxford, 1982).

DUMVILLE, D. N., '"Nennius" and the *Historia Brittonum*', *Studia Celtica* 10–11 (1975–6) 78–95.

EARLE, J. and PLUMMER, C., *Two of the Saxon Chronicles Parallel* 2 vols. (Oxford, 1899).

ECKENSTEIN, L., *Woman under Monasticism* (Cambridge, 1896).

EHWALD, R., *Aldhelmi Opera* MGH Auctorum Antiquissimorum 15 (Berlin, 1919, reprinted 1961).

EMERTON, E. trans. *The Letters of Saint Boniface* (New York, 1940).

ERICKSON, C. and CASEY, K., 'Women in the Middle Ages: a Working Bibliography', *Medieval Studies* 37 (1975), pp. 340–59.

FELL, C. E. trans. *Egils saga* (London, 1975).

FELL, C. E., 'Old English *beor*', *Leeds Studies in English* n.s. 8 (1975) 76–95.
FELL, C. E., 'Hild, abbess of Streonæshalch', *Hagiography and Medieval Literature: a Symposium* (Odense, 1981) 76–99.
FELL, C. E., 'A *friwif locbore* revisited', *Anglo-Saxon England* 13 (1984) forthcoming.
FELL, C. E., 'Some domestic problems', *Leeds Studies in English* 16 (1986) forthcoming.
FELLOWS-JENSEN, G., *Scandinavian Personal Names in Lincolnshire and Yorkshire* (Copenhagen, 1968).
FRANTZEN, A. J., 'The tradition of penitentials in Anglo-Saxon England', *Anglo-Saxon England* 11 (1983), 23–56.
GARMONSWAY, G. N. ed. *Ælfric's Colloquy* (London, 1939, reprinted 1965).
GARMONSWAY, G. N. trans. *The Anglo-Saxon Chronicle* (London, 1953).
GELLING, M., *Signposts to the Past* (London, 1978).
GIES, F. and J., *Women in the Middle Ages* (New York, 1978).
GOLLANCZ, I. and MACKIE, W. S., *The Exeter Book* Early English Text Society 104 and 194 (Oxford, 1895 and 1934, reprinted 1975).
GRAHAM-CAMPBELL, J., *The Viking World* (London, 1980).
GRAHAM-CAMPBELL, J., *Viking Artefacts: A Select Catalogue* (London, 1980).
GRATTAN, J. H. G. and SINGER, C., *Anglo-Saxon Magic and Medicine* (Oxford, 1952).
GREENFIELD, S. B. and ROBINSON, F. C., *A Bibliography of Publications on Old English Literature to the End of 1972* (Toronto, 1980).
GRUNDMANN, H., 'Die Frauen und die Literatur im Mittelalter', *Archiv für Kulturgeschichte* 26 (1936) 129–161.
HALL, Mrs. Matthew, *The Queens before the Conquest* 2 vols (London, 1854).
HARMER, F. E., *Select English Historical Documents* (Cambridge, 1914).
HARMER, F. E., *Anglo-Saxon Writs* (Manchester, 1952).
HART, C. R. *The Early Charters of Northern England and the North Midlands* (Leicester, 1975).
HEALEY, A. DIPAOLO and VENEZKY, R. L., *A Microfiche Concordance to Old English* (Toronto, 1980).
HILL, R., 'Marriage in Seventh-Century England', in *Saints Scholars and Heroes Studies…in honour of Charles W. Jones*, ed. M. H. King and W. M. Stevens (Minnesota, 1979) 67–75.
HOLT, E. S., *Imogen: A story of the Mission of Augustine* (London, n.d.).
JENKINS, D. and OWEN, M. E., *The Welsh Law of Women* (Cardiff, 1980).
JOHNSTON, G., trans. *The Saga of Gisli* (London, 1963).
JONES, G. trans. *Eirik the Red and other Icelandic Sagas* (London, 1961).
KEMBLE, J. M., *The Saxons in England* 2 vols (London, 1849).
KER, N., *Catalogue of Manuscripts containing Anglo-Saxon* (Oxford, 1957).
KER, N. R. *Medieval Libraries of Great Britain: a List of Surviving Books* 2nd edn (London, 1964).
KEYNES, S. and LAPIDGE, M., *Alfred the Great: Asser's Life of King Alfred and other contemporary sources* (London, 1983).
KLÆBER, F., *Beowulf and the Fight at Finnsburg* (3rd ed.) Lexington, Massachusetts, 1950).
KLIMAN, BERNICE W., 'Women in Early English Literature, "Beowulf" to the "Ancrene Wisse"', *Nottingham Mediaeval Studies* 21 (1977), pp. 32–49.
KLINCK, A. L., 'Anglo-Saxon women and the law', *Journal of Medieval History* 8 (1982), 107–121.
KRAPP, G. P. and DOBBIE, Elliott van Kirk, eds. *The Anglo-Saxon Poetic Records* vols 1–6 (New York and London, 1931–1942, reprinted 1968).
LAING, S. trans. *Snorri Sturluson: Heimskringla* 3 vols. (rev. ed. London 1961 and 64).
LANCASTER, L. 'Kinship in Anglo-Saxon Society', parts I and II *British Journal of Sociology* 9 (1958), 234–48 and 359–77.
LAPIDGE, M, and HERREN, M., *Aldhelm: The Prose Works* (Cambridge, 1979).

LAPIDGE, M., 'Some remnants of Bede's lost Liber Epigrammatum', *The English Historical Review* 90 (1975), 799–820.

LESLIE, R. F., *Three Old English Elegies: The Wife's Lament, The Husband's Message, The Ruin* (Manchester, 1961).

LEVISON, W., *England and the Continent in the Eighth Century* (Oxford, 1946).

LIEBERMANN, F., *Die Gesetze der Angelsächsen* (Halle, 1903–16).

LOYN, H. R., 'Kinship in Anglo-Saxon England', *Anglo-Saxon England* 3 (1974), 197–209.

LOYN, H. R., *The Vikings in Britain* (London, 1977).

LUCAS, A. M., *Women in the Middle Ages. Religion, Marriage and Letters* (Brighton, 1983).

MALONE, K. ed. *Deor* (Exeter, 1977).

McNULTY, J. B., 'The Lady Aelfgyva in the Bayeux Tapestry', *Speculum* 55 (1980), 659–668.

MEANEY, A. L., *Anglo-Saxon Amulets and Curing Stones* BAR British Series 96 (Oxford, 1981).

MEYER, M. A., 'Women and the Tenth Century: English Monastic Reform', *Revue Bénédictine* 87 (1977), 34–61.

MONTALEMBERT, Le Comte de, *Les Moines d'Occident* 5 vols (rev. ed. Paris, 1863–7).

MORRIS, J., (general editor) *Domesday Book: A Survey of the Counties of England* (an ongoing series issued by county).

MORRIS, J. ed. *Nennius: British History and the Welsh Annals* (London, 1080).

NICHOLSON, J. see BAKER, D. (Bibliography, Chapter 9).

OKASHA, E., *Hand-List of Anglo-Saxon Non-Runic Inscriptions* (Cambridge, 1971).

OWEN, G., 'Wynflæd's wardrobe', *Anglo-Saxon England* 8 (1979), 195–222.

OWEN, G. R., *Rites and Religions of the Anglo-Saxons* (London, 1981).

PAGE, R. I., *An Introduction to English Runes* (London, 1973).

PAGE, R. I., *Life in Anglo-Saxon England* (London, 1970).

PAGE, R. I., 'The Manx rune-stones' in *The Viking Age in the Isle of Man* ed. Fell et al. (London, 1983), 133–146.

PÁLSSON, H. and EDWARDS, P. trans. *Orkneyinga Saga* (London, 1981).

PHILLPOTTS, B. S., *Kindred and Clan* (Cambridge, 1913).

PHILP, B., *Excavations in West Kent 1960–1970* Second Research Report in the Kent Series published by the Kent Archaeological Rescue Unit (1973).

POPE, J. C. ed. *Homilies of Ælfric: A supplementary Collection* 2 vols. Early English Text Society 259 and 260 (Oxford, 1967–8).

PRESS, M. trans. *The Laxdale Saga* (rev. ed. London, 1964).

RIVERS, T. J., 'Widows' Rights in Anglo-Saxon Law', *The American Journal of Legal History* 19 (1975) 208–215.

ROBERTSON, A. J., *Anglo-Saxon Charters* 2nd ed. (Cambridge, 1956).

SAWYER, P., *Anglo-Saxon Charters: An Annotated List and Bibliography* (London, 1968).

SEDGEFIELD, W. J. ed. *King Alfred's Old English Version of Boethius De Consolatione Philosophiae* (Oxford, 1899).

SIMS-WILLIAMS, P., 'Cuthswith, seventh-century abbess of Inkberrow, near Worcester, and the Würzburg manuscript of Jerome on Ecclesiastes', *Anglo-Saxon England* 5 (1976), 1–21.

SIMS-WILLIAMS, P. 'The settlement of England in Bede and the *Chronicle*', *Anglo-Saxon England* 12 (1983), 1–41.

SKEAT, W. W. ed. *Ælfric's Lives of Saints* Early English Text Society 76, 82, 94, 114, (Oxford 1885–1900, reprinted 1966).

SMITH, A. H., *English Place-Name Elements* English Place-Name Society 25 & 26 (Cambridge, 1956).

STAFFORD, P., 'The laws of Cnut and the history of Anglo-Saxon royal promises', *Anglo-Saxon England* 10 (1982) 173–190.

STAFFORD, P., *Queens, Concubines and Dowagers: The King's Wife in the Early Middle Ages* (London, 1983).

STANLEY, E. G., 'Did Beowulf commit "Feaxfeng" against Grendel's mother?', *Notes and Queries* 221 (1976) 339–40.

STENTON, D. M., *The English Woman in History* (London, 1957).

STENTON, F. M., 'The Historical Bearing of Place-Name Studies: The Place of Women in Anglo-Saxon Society', *Transactions of the Royal Historical Society* 4th series 25 (1943), 1–13.

SWANTON, M. ed. *The Dream of the Rood* (Manchester, 1970).

SWANTON, M., *Anglo-Saxon Prose* (London, 1975).

TALBOT, C. H., *The Anglo-Saxon Missionaries in Germany* (London, 1954).

TALBOT, C. H., *Medicine in Medieval England* (London, 1967).

TANGL, M. ed. *Die Briefe des Heiligen Bonifatius und Lullus* MGH Epistolae Selectae I (Berlin, 1955).

TIMMER, B. J. ed. *The Later Genesis* (Oxford, 1948).

THORPE, B. ed. *The Homilies of the Anglo-Saxon Church* 2 vols. (London, 1844–6).

THRUPP, J., *The Anglo-Saxon Home* (London, 1862).

TURNER, S., *History of the Anglo-Saxons* (London, 1799–1805). (Frequent editions and reprints, 7th ed. 1852.)

WAINWRIGHT, F. T., 'Æthelflæd, Lady of the Mercians' in *The Anglo-Saxons: Studies...presented to Bruce Dickins* ed. P. Clemoes (London, 1959), 53–70.

WHITELOCK, D., *Anglo-Saxon Wills* (Cambridge, 1930).

WHITELOCK, D., *The Anglo-Saxon Chronicle: A Revised Translation* (London, 1961).

WHITELOCK, D., *English Historical Documents c. 500–1042*, 2nd ed. (London and Oxford, 1979).

WHITELOCK, D. et al., *The Will of Æthelgifu* (Oxford, 1968).

WILSON, D. M. ed. *The Archaeology of Anglo-Saxon England* (London, 1976, and Cambridge, 1981). See also BERSU AND WILSON.

WILSON, D. M., *The Northern World* (London, 1980).

WOOLF, R. ed. *Juliana* (London, 1955).

WRIGHT, T., *Womankind in Western Europe* (London, 1869).

WORMALD, C. P., 'The Uses of Literacy in Anglo-Saxon England and its Neighbours', *Transactions of the Royal Historical Society* 5th series 27 (1977), 95–114.

## CHAPTER 8

ABRAM, A. 'Women traders in medieval London', *Economic Journal* 26 (1916), pp. 276–83.

ADAMS, N and DONAHUE, C. eds *Select Cases from the Ecclesiastical Courts of the Province of Canterbury c. 1200–1301*, Publications of the Selden Society 95 (London, 1981).

BANDEL, B. 'The English chroniclers' attitude toward women', *Journal of the History of Ideas* 16 (1955), pp. 113–18.

BATESON, M. ed. *Borough Customs*, 2 vols, Publications of the Selden Society 18 and 21 (London, 1904–1906).

BRITTON, E. *The Community of the Vill: a Study in the History of the Family and Village Life in Fourteenth-century England* (Toronto, 1977).

BROOKE, C. N. L. 'Gregorian Reform in action: clerical marriage in England 1050–1200', *Cambridge Historical Journal* 12 (1956), pp. 1–21 and 187–8.

BUGGE, J. *Virginitas: an Essay on the History of a Medieval Ideal* (The Hague, 1975).

BULLOCK-DAVIES, C. *Menestrellorum Multitudo: Minstrels at a Royal Feast* (Cardiff, 1978).

BURTON, J. E. *The Yorkshire Nunneries in the Twelfth and Thirteenth Centuries*, Borthwick Papers 56 (York, 1979).

CHIBNALL, M. ed. and trans. *The Ecclesiastical History of Orderic Vitalis* 6 vols (Oxford, 1969–1980).

C[OKAYNE,] G. E., *et al.*, *The Complete Peerage*, 12 vols (London, 1910–1959).

*Collectanea Stephan Kuttner II*, Studia Gratiana 12 (Bologna, 1967).

CONSITT, F. *The London Weavers' Company* (Oxford, 1933).

DALE, M. K. 'The London silkwomen of the fifteenth century', *Economic History Review* 4 (1932–1934), pp. 324–35.

DELISLE, L., ed. *Rouleau mortuaire du B. Vital, abbé de Savigni…1122–1123* (Paris, 1909).

DUBY, G. (tr. FORSTER, E.), *Medieval Marriage: Two Models from Twelfth-Century France* (Baltimore, 1978).

DUMONT, C., ed. and trans. *Aelred de Rievaulx: La Vie de recluse; la prière pastorale* (Paris, 1961).

EKWALL, E. ed. *Two Early London Subsidy Rolls*, Acta Regiae Societatis Humaniorum Litterarum Lundensis 48 (Lund, 1951).

ERENS, A. 'Les soeurs dans l'Ordre de Prémontré', *Analecta Praemonstratensia* 5 (1929), pp. 5–26.

*LA FEMME*, Recueils de la Société Jean Bodin 11 and 12 (Brussels, 1959–1962).

*LA FEMME dans les civilisations des $x^e$ – $xiii^e$ siècles: actes du colloque tenu à Poitiers les 23–25 septembre 1976*, Publications du Centre d'Etudes Supérieures de Civilisation Médiévale 8 (Poitiers, 1977).

FINUCANE, R. C. *Miracles and Pilgrims* (London, 1977).

FRANSSON, G. *Middle English Surnames of Occupation*, Lund Studies in English 3 (Lund, 1935).

GIVEN, J. B. *Society and Homicide in Thirteenth-Century England* (Stanford, California, 1977).

GÖSSMANN, E. 'Anthropologie und soziale Stellung der Frau nach Summen und Sentenzenkommentaren des 13. Jahrhunderts', in ZIMMERMANN, A., ed. *Soziale Ordnungen im Selbstverständnis des Mittelalters*, Miscellanea Mediaevalia 12/i (Berlin, 1979), pp. 281–97.

GRAHAM, R. S. *Gilbert of Sempringham and the Gilbertines* (London, 1901).

GROSS, C. *The Gild Merchant*, 2 vols (Oxford, 1890).

HALL, G. D. G., ed. and trans. *The Treatise on the Laws and Customs of the Realm of England commonly called Glanvill* (London, 1965).

HALLAM, H. E. *Rural England 1066–1348* (London, 1981).

HAMILTON, N. E. S. A. ed *Willelmi Malmesbiriensis Monachi de Gestis Pontificum Anglorum Libri Quinque*, Rolls Series (London, 1870).

HELMHOLZ, R. H. *Marriage Litigation in Medieval England* (Cambridge, 1974).

HOLT, J. C. *Magna Carta* (Cambridge, 1965).

HOMANS, G. C. *English Villagers of the Thirteenth Century* (Cambridge, Mass., 1941).

HUNNISETT, R. F. ed. *Bedfordshire Coroners' Rolls*, Publications of the Bedfordshire Historical Record Society 41 (Streatley, 1961).

HUNNISETT, R. F. *The Medieval Coroner* (Cambridge, 1961).

HUNT, N. 'Notes on the history of Benedictine and Cistercian nuns in Britain', *Cistercian Studies* 8 (1973), 157–77.

HYAMS, P. R. *Kings, Lords and Peasants in Medieval England: the Common Law of Villeinage in the Twelfth and Thirteenth Centuries* (Oxford, 1980).

*IL MATRIMONIO nella società altomedievale*, Settimane di Studio del Centro italiano di Studi sull' Alto Medioevo 24, 2 pts continuously paginated (Spoleto, 1977).

KEALEY, E. J. *Medieval Medicus: a Social History of Anglo-Norman Medicine* (Baltimore, 1981).

LABARGE, M. W. *A Baronial Household of the Thirteenth Century* (London, 1965).

LE BRAS, G. 'Le mariage dans la théologie et le droit de l'Eglise du $xi^e$ au $xiii^e$ siècle', *Cahiers de civilisation médiévale* 11 (1968), pp. 191–202.

LEGGE, M. D. *Anglo-Norman in the Cloisters* (Edinburgh, 1950).

LEGGE, M. D. *Anglo-Norman Literature and its Background* (Oxford, 1963).

MACBAIN, W., ed. *The Life of St Catharine by Clemence of Barking*, Anglo-Norman Texts 18 (Oxford, 1964).

METCALFE, W. M., re-ed. *Pinkerton's Lives of the Scottish Saints*, 2 vols (Paisley, 1889).

MEYER, P. ed. *L'Histoire de Guillaume le Maréchal*, 3 vols, Société de l'Histoire de France (Paris, 1891–1901).

MILLETT, B. ed. *Hali Meiðhad*, Early English Text Society: Original Series 284 (Oxford, 1982).

MOREY, A. and BROOKE, C. N. L. eds *The Letters and Charters of Gilbert Foliot* (Cambridge, 1967).

NOONAN, J. T. *Contraception: a History of its Treatment by the Catholic Theologians and Canonists* (Cambridge, Mass., 1966).

OGDEN, M. S. ed. *The Cyrurgie of Guy de Chauliac*, vol. 1, Early English Text Society: Original Series 265 (Oxford, 1971).

OSCHINSKY, D., ed. and trans. *Walter of Henley* (Oxford, 1971).

OWEN, A. ed. *Le Traité de Walter de Bibbesworth sur la langue française* (Paris, 1929).

PENELOPE (STANLEY), J. and McGOWAN, C., 'Woman and *wife*: social and semantic shifts in English', *Papers in Linguistics* 12 (1979), pp. 491–502.

POTTER, K. R. ed. *The Historia Novella by William of Malmesbury* (London, 1955).

POTTER, K. R., and DAVIS, R. H. C. eds *Gesta Stephani* (Oxford, 1976).

POWER, E. 'Some women practitioners of medicine in the Middle Ages'. *Proceedings of the Royal Society of Medicine* 15 (1921–22), Section of the History of Medicine pp. 20 – 3.

POWICKE, F. M. 'Loretta, countess of Leicester', in his *The Christian Life in the Middle Ages* (Oxford, 1935), pp. 147–68.

RAFTIS, J. A. *Tenure and Mobility: Studies in the Social History of the Mediaeval English Village*, Pontifical Institute of Mediaeval Studies: Studies and Texts 8 (Toronto, 1964).

RAFTIS, J. A. *Warboys: Two Hundred Years in the Life of an English Medieval Village*, Pontifical Institute of Mediaeval Studies: Studies and Texts 29 (Toronto, 1974).

ROUND, J. H. ed. *Rotuli de Dominabus et Pueris et Puellis de XII Comitatibus [1185]*, Publications of the Pipe Roll Society 25 (London, 1913).

ROWLAND, B., ed. and trans. *Medieval Woman's Guide to Health: the First English Gynaecological Handbook* (London, 1981).

SEYMOUR, M. C., ed. *On the Properties of Things: John Trevisa's Translation of Bartholomaeus Anglicus de Proprietatibus Rerum*, 2 vols (Oxford, 1975).

SHEEHAN, M. M. 'The influence of canon law on the property rights of married women in England', *Mediaeval Studies* 35 (1963), pp. 109–24.

THURESSON, B. *Middle English Occupational Terms*, Lund Studies in English 19 (Lund, 1950).

TOBIN, R. B. 'Vincent de Beauvais on the education of women', *Journal of the History of Ideas* 35 (1974), pp. 485–9.

TOLHURST, J. B. L., ed. *The Ordinale and Customary of the Benedictine Nuns of Barking Abbey* 2 vols, Henry Bradshaw Society 65 and 66 (London, 1927–1928).

CHAPTER 9

BENNETT, H. S., *Six Medieval Men and Women* (Cambridge, 1955), esp. pp. 100–50 on Margaret Paston and Margery Kempe.

BREWER, D. *English Gothic Literature* (London, 1983).

BROOK, G. L. ed. *The Harley Lyrics* (Manchester, 1948; 4th ed. 1968).

BROWN, C. ed. *English Lyrics of the XIIIth Century* (Oxford, 1932; repr. 1965).

BROWN, C. ed. *Religious Lyrics of the XIVth Century*, 2nd ed., revised by G. V. Smithers (Oxford, 1957, repr. 1965).

BROWN, C. ed. *Religious Lyrics of the XVth Century* (Oxford, 1939; repr. 1967).

BURROW, J. A., *Medieval Writers and their Work. Middle English Literature and its Background 1100–1500* (Oxford, 1982).

BUTLER-BOWDON, W. trans. *The Book of Margery Kempe* (London, 1936; reissued in The World's Classics, London, 1954).

CAWLEY, A. C. ed. *Everyman and Medieval Miracle Plays* (London, 1956; new ed., revised, 1977.)

CLIFFORD, P., *Marie de France. Lais*, Critical Guides to French Texts 16 (London, 1982).

COGHILL, N. trans. *Geoffrey Chaucer. The Canterbury Tales* (Harmondsworth, 1951; revised ed. 1977).

COGHILL, N. trans. *Geoffrey Chaucer. Troilus and Criseyde* (Harmondsworth, 1971; repr., 1982).

COLLEDGE, E. and WALSH J. eds. *A Book of Shewings to the Anchoress Julian of Norwich*, 2 vols. (Toronto, 1978).

CORRIGAN, M., 'Chaucer's Failure with Woman: the Inadequacy of Criseyde', *Western Humanities Review* 23 (1969), pp. 107–20.

DAVIES, R. T. ed. *Medieval English Lyrics. A Critical Anthology* (London, 1963; repr. 1966).

D'EVELYN, C. and MILL A. J. eds. *The South English Legendary*, 3 vols., Early English Text Society, Original Series 235, 236, 244 (London, 1956, 1956, 1959; repr. 1967, 1967, 1969).

DIAMOND, A., 'Chaucer's Women and Women's Chaucer', *The Authority of Experience: Essays in Feminist Criticism*, ed. A. Diamond and L. R. Edwards (Amherst, Mass., 1977), pp. 60–83.

DONALDSON, E. T. *Speaking of Chaucer* (London, 1970; repr. 1977), esp. Ch. 4.

ERICKSON, C., *The Medieval Vision. Essays in History and Perception* (New York, 1976), esp. Ch. 8.

EWERT, A. ed. *Marie de France: Lais* (Oxford, 1947; repr. 1952).

FERRANTE, J. M. *Woman as Image in Medieval Literature from the Twelfth Century to Dante* (New York and London, 1975).

FRENCH, W. H. and HALE, C. B. eds *Middle English Metrical Romances*, 2 vols. (New York, 1930; repr. as 1 vol., 1964).

FRIES, M., 'The Characterization of Women in the Alliterative Tradition', *The Alliterative Tradition in the Fourteenth Century*, ed. B. S. Levy and P. E. Szarmach (Kent, Ohio, 1981).

GIST, M. A., *Love and War in the Middle English Romances* (Philadelphia and London, 1947).

GOODRIDGE, J. F. trans. *Piers the Plowman* (Harmondsworth, 1959; revised ed. 1966).

GREEN, R. F., 'The *Familia Regis* and the *Familia Cupidinis*', *English Court Culture in the Later Middle Ages*, ed. V. J. Scattergood and J. W. Sherborne (London, 1983), pp. 87–108.

HALL, J. ed. *King Horn. A Middle-English Romance* (Oxford, 1901).

HANNING, R. W., 'From *Eva* and *Ave* to Eglentyne and Alisoun: Chaucer's Insight into the Roles Women Play', *Signs. Journal of Women and Society* 2 (1977), pp. 580–99.

JACOBUS DE VORAGINE, *The Golden Legend*, trans. G. Ryan and H. Ripperger (New York, 1941; repr. 1948).

KELLY, H. A., 'Marriage in the Middle Ages: 2. Clandestine Marriage and Chaucer's "Troilus"', *Viator* 4 (1973), pp. 435–57.

KEMP-WELCH, A., *Of Six Mediaeval Women* (London, 1913).

MANN, J., *Chaucer and Medieval Estates Satire. The Literature of Social Classes and the 'General Prologue' to the 'Canterbury Tales'* (Cambridge, 1973), esp. Ch. 5.

MASON, E. trans. *Lays of Marie de France* (London, 1911).

MEECH, S. B. and ALLEN, H. E. eds. *The Book of Margery Kempe*, Early English Text Society, Original Series 212 (1940; repr. 1961).

MEHL, D., *The Middle English Romances of the Thirteenth and Fourteenth Centuries* (London, 1969).

MICKEL, E. J. Jr. 'A Reconsideration of the *Lais* of Marie de France', *Speculum* 46 (1971), pp. 39–65.

MORSE, R., 'The "*Granz Bienz*" again', *Neuphilologische Mitteilungen* 81 (1980), pp. 361–5.

MURTAUGH, D. M., 'Women and Geoffrey Chaucer', *Journal of English Literary History* (ELH), 38 (1971), pp. 473–92.

MUSCATINE, C., *Chaucer and the French Tradition* (Berkeley and Los Angeles, 1957; repr. 1969).

NOONAN, J. T. Jr. 'Marriage in the Middle Ages: 1. Power to Choose', *Viator* 4 (1973), 419–34.

OWST, G. R., *Literature and Pulpit in Medieval England*, 2nd. ed. (Oxford, 1961; repr. 1966), esp. Ch. VII.

PEARSALL, D., *Old and Middle English Poetry* (London, 1977).

PEARSALL, D. ed. *Piers Plowman by William Langland. An Edition of the C-Text* (London, 1978).

POPE, M. K. ed. *The Romance of Horn by Thomas*, Vol. I, Anglo-Norman Texts, 9–10 (Oxford, 1955); Vol. II, revised and completed by T. B. W. Reid, Anglo-Norman Texts, 12–13 (Oxford, 1964).

POWER, E., *Medieval Women*, ed. M. M. Postan (Cambridge, 1975).

POWER, E., 'The Position of Women', *The Legacy of the Middle Ages*, ed. C. G. Crump and E. F. Jacob (London, 1926; corrected, 1932; repr. 1951), pp. 401–33.

ROBBINS, R. H. ed. *Secular Lyrics of the XIVth and XVth Centuries*, 2nd. ed. (Oxford, 1955; repr. 1964).

ROBINSON, F. N. ed. *The Works of Geoffrey Chaucer*, 2nd. ed. (Boston, Mass., 1957; repr. Oxford, 1979).

SALU, M. B. trans. *The Ancrene Riwle* (London, 1955).

SANDS, D. B. ed. *Middle English Verse Romances* (New York, 1966).

SCHMIDT, A. V. C. ed. *The Vision of Piers Plowman. A Complete Edition of the B-Text* (London, 1978).

STANLEY, E. G. ed. *The Owl and the Nightingale* (London, 1960; repr. Manchester, 1972, 1981).

STEVENS, J., 'The *granz biens* of Marie de France', *Patterns of Love and Courtesy. Essays in Memory of C. S. Lewis*, ed. J. Lawlor (London, 1966), pp. 1–25.

STEVENS, J., *Medieval Romance. Themes and Approaches* (London, 1973).

STONE, B. trans. *The Owl and the Nightingale, Cleanness, St Erkenwald* (Harmondsworth, 1971).

TALBOT, C. H. ed. and trans. *The Life of Christina of Markyate* (Oxford, 1959).

TOLKIEN, J. R. R. ed. *Ancrene Wisse. Edited from MS Corpus Christi College Cambridge 402*, with an introduction by N. R. Ker, Early English Text Society 249 (1962).

WEISSMAN, H. P., 'Antifeminism and Chaucer's Characterization of Women', *Geoffrey Chaucer. A Collection of Original Articles*, ed. G. D. Economou (New York, 1975), pp. 93–110.

WILSON, K. M. ed. *Medieval Women Writers* (Manchester, 1984). (Essays with translated extracts.)

WOLTERS, C. trans. *Julian of Norwich: Revelations of Divine Love* (Harmondsworth, 1966; repr. 1982).

# Photographic Sources

*Frontispiece* Trinity College Cambridge, MS 0.3.7, f. 1 (Courtesy of the Master and Fellows of Trinity College).

1. Photo British Library
2. Photo British Library
3. Photo British Museum Publications
4. Photo British Library
5. Corpus Christi College, Cambridge, MS 23, f. 39v (photo Courtauld Institute)
6. Oxford Archaeological Unit
7. British Museum, Dept of Medieval and Later Antiquities
8. Corpus Christi College, Cambridge, MS 23. f. 13r (photo Courtauld Institute)
9. British Museum, Dept of Medieval and Later Antiquities
10. British Museum, Dept of Medieval and Later Antiquities
11. British Library, Harley 603, f. 26r
12. British Museum, Dept of Medieval and Later Antiquities
13. British Library, Harley 603, f. 33
14. Phaidon Press, London (photo A. C. Cooper Ltd)
15. British Library, Cotton Tiberius C VI, f. 5v
16. Corpus Christi College, Cambridge, MS 23, f. 13r (photo Courtauld Institute)
17. British Library, Cotton Vitellius C III, f. 23v
18. British Library, Harley 603, f. 24v
19. British Library, Cotton Claudius B IV, f. 27v
20. British Museum, Department of Medieval and Later Antiquities
21. Phaidon Press, London (photo A. C. Cooper Ltd)
22. Corpus Christi College, Cambridge, MS 23, f. 18v (photo Courtauld Institute)
23. Corpus Christi College, Cambridge, MS 23, f. 6v (photo Courtauld Institute)
24. British Museum, Department of Medieval and Later Antiquities
25. British Library, Harley 603, f. 67v
26. The Dean and Chapter of Exeter Cathedral
27. British Library, Cotton Claudius B IV f. 57r
28. British Library, Harley 603, f. 58r
29. British Library, Cotton Claudius B IV, f. 57
30. British Museum, Dept of Coins and Medals
31. British Museum, Dept of Medieval and Later Antiquities
32. British Museum, Dept of Medieval and Later Antiquities
33. Photo British Museum Publications
34. Dean and Chapter of Exeter Cathedral
35. British Museum, Dept of Medieval and Later Antiquities
36. British Library

37, 38. British Museum, Dept of Medieval and Later Antiquities
39. British Library, Cotton Claudius, B IV, f. 77r
40. British Library, Add. MS 49598, f. IV
41. Bodleian Library, Oxford, MS Bod. 577, f. IV
42. Corpus Christi College, Cambridge, MS 23, f. 33v (photo Courtauld Institute)
43. Kungliga Biblioteket, Stockholm
44. Photo D. Tweddle and M. Budny
45. British Library, Add. MS 49598, f. 90v
46. Museum of Antiquities of the University and the Society of Antiquaries of Newcastle-upon-Tyne
47. Whitby Museum (photo Tindale's)
48. Corpus Christi College, Cambridge, MS 23, f. 23v (photo Courtauld Institute)
49. The Society of Antiquaries
50. York Archaeological Trust
51, 52. British Museum, Dept of Medieval and Later Antiquities
53. English Place-Name Society
54. British Library, Stowe 944, f. 6
55, 56. Photo by courtesy of the Manx Museum
57. Statens Historiska Museer, Stockholm (photo Antikvarisk-Topografiska Arkivet, Stockholm)
58. King's College, Cambridge, MS 19, f. 21v
59. National Monuments Record, London
60. Batsford Press, London (photo National Monuments Record)
61. British Library, Lansdowne 383, f. 165v
62. Photo British Museum Publications
63. Batsford Press, London (photo National Monuments Record)
64. Private Collection (photo Courtauld Institute)
65. British Library, Royal MS 2.B.VII, f. 74v
66. Bibliothèque Nationale, Paris, MS Fr. 3142, f. 256
67. Batsford Press, London (photo National Monuments Record)
68. British Library, Royal MS 10. E. IV, f. 187
69. British Library, Add. MS 42130, f. 60r
70. British Library, Add. MS 42130, f. 63
71. British Library, Add. MS 42130, f. 44r
72. Victoria and Albert Museum
73. British Library, Royal MS 2.B.VII, f. 153

# Index

*Figures in italic refer to illustrations*